D1281949

INTERMEDIATE READER IN MODERN CHINESE

INTERMEDIATE
READER *in*
MODERN
CHINESE

VOLUME III

by Harriet C. Mills

with P. S. Ni

CORNELL UNIVERSITY PRESS
ITHACA, NEW YORK

Copyright © 1967 by Cornell University

All rights reserved. Except for brief quotations in a review, this book, or parts thereof, must not be reproduced in any form without permission in writing from the publisher.

Cornell University Press

First published 1967

Library of Congress Catalog Card Number: 67-23068

Printed in the United States of America

by Valley Offset, Inc.

PL
1117
.M5
V.3

To

L. T. C.

whose book this is

YOUNGSTOWN STATE UNIVERSITY
LIBRARY

181319

C O N T E N T S

Volume I

Preface   xiii

I n d e x e s

Key to Use   I

1. Index to the 1,000 New Characters by Yale Romanization   III

2. Radical Index of New Characters and Radical Chart   XV

3. List of Items Noted in the "Structure Notes"   XXIX

4. Basic Vocabulary in Read Chinese I, II, III and Read About China   XXXVII

5. Comparative Romanization Table   XCIII

T e x t s

I. 中國的三種發明
THREE CHINESE INVENTIONS

    A. 指南針
    THE COMPASS   [1]

    B. 造紙和印刷術
    THE MAKING OF PAPER AND THE ART OF PRINTING   [4]

    C. 火藥
    GUNPOWDER   [9]

II. 中國共產黨的產生   廖蓋隆
THE BIRTH OF THE CHINESE COMMUNIST PARTY   Liao Kai-lung   [11]

III. 論共產黨員的修養   劉少奇
ON THE CULTIVATION OF A COMMUNIST   Liu Shao-ch'i   [16]

IV. 我們對於推行新文字的意見 蔡 元 培
OUR IDEAS ON THE PROMOTION OF THE NEW WRITING Ts'ai Yuan-p'ei [24]
and others

V. 中華人民共和國憲法
THE 1954 CONSTITUTION OF THE CHINESE [30]
PEOPLE'S REPUBLIC

VI. 建立無產階級人口學 董 杰
ESTABLISHING A PROLETARIAN DEMOGRAPHY Tung Chieh [41]

VII. 三民主義 孫 中 山
THE THREE PEOPLE'S PRINCIPLES Sun Yat-sen [51]

VIII. 周恩來在政協會上報告國共會談經過 周 恩 來
REPORT TO THE POLITICAL CONSULTATIVE Chou En-lai [65]
CONFERENCE ON NATIONALIST-COMMUNIST
NEGOTIATIONS

IX. 我們對於文化運動的意見
OUR IDEAS ON THE CULTURAL MOVEMENT [74]

X. 我們走那條路？ 胡 適
WHICH ROAD SHALL WE TAKE? Hu Shih [79]

XI. 中國革命和中國共產黨 毛 澤 東
THE CHINESE REVOLUTION AND THE CHINESE Mao Tse-tung [92]
COMMUNIST PARTY

XII. 和平建國方針 蔣 介 石
A POLICY OF PEACEFUL NATIONAL Chiang Kai-shek [97]
CONSTRUCTION

XIII. 中國社會各階級的分析 毛 澤 東
ANALYSIS OF CLASSES IN CHINESE SOCIETY Mao Tse-tung [101]

XIV. 追述我們努力建立「聯合政府」的用意 張 東 蓀
AN ACCOUNT OF OUR PURPOSE IN WORKING TO Chang Tung-sun [109]
ESTABLISH A "COALITION GOVERNMENT"

XV.   不平等條約對經濟的影響   蔣 介 石
       ECONOMIC EFFECTS OF THE UNEQUAL TREATIES   Chiang Kai-shek [116]

XVI.   中國人民解放軍總部宣佈約法八章
       EIGHT ARTICLES PROMULGATED BY THE   [120]
       HEADQUARTERS OF THE CHINESE PEOPLE'S
       LIBERATION ARMY

XVII. 我參加了革命   馮 友 蘭
       I PARTICIPATED IN THE REVOLUTION   Fung Yu-lan   [124]

XVIII. 鄉土本色   費 孝 通
       BASIC RURAL FEATURES   Fei Hsiao-t'ung [134]

XIX.   「中國本位的文化建設」宣言   陶 希 聖
       PROCLAMATION ON "CULTURAL CONSTRUCTION ON   T'ao Hsi-sheng [142]
       A CHINESE BASIS"   and others

XX.   五四運動   陶 菊 隱
       THE MAY FOURTH MOVEMENT   T'ao Chü-yin   [149]

XXI.   平民文學   周 作 人
       POPULAR LITERATURE   Chou Tso-jen   [160]

XXII. 隨感錄（三十八）   魯 迅
       RANDOM THOUGHTS - NO. 38   Lu Hsun   [165]

XXIII. 李自成起義   宋 揚
       THE UPRISING OF LI TZU-CH'ENG   Sung Yang   [170]

Volume II

Notes: Selections I - VIII

       Abbreviations   xiii

  I.   THREE CHINESE INVENTIONS

       A.   THE COMPASS   1

B. THE MAKING OF PAPER AND THE ART OF PRINTING   37

C. GUNPOWDER   71

II.   THE BIRTH OF THE CHINESE COMMUNIST PARTY   Liao Kai-lung   83

III. ON THE CULTIVATION OF A COMMUNIST   Liu Shao-ch'i   115

IV.   OUR IDEAS ON THE PROMOTION OF THE NEW WRITING Ts'ai Yuan-p'ei 155
                                                     and others

V.   THE CONSTITUTION OF THE CHINESE   189
      PEOPLE'S REPUBLIC

VI.   ESTABLISHING A PROLETARIAN DEMOGRAPHY   Tung Chieh   225

VII. THE THREE PEOPLE'S PRINCIPLES   Sun Yat-sen   273

VIII. REPORT TO THE POLITICAL CONSULTATIVE   Chou En-lai   321
      CONFERENCE ON NATIONALIST-COMMUNIST
      NEGOTIATIONS

Volume III

Notes: Selections IX - XXIII

IX.   OUR IDEAS ON THE CULTURAL MOVEMENT   367

X.   WHICH ROAD SHALL WE TAKE?   Hu Shih   395

XI.   THE CHINESE REVOLUTION AND THE CHINESE   Mao Tse-tung   449
      COMMUNIST PARTY

XII. A POLICY OF PEACEFUL NATIONAL CONSTRUCTION   Chiang Kai-shek 469

XIII. ANALYSIS OF CLASSES IN CHINESE SOCIETY   Mao Tse-tung   487

XIV.   AN ACCOUNT OF OUR PURPOSE IN WORKING TO   Chang Tung-sun   523
        ESTABLISH A "COALITION GOVERNMENT"

XV.   ECONOMIC EFFECTS OF THE UNEQUAL TREATIES   Chiang Kai-shek   549

XVI.   EIGHT ARTICLES PROMULGATED BY THE HEADQUARTERS   569
        OF THE CHINESE PEOPLE'S LIBERATION ARMY

XVII.   I PARTICIPATED IN THE REVOLUTION   Fung Yu-lan   585

XVIII. BASIC RURAL FEATURES   Fei Hsiao-t'ung   607

XIX.   PROCLAMATION ON "CULTURAL CONSTRUCTION ON   T'ao Hsi-sheng   637
        A CHINESE BASIS"   and others

XX.   THE MAY FOURTH MOVEMENT   T'ao Chü-yin   655

XXI.   POPULAR LITERATURE   Chou Tso-jen   689

XXII.   RANDOM THOUGHTS - NO. 38   Lu Hsun   703

XXIII. THE UPRISING OF LI TZU-CH'ENG   Sung Yang   715

INTERMEDIATE READER IN MODERN CHINESE

Notes: Selections IX - XXIII

The rising tide of conservatism, which in the mid-1930's manifested itself partly in renewed official sponsorship of Confucianism and renewed promotion of the classical language, elicited this protest from a distinguished group of liberals and liberal publications which insisted that China's hope lay in change, not in imitation of the past.

Chang Ching-lu, ed., <u>Source Materials on Contemporary Chinese Publishing</u> (Chung-kuo hsien-tai ch'u-pan shih-liao), Peking, 1955, Vol. II, pp. 105-108.

74:3	日益		S1	A: increasingly, more and more
	處在 . . . 地位		(VII:NM9)	PT: to be in the situation of ...
	自			A: (short form of) 自然
4	當兒			N: the very moment
	議論			V/N: to discuss; discussion, opinions (in sense of appraising)
	症候	jèng--	1	N: symptoms
	如何		S2	V/A: (literary form of) 怎麼樣
	胡亂	hú--	2	A: recklessly, at random
5	瀰漫	mìmàn		V/N: to pervade; pervasion
	呼聲	hū--	3	N: clamor, cry, voice
	味		NM1	M: for ingredient in Chinese medicine
6	戊戌	wùsyū		N: (cyclical characters for) 1898
	維新			N: reform (75:2)

維新運動　N: reform movement

明治維新　N: Meiji restoration

維新變法　N: reform program

7	中學爲體西學爲用			EX: Chinese learning as a base; Western learning for practical application.
	李鴻章	--húng--		N: Li Hung-chang

	推演			V/N: to evolve to, to develop to; development
8	到····地步		S3	PT: to come to the stage or state of (as of development, situation)
	庸妄	yūngwàng	4,5	SV: foolish, absurd, vainglorious
	呼號	hū(háu)	3,NM2	V/N: (to) cry, (to) appeal, call
9	癥結	jēng--		N: difficulty, core of a problem
	所在			V/N: to go, lie, be located; location
	反省	--(syǐng)	NM3	V/N: to examine and think over one's thoughts, plans, intentions, etc.; introspection, self-examination
10	奴隸	núlì		N: slave
	次殖民地		(VII:NM12)	N: sub-colony
	掙扎	jēngjá	6,7	V/N: (to) struggle; to twist and strain in struggling for release (from bondage, ropes, etc.)
	功業			N: meritorious task; great deeds
11	憧憬	chūngjǐng		V/N: to day-dream, to look forward to, to envisage; expectation
	破落戶	-----hù	8	N: families now fallen from high position and wealth
	捧着	pěng--	9	V: to hold up with both hands
	廢址	fèi--	10	N: ruins of (an old site)
	殘磚碎瓦	--jwān swèiwǎ	11,12,13	EX: broken bricks and shattered tiles
75:1	樓台			N: building, structure
	愚妄	yúwàng	14,5	SV/N: stupid, foolish; stupidity (77:10)
3	故步自封			EX: to be content in one's old ways; to be extremely conservative
	一切···惟有··· 却···		S4	PT: everything ... with the exception of ...
5	希臘	--là	15	N: Greece

6	純粹	--tswèi	(VII:4)	SV: pure
	國粹	--tswèi	(VII:4)	N: "National Essence," the quintessence of the culture of a nation
	國樂器			N: Chinese musical instruments
	胡琴	húchín	2,16	N: (lit. violin of barbarians) Chinese violin
	(疆)胡物	--hú--	2	N: articles used by barbarians
	長袍馬褂	--páu--gwà	17	N: traditional Chinese long gown and jacket type of dress (formal dress for males)
	禮服			N: formal dress
7	胡服	hú--	2	N: barbarian attire
	床			alternate form of 牀
	胡床	hú--	2	N: light chair (something like a rocking-chair)
	民間			N: folk (as in "folk literature"); people; (among) the people
	燒餅	--bǐng	18	N: type of unleavened bread usually salty and topped with sesame
	胡餅	húbǐng	2,18	N: barbarian bread
8	鼎食	dǐng--	19	V: to eat out of ding or metal tripod
	漢衣冠	----gwān	20	N: Chinese costume (lit. Han clothes and caps)
11	古文			N: classical language (76:10; 77:1)
	春秋			N: Spring and Autumn Annals (of roughly the eighth to fifth centuries B.C.)
12	方術			N: magic formula
	淺妄	--wàng	5	SV: stupidly shallow, superficial
76:1	結集			V/N: to collect together; collection

2 解釋	--shr̀	21	V/N:	to explain; explanation
3 道德			N:	morality, ethical code, ethics (76:4)
立身處世		(VII:NM9)	EX:	to establish oneself and assume one's place in the world
妄想	wàng--	5	V/N:	to indulge in wild thoughts; wild ideas or foolish thoughts
5 近世			N:	modern times
倫理		NM4	N:	ethics
金科玉律	----yù--	22	N:	precepts; sacred and inviolable rules and codes
退化			V/N:	to retrogress; retrogression
人羣			N:	(group of) people; mass
6 溫故			V:	to review, go over the past/old
8 通力合作			EX:	to make a concerted effort, to cooperate smoothly
10 文言文			N:	writing in the classical (or <u>wen-yen</u>) style (76:12)
僵硬	jyāngyìng	23	SV:	moribund, dead, rigid, fixed, stiff, set
11 (不)足以		S5	AV:	(in)sufficient to
口頭語			N:	colloquial speech
國語文			N:	vernacular writing
修辭學			N:	rhetoric (i.e. the art of using words)
12 淺陋	--lòu	24	SV:	shallow
苟簡	gǒu--		SV:	superficial, unsophisticated
77:1 國文			N:	Chinese (used as in the study of "Chinese")
2 詞	tsź	25	N:	type of poetry (77:3)
賦	fù	26	N:	type of poetry

愚蠢	yúchwǔn	14,27	SV: stupid, dumb, foolish
3 通		NM5	V/SV: to be versed in
表白			V/N: to make clear, to express; vindication
4 情思			N: sentiments; feelings and thoughts
5 諸子百家			N: the various schools of philosophy
專(門)家			N: specialist
			(專門) SV/A: specialized; particularly
6 鼓吹	--(chwèi)		V/N: to encourage, promote, push, advocate; promotion, advocacy
7 危急			SV/N: dangerous, hazardous, critical; danger
王道			SV/N: royal; (to act in a) kingly way (opposite of 霸道)
同輩			N: comrades, associates
9 一服毒藥	--(fù)dú--	NM6,28	N: dose of poison
功效			N: effect, efficacy; power to, power of
10 不忍	--rěn	29	AV: not having the heart to
日漸		S1	A: day after day, gradually
竭其微忱	jyé--wéichén		EX: to put forth one's effort or strength
如右			ex: (lit. to the right) as is stated above

(No notes for individual or group signatures)

CHARACTERS TO BE LEARNED

1. 症 jèng   N: disease, symptom

   症候   N: symptom of ailment (74:4)

   對症 V/SV: to administer or be a specific remedy (74:5; 168:7)

YOUNGSTOWN STATE UNIVERSITY
LIBRARY

181319

對症下藥　EX: to suit the remedy to the symptoms (used more figuratively than literally)

病症　N: disease, ailment

2. 胡 hú　(1) BF: recklessly; foolishly; blindly

胡亂　A: blindly, confusedly; recklessly (74:4)

胡作非爲　EX: to do exactly as one pleases without regard to (and with the implication of being at the expense of) others' interests (171:2)

胡說 V/N: to speak irresponsibly or recklessly ; nonsense

胡說八道　V/N: (to talk) "nonsense"

胡思亂想 V/N: (to indulge in) wild imaginings

胡鬧 V/N: to act wildly; (to raise a) fuss

(2) BF: barbarian, foreigner (applied especially to the Mongol, Tartar and other border peoples)

胡物　N: barbarian articles (75:6)

胡床（牀）　N: light chair somewhat like a rocking chair (75:7)

胡服　N: barbarian dress (75:7)

(3) Surname

胡適　N: Hu Shih (79:T)

3. 呼 hū　(1) BF: call out

呼聲　N: sound, cry (74:5)

打個招呼　VO: to nod to (by way of saying hello) (139:8)

呼號　N: call sign (as call letters of a radio station)

呼救 V/N: (to) cry for help

呼痛　V: to cry out in pain

稱呼 V/N: to address; title

(2) BF: exhale

呼吸 V/N: to breathe; breath

4. 庸 yūng (1) BF: commonplace, ordinary; usual

庸人 N: simple, ordinary person

庸人自擾 EX: the fool makes trouble for himself

平庸 SV: common, inferior, ordinary

庸俗 SV: commonplace, ordinary; vulgar

庸醫 N: quack doctor

昏庸 SV: muddle-headed and stupid

(2) BF: use, need

毋庸顧慮 ex: to have no need to worry about; don't worry (58:8)

毋庸說明／掛念／遠慮 ex: don't (or to have no need to) explain/think about/worry

5. 妄 wang BF: wild, false, absurd, fantastic

庸妄 SV: foolish, absurd (74:8)

淺妄 SV: stupidly shallow (75:12)

妄想 V/N: (to indulge in) vain hopes (103:6)

妄取 V: to misappropriate (123:3)

輕信妄斷 EX: to be gullible and make snap judgments (171:12)

妄言 V/N: to speak recklessly; irresponsible or boastful talk

妄費心機 EX: to scheme or plot in vain

妄作妄爲 EX: to act in an unseemly manner

輕舉妄動 EX: to act heedlessly or recklessly

妄自尊大 EX: to boast of oneself; be self-opinionated; self-conceit, self-exaltation

6. 掙 jēng   (1) V: to wrench off or apart (74:10)

               掙脫 RV: to wrench off (as bonds, etc.)

               掙開 RV: to wrench apart

   (jèng)   掙命 V: to struggle for one's life; to struggle desperately

   (jèng) (2) V: to earn (as money or a living)

               掙錢 VO: to earn money

7. 扎 já   (1) BF: pull up or out

               掙扎 V/N: (to strain or) struggle to get free of (bonds, etc.) (74:10; 142:5)

                  掙扎出來 RV: to extricate oneself; to struggle free

                  做最後的掙扎 VO: to be engaged in a life and death struggle

             扎營 VO: to encamp (as military)

   (jā)   (2) V: to prick, stab

             扎破 RV: to prick or pierce a hole in (and ruin)

             扎針 VO/N: to give an injection (colloq.); needle used in acupuncture

8. 戶 hù   (1) N: door   Rad. 63

             門戶 N: door (119:7); (here used in the special sense of port)

               門戶開放 EX: Open Door Policy (99:12)

     (2) N/M: (for) household

           破落戶 N: family declining in wealth and influence; impoverished or ruined family (74:11)

            大戶 N: important or rich homes or families (172:7)

            戶口 N: population, register of population

         一戶人家 N: a family household

門當戶對　EX: well-matched (in marriage); (i.e. of similar and congenial backgrounds and estate)

開戶頭　VO: to open an account

9. 捧 pěng　(1)　V: to hold in the hands, to offer respectfully; to scoop up

捧(着)　V: to carry or cup in the hands (74:11)

(2)　V: to bolster or flatter, support

捧...　V: to flatter

他在政治上很有地位，所以捧他的人不少。
Quite a few people flatter him because he is influential in politics.

捧場　VO: to applaud or cheer someone (at a performance or show; often with the implication of encouraging the performers because they are friends)

10. 廢 fèi　(1)　V: to abolish, cast aside or abrogate

廢止　V: to declare null and void; to rescind or discard (56:10; 149:2)

廢址　N: ruins (as of an ancient city) (74:11)

撤廢　V: to abrogate (97:6)

廢除　V/N: to eliminate; to abrogate; abrogation (122:5)

廢棄　V/N: to discard; discarding

作廢　V/N: to declare void; to make useless; rescinding; invalidation

殘廢　V/N: (to be) disabled (as veterans, etc.)

(2)　BF: useless

廢話　V/N: (to talk) nonsense; stupid sayings or utterances

廢物　N: useless thing (applied figuratively to people); trash, garbage

廢物利用　EX: to put a useless thing to good use

廢紙　N: wastepaper

報廢 V/N: to nullify; to declare obsolete

廢鐵　N: scrap iron

廢料　N: ruined materials that may be salvaged for another purpose

11. 磚 jwān　　N: brick (74:11)

磚頭　N: brick (塊)

12. 碎 swèi　　V/SV: to break; broken, fragmentary (74:11)

打碎　RV: to break something into pieces

零碎 SV/N: miscellaneous; bits and pieces

零七八碎　EX: in a mess, odd pieces; bits and pieces

零零碎碎　EX: bits and pieces, odds and ends

破碎　V: to be broken into pieces

碎片　N: fragments, shards

心碎　SV: brokenhearted

13. 瓦 wǎ　　(1)　N: tiles, pottery, earthenware　Rad. 98

殘磚碎瓦　EX: broken bricks and tiles (74:11)

磚瓦　N: bricks and tiles; building materials

瓦房　N: tiled-roof house (所)

瓦解 V/N: (lit. to become loosened or disintegrate as tiles do); to disintegrate, undermine; collapse; disintegration; breakup

弄瓦之喜　EX: congratulations on the birth of a daughter

(2) Used in transliteration

瓦特 N/M: Watt; watt of electricity (85:3)

14. 愚 yú　　SV: stupid, foolish

愚妄　SV: stupid, foolish, ignorant (75:1)

庸愚 SV: simple and stupid (of the masses)

愚弄 V/N: to fool, deceive, to make a fool of; to play tricks on

昏愚 SV: ignorant, stupid

昏愚無知 EX: to be very ignorant and unenlightened

愚民 V/N: to fool the people (by a ruler); stupid or ignorant people

愚民政策 N: policy designed to keep the people ignorant, stupid, unenlightened

愚笨 SV/N: foolish, stupid; foolishness

15. 臘 là (1) BF: the end of lunar year; preserved, dried (of meats originally prepared as special foods for the year-end season)

臘肉 N: dehydrated meat (usually pork)

臘月 N: last month of the lunar year

臘味 N: dehydrated and salted food (usually meat)

(2) Used in transliteration

希臘 N: Greece (75:5; 81:8; 143:10)

16. 琴 chín N: stringed instrument

(拉) 胡琴 VO/N: (to play a) Chinese violin (75:6)

(吹) 口琴 VO/N: (to play an) harmonica

風琴 N: organ, harmonium (架)

(拉) 手風琴 VO/N: (to play) accordion

(拉) 提琴 VO/N: (to play) violin

鋼琴 N: piano (鋼 gāng N: steel) (架)

古琴 N: seven-stringed lute (張)

17. 袍 páu BF: traditional long Chinese gown (件)

長袍／袍子　N: Chinese long gown (worn by man) (75:6)

黃袍　N: Emperor's gown (of imperial yellow)

旗袍　N: traditional slit sheath dress of well-born Chinese women (currently known in the West under the Cantonese pronunciation of <u>cheong-sam</u>).

睡袍　N: pajama housecoat

18. 餅 bǐng　　N: cakes, pastry (usually disc-shaped)

燒餅　N: kind of unleavened biscuit sprinkled with sesame seeds (75:7)

月餅　N: mooncakes (eaten at Mid-Autumn Festival)

餅乾　N: cookies, crackers (塊)

19. 鼎 dǐng　(1)　N: two-handled, bronze tripod; sacrificial cauldron regarded as symbol of imperial power (75:8) Rad. 206

鐘鼎　N: bells and vessels engraved with inscriptions (161:4,6)

紋鼎　N: cauldron carved with various designs

(2) BF: divide into three

鼎立　EX: three (opposing) forces standing in equilibrium

三國鼎立　EX: stabilized coexistence of three opposing political states

鼎足而立　ex: divided into three opposing forces or powers

(3) BF: great, powerful

鼎鼎大名　EX: of great reputation or fame

鼎力相助　EX: to help with great strength or effort

20. 冠 gwān　(1)　N: cap

衣冠　N: dress; clothing (lit. Han cap and clothes)

漢衣冠　N: Han dress or clothing (75:8)

衣冠不整　EX: sloppy of dress

(怒髮)衝冠　V: to get so angry that one's hair stands on end (174:8)

皇/王冠　N: crown

冠冕堂皇　EX: elegant, attractive, dressed up (of places, speeches, promises, etc.) (冕 myǎn: ceremonial cap)

掛冠而去　EX: (lit. to hang up hat of official rank and depart); to resign without notice

(gwàn)　(2) BF: head

冠軍　N: first in the traditional triennial examinations; winner in a competition

全班之冠　N: top of the class

21. 釋 shr̀　(1) BF: release, set free

釋放 V/N: (to) release (as from prison) (154:4,5)

釋出　V: to set free, release (158:12)

(2) BF: explain

解釋 V/N: to explain; explanation (76:2; 102:7; 110:3,4)

注釋 V/N: to make explanatory notes; explanatory notes; footnotes

釋疑　V: to explain what is not understood, to clear doubt, misunderstanding or suspicion

以釋群/其疑　ex: to remove or clear up group or individual suspicion or misunderstanding

22. 玉 yù　N: jade, gem　Rad. 96

金科玉律　N: sacred and inviolable codes or truths (76:5)

金玉其外　EX: all that glitters is not gold

玉器　N: ornaments of jade

玉女　N: fairy lady; beautiful teenage girl

玉體　　N: body (of a woman)

玉手　　N: white and fine-skinned hand (of a woman)

玉照　　N: your portrait (polite term)

拋磚引玉　EX: (lit. to throw out a brick to attract jade)
　　　　　　　polite phrase used to preface one's own ideas
　　　　　　　implying others will offer theirs

玉成其事　V: to assist in completing a job or matter

(老)玉米　N: maize, corn

23. 硬 yìng　(1) SV: hard (lit. and fig.) (76:10)

強硬　SV: very strong, determined, inflexible (167:2)

硬水　　N: hard water

硬度　　N: degree of hardness

堅硬　　SV: inflexible, hard

生硬　　SV: very harsh, raw, uncouth (of manner, etc.);
　　　　　　not fluent (as in a foreign language)

硬漢　　N: firm and tough man

(2)　A: perversely, stubbornly

硬+VERB　V: to insist forcibly or stubbornly on (against
　　　　　　　advice of others)

硬定　　V: to insist on designating (88:11)

硬給　　V: to insist on giving (129:1)

硬說/幹　V: to insist on saying/doing

硬着頭皮　EX: to act without regard for shame or
　　　　　　　embarrassment

24. 陋 lòu　　BF: low, humble, uncultured

淺陋　SV: shallow (76:12)

簡陋　SV: simple; disparaging (of one's own hospitality)

陋規　N: simple practices; base practices

陋習　　N: uncouth or vulgar custom; bad habits

25. 詞 tsz　(1)　N: type of poetry of unequal lines with fixed tonal patterns (首)

詩詞　　N: a general term for poetry (77:2,3)

歌詞　　N: text of a song

(2)　N: phrase, term, word (as a linguistic unit)

名詞　　N: term, noun (87:7)

無詞可答　V: to have nothing to say in reply (156:4)

新/生詞　N: new vocabulary items

動詞　　N: verb

形容詞　N: adjective

副詞　　N: adverb

連接詞　N: conjunction

前置詞　N: preposition (also 介詞)

詞典　　N: dictionary

措詞 V/N: to turn phrases; wording

詞不達意　EX: not to get one's ideas across (because of inadequate ability to express them)

26. 賦 fù　(1) V/N: to write poetry; type of poetry

詩詞歌賦　N: four types of Chinese poetry (sometimes used as general term for poetry) (77:2)

賦詩　VO: to compose poems

賦　　N: song of ... (as Ouyang Hsiu's 秋聲賦)

(2) BF: wealth; bestow

天賦　　N: natural talent

賦與　　V: to give to, bestow on

賦性　　N: natural character

賦有   V: to be endowed with

他賦有音樂的天才。
He is endowed with talents of music.

27. 蠢 chwǔn   SV: stupid, blunt, tactless

愚蠢   SV: stupid, dumb, foolish, ignorant (77:2)

蠢才   N: stupid fool, dolt

28. 毒 dú   (1) SV/N: poisonous, poison

毒藥   N: poison (77:9)

病毒   N: virus; infection (158:7)

毒氣   N: poison gas

中毒   VO: to be poisoned (中 read jùng)

消毒   VO: to sterilize, counteract poison

下毒   VO: to poison (as food, water, etc.)

解毒   V: to counteract poison; to sterilize

解毒藥   N: antidote

流毒   N: baneful influences, harmful effects

以毒攻毒   EX: to attack one poison with another; to fight fire with fire

(2) SV: cruel, mean, dangerous (of a person)

毒計   N: malicious or cruel scheme

29. 忍 rěn   V: to endure, to bear; to contain oneself

不忍   AV: not to have the heart to (77:10)

不忍(得)說/作 can't bear to say/do, etc.

心有不忍   EX: to be unable to bring oneself to (as kill someone)

殘忍 SV/N: cruel; cruelty (89:7)

忍受   V: to endure patiently (94:3)

不堪忍受　　ex: unbearable, unendurable

容忍 V/N: to endure, tolerate; tolerance (149:11)

堅忍　 V: steadfastly to endure

　　堅忍不移/拔 EX: steadfast and unshakeable

忍心　 A: to be hard-hearted; to be callous or unfeeling
　　　　enough to

你忍心看你的父母受苦嗎？

Could you bear to see your parents suffer?

忍痛　V: to bear pain

忍無可忍 EX: no longer bearable

忍辱負重 EX: long suffering and patient under onerous
　　　　　responsibility and criticism

NEW MEANINGS

1. 味
M: for each element in Chinese herb medicine prescription
(74:5; 168:5)

一味藥　 N: one ingredient (in a Chinese herb prescription)

2. 號 háu
V: to call out

呼號 V/N: (to) shout (74:8)

號哭　 V: to wail

3. 省 sy̆ing
BF: examine, look into; be on the alert

反省 V/N: to think over or reflect; reflection,
　　　　introspection (Communist term for reflecting
　　　　upon one's social or political ideas and
　　　　errors) (74:9)

自省 V/N: (to make a) self-examination

省察　 V: to examine, look into

4. 倫
(1) BF: right principles; human relationships

倫理　 N: moral principles; ethics (76:5)

倫理學   N: ethics, moral philosophy

倫常 or 五倫   N: moral obligations; the five human relationships of (1) overlord and minister; (2) father and son; (3) husband and wife; (4) brothers; (5) friends

(2) Used in transliteration

哥倫布   N: Christopher Columbus

5. 通   V: to be versed in (77:3)

你通幾種語言？
How many languages do you know?

中國通   N: China specialist; Old China Hand

通文墨   EX: to be familiar with writing or literature; to be educated

精通 V/SV: (to be) well versed in

精通中文／英文／etc.   VO: well versed in Chinese/English, etc.

一通百通   EX: (lit. to understand one thing and thus to understand a hundred); suddenly to understand something one has not previously understood

似通非通   EX: seemingly but not actually a master of (some skill, branch of learning, style, etc.)

6. 服 fù   (1) M: dose (of medicine) (77:9)

一服藥   N: a dose of medicine

這一服藥裏面有十味藥。
This dose of medicine contains ten ingredients.

(fú)   (2) V: to take (medicine)

服藥   VO: to take medicine

服毒   VO: to take poison

STRUCTURE NOTES

1. 日益   **A: increasingly; more and more ... everyday**

    日加   **A: common variant of** 日益

    日漸   **A: gradually**

    <u>Notes:</u>

    The series 日益／加   (a) is not followed by monosyllabic verbs.

    (b) is frequently followed by verbs like 減少，增加，擴大，etc.

    (c) can precede a main verb or a CV+O+V.

2. 如何   <u>**V/A: (literary form of)**</u> 怎樣／麼

    A.

    $$\boxed{S_1 + VP_1 + \left[\,S_2 + 如何\,\right]} \longrightarrow \boxed{\left[\,S_2 + 如何\,\right] + S_1 + VP_1}$$

    沒有人敢說結果如何 → 結果如何沒人敢說。
    What the results will be no one dares say.

    <u>Notes:</u>

    1. In 結果如何 ，如何 operates as a predicate verb.

    2. In the example above the construction 結果如何 operates as the object of 說 .

    B.

    $$\left.\begin{matrix} S_1 + VP_1^* \\ S_2 + VP_2 \end{matrix}\right\} \longrightarrow \boxed{不 \begin{Bmatrix} 管 \\ 問 \\ \text{etc.} \end{Bmatrix} + S_1 + VP_1 + S_2 + (都) + VP_2}$$

    * where VP_1 must be 如何 or 如何 + V + (O).

1. 病人的症候如何
    我們要救濟他。 $\Big\} \rightarrow$ 不問病人的症候如何我們都要救濟他。

    We helped him without asking what the patient's symptoms were.

2. 你如何強辯。
    你無法抵賴。 $\Big\} \rightarrow$ 不管你如何強辯你都無法抵賴。

    No matter how you argue, you have no way to deny your
    responsibility.

Note:

   In (1) above 如何 operates as a verb while in (2) it operates
   as an adverb.

3. 到 ... 地步   PT: to come to the point where/of ...

   到 ... 地步 is essentially a VO construction in which the object, must
   be modified, frequently only by 這個 implying an emphatic __this__ or __such__
   __a (state)__.

      沒想到時局已經發展到這個地步。

      I had not realized that the current (political/military) situation
      had already developed to this state.

4. 一切 ... 惟有 ... （却） ...   PT: everything is ... except for ...

$$S_1+VP_1 \text{ (general rule)} \atop S_2+VP_2 \text{ (exception)} \Big\} \rightarrow \left[{一切 \atop 所有} \right] + \left[{S_1+都+VP_1 \atop O_1+S+都+V_1} \right] + \left[{惟有 \atop 只有} \atop \text{etc.} \right] + \left[{S_2+却+VP_2 \atop O_2+S+却+V_2} \right]$$

      學生喜歡數學。
      他不喜歡（數學）。 $\Big\} \rightarrow$ 所有學生都喜歡數學惟有他不喜歡（數學）

   All students like mathematics except for him.

      他不喜歡功課。
      他喜歡數學。 $\Big\} \rightarrow$ 一切功課他都不喜歡，只有數學他却喜歡。

   He dislikes all his studies except for mathematics.

開辦進出口公司事，一切都已籌備就緒，惟有向政府登記一項却未開始
辦理。

Everything is in order for the opening of the import-export
company except that the matter of registering with the government
has not been taken up.

Notes:

    1.   In the above pattern one but not both of the verbs must be
       negative, i.e. the verbs must maintain a contrastive semantic
       relationship.

    2.   This is not a pattern in the strictest sense but the
       juxtaposition of two separate sentences.

5.   足以   <u>AV: sufficient or enough to</u>

足以 is a compound consisting of SV + 以. Like 能夠 or 足夠 it
functions as an AV in that it must always be followed by a verb.

我們的力量足以戰勝敵人。

Our strength is enough to overcome the enemy.

難以   <u>AV: difficult to</u>

難以 functions like 足以.

鐵路太少使中國交通問題難以解決。

The paucity of China's railroads makes China's communication
problem hard to solve.

E X E R C I S E S

I. Correlative Structures

A. 一切 ... 惟有 ... 却 ...

1. 他們興建工人宿舍的計劃已經決定，一切應辦事項也已籌備妥當，
惟有基金却未籌到預計的數目。

2. 新政府成立後一切措施都已依照所計劃的步驟進行辦理，惟有開墾
邊區和減少田賦却未着手進行。

3. 張先生準備明年夏天到埃及去研究當地土人的語言，他已將一切出
國手續辦理完善，惟船期却未決定。

B. 不但不 ... 甚至 ...

1. 不用科學方法作事，不但不發生效力，甚至會生出反作用。

2. 關於這件事的處理，由於他的態度過於強硬，不但得不到別人的諒
解甚至引起更多的糾紛。

3. 所謂「庸醫誤人」，他們不但不能對症下藥，使病人早日康復，甚
至給病人以更多的痛苦。

II. Structure Words

A. 如何

1. 據說前方敵人分三路進攻我軍，戰事危急，究竟我軍情況如何，尚
未查明。

2. 你當時又不在那兒，他又沒有告訴過你，你如何知道這是他做的事？

3. 關於這種奇怪的病，症候如何，連醫生也不能斷定。

4. 那個人眞討厭，常常跑到我這兒來說張三如何壞，李四如何好，弄
得我事情也沒法做下去。

5. 政治協商會議進行商談已有兩月之久，商談結果如何還不得而知。

B. 足以

1. 封建社會受傳統思想的支配很利害，豈只是大戶在婚姻上講究門當
戶對，即使小戶人家也如此，這種思想是否足以影響社會的進步乃

是一個極待詳細研究的問題。

2. 治理國家需要有才幹的人。但只有才幹而沒有節操也足以禍國。

3. 胡作非為是犯法的行為，然而胡思亂想也足以構成犯法的動機。

III. Miscellaneous

A. 日益

1. 隋朝末年，由於大興土木並且三次遠征高麗（朝鮮）以致賦稅日益繁重，並且人民被征集服役感到痛苦不堪，漸漸的叛變起來。

2. 在科學日益進步的社會尚妄想以魔教取信於人，倘不是鄉愚無知，豈肯為他所愚弄？

3. 印度政府為了解決本身的經濟困難，特別是資金的困難，修改了對外資的政策。許多重要工業部門的外資開放，政府更加依賴外援，結果印度同西方國家的關係日益密切。

B. 到...地步

1. 共產黨要人人省吃省用，把錢都拿去製造原子彈，以致人民到了無法生活的地步。

2. 到了這個地步，你還是把真實的情形告訴他吧！也許他因同情而不致於怪你。

3. 國家到了這樣危險的地步，你們還在那兒醉生夢死，一天到晚只想發財，真是豈有此理！

I. Correlative Structures

A. 一切 . . . 惟有 . . . 却 . . .

1. After the liberation all social systems on the
    mainland changed. Only the thinking of a part of
    the older generation did not change easily.

2. No questions were resolved as a result of Communist-
    Kuomintang negotiations at the Political Consultative
    Conference except the question of the nationalization
    of the army on which both sides agreed.

3. There was agreement by all sides on all questions
    discussed at the last meeting of the Executive
    Yuan except for a still unresolved divergence of
    opinion on the question of tax collection.

B. 不但不 . . . 甚至 . . .

1. Their line (論調) on arms reduction not only does
    not enjoy public sympathy, it even arouses the
    opposition of prominent figures in the government.

2. Although he has made a special study of Chinese
    philosophy and history, he not only does not
    understand the theories of the various philosophers,
    he does not even understand the central ideas of
    Confucian thought.

3. Owing to his excessively harsh attitude, the
    disposition of this matter not only failed to win
    others' understanding, but aroused even more
    discord.

II. Structure Words

A. 如何

1. The exam questions this time were rather difficult,
    although I was amply prepared. What the results of
    the examination are won't be known until next week.

2. I am most fond of my second daughter. Now she has
    left home and gone abroad but we haven't had a letter
    in over a month. How can I help not thinking of
    her?

3. They have been debating moral questions for a long
    time, but what is a moral standard and what should
    one use to determine it?

4. In teaching, the most important thing is to know how
    to raise the interest of the students and how to
    trigger their motivation (動機) to study.

5. I have not corresponded with my parents since the
    Chinese Communists took over the mainland. What
    their present life is like and what the state of
    their health is, I simply do not know.

B. 足以

1. Even bits of broken bricks and tiles can be used to
    build tall buildings.

2. When the situation is tense, even a chance remark
    can be sufficient to undermine morale.

3. He feels that everything his father says is sacred
    and the inviolable truth which is to be honored. He
    says this is "being earnest or sincere" (誠), but
    I feel it is sincerity which can destroy what he
    undertakes.

III. Miscellaneous

A. 日益

1. To satisfy the steadily growing transportation
    demands, in addition to increasing the number of
    roads and improving equipment, it will be necessary
    to improve management.

2. Since the founding of that one party government,
    politics have been decadent and social order confused,
    which has meant that the suffering of the people
    and the danger to the state steadily increased.

3. There are some societies where in actuality workers
    are not enjoying the results of industrialization
    or scientific progress although there is steadily
    increasing progress on both fronts.

B. 到 . . .地步

1. When one has already gotten into an impossible
    situation, it's much too late to try to figure a
    way out.

2. Let me tell you something, you got yourself into
    this mess and you needn't come to me in the future.

3. If you had only listened to others when they urged
    you to do a good job, you would not be in this
    position today.

IV. Review Sentences

Use:

假如 . . . 則 . . .   如何 . . . 便 . . .   只有 . . . 才 . . .

如何 . . . 才 . . .   不是 . . . 而是 . . .

難以   只要 . . . 便 . . .

1. a. As long as you use your common sense and
    intelligence, keep your feet firmly on the ground, and
    do not act recklessly, you will accomplish something.

    b. Only if you use your common sense and intelligence,
    keep your feet firmly on the ground, and do not act
    recklessly, can you have hope to accomplish something
    and realize the confidence people have in you.

2. a. Although the philosophy of the various schools may
    be deep and difficult to comprehend, so long as you are
    willing to work for a few years on it, you will be able
    to understand the general idea of the various groups
    and schools.

    b. Because the philosophy of the various schools is
    deep and hard, only if you are willing to work for a
    few years on it can you understand the general idea of
    the various groups and schools.

3. a. To undermine the political power of the enemy, one
    must adopt all sorts of measures including underground
    (clandestine) activities.

    b. To undermine the political power of the enemy is
    not easy. Only by adopting all sorts of measures,
    including clandestine activities, can the goal be reached.

4. If disabled veterans cannot be provided with a way to
    make a living, society may be in trouble in the future.

5. a. How to persuade him to change his harsh attitude is
    a problem I cannot resolve.

b.   Let's not worry about anything else for the moment. The first question we have to solve is how to persuade him to change his harsh attitude.

6.   Old man, you are wrong; Marx is not revered by the Americans as the savior of mankind but is the saint of the Communists.

7.   a.   How he can be so heartless as to let his child cry all day long I certainly cannot explain.

b.   How to make him not be so heartless as to let his child cry all day long is the matter we should first take into consideration.

8.   Of the students who went abroad to study in the fiscal year of 1963, about eighty per cent were self-supporting.

9.   他對人的態度本來就驕傲無禮，近來更變本加厲以至放肆。

10.   倘若你不那麼驕傲自大，常常對人以誠，常常反省自己的思想和行為，那麼就很容易與人相處了。

11.   假如一個中國共產黨員不奉毛澤東的新民主主義為金科玉律，那麼該黨員必要受制裁。

12.   處人處事總須有自省 self-reflection 的工夫，才能發現自己的短處，他人的長處，以他人之長補自己之短才能有所進步。

In this famous April 1930 article, Hu Shih identifies Poverty, Disease, Ignorance, Corruption and Disorder as China's five great enemies. For denying that feudalism, imperialism and capitalism were responsible for China's plight he was quickly attacked from the left.

The essential ideas in this piece were originally presented as a paper to a discussion group consisting largely of Western-trained liberals connected with the Crescent Moon (Hsin Yueh) magazine. In 1930 the group had taken as its central theme the question, "How Should China's Problems be Solved?" The original essay was very long and has been cut here to preserve the original argument within a reasonable length.

Hu Shih, Recent Discussions by Hu Shih (Hu Shih lun hsueh chin-chu), Shanghai, 1935, Vol. 1, pp. 440-453.

79:2	探路	tàn--	1	V: to explore the road (79:2)
5	在於			V: to lie or consist in (80:1) (於 can be omitted as in 79:10)
8	頗	pwō	2	A: rather, quite
	史大林			N: Stalin
	托洛斯基	twōlwòsz̄--	3	N: Trotsky
10	意氣			N: arbitrary or reckless emotions
80:3	剷除	chǎn--	4	V/N: to weed out, get rid of, eradicate; eradication (81:2; 86:1; 87:12)
4	仇敵	chóu--	5	N: enemy (80:10; 82:9; 83:1,2)
6	疾病	jí--	6	N: disease (81:6,7; 82:11; 89:10)
7	愚昧	--mèi	7	SV/N: ignorant; ignorance (82:3,5; 89:10)
8	貪污	tānwū	8,9	V/N: to be corrupt; corruption (82:7,8,12; 89:10)
9	擾亂	(rǎu--)	(VII:32)	V/N: to disturb; disturbance, disorder
11	富人	fù--	10	N: rich person
	崩壞	bēng--	11	V/N: to collapse, disintegrate; collapse, ruin (88:7)

12	在內		V: to be included
81:1	偏愛	NM1	AV: to make a stubborn point of
	光顧		V/N: (to be honored with a) visit by (here sarcastic)
	惡魔	è--	12	N: devil (89:10)
3	余天休	yú----	N: Yü T'ien-hsiu
	張振之	(--jèn--)(VII:16)	N: Chang Chen-chih
4	貧民		N: the poor
5	竟		A: after all; actually; suprisingly, unexpectedly (also 竟然 156:2)
6	瘟疫	wēnyì	N: epidemic, pestilence, contagion
	肺結核	fèi--hé	13,14	N: pulmonary tuberculosis (81:10)
	花柳病	--lyǒu--	N: syphilis (81:10)
	滅族		VO: to wipe out clan, race, etc. (81:12)
7	(不)明白		A: (here) (not) obviously or clearly
	衰弱	shwāi--	15	V/SV: to weaken; weak
	瘧疾	nywèjí	16,6	N: malaria (81:7,8,9,10)
8	衰亡	shwāi--	15	V/N: (to) decline, (to) collapse, destruction
	眼見		V: to witness (82:10)
9	村莊	NM2	N: village
	荆棘(地)	jīngjí--	N: thorny ground; desolated area
	害	NM3	V: to be sick with, suffer from
	人家		N: family (in this meaning pronounced with equal stress on both syllables; contrast with 90:8)
	人丁	NM4	N: people
	絕滅		V/N: to be extinct, to wipe out; extinction

10	與生俱來	--jyū--	S1,17	EX: innate, inborn
	避免			V: to avoid
	病痛			N: illness
	甚於		S2	V: to be greater or more than (86:2)
11	致死			V: to be fatal, cause death
	故			A: therefore (81:11,12; 82:5,6; 84:6)
	牠			PN: alternate form of 它 (81:12)
	可怕			SV: fearful, frightful (81:12)
	苟延生命	gǒu-----	18	V: to hold on to life with difficulty
12	立死			V: to be instantly fatal (立 short literary form of 立刻，立即)
	痕	hén	19	N: scar, trace (85:1)
	格外			A: all the more
	況且			CJ: moreover
82:1	超過	chāu--	20	V: to exceed
4	生存			V/N: to exist; life, existence
5	低微	--wéi	21	SV/N: low (of social origin, productive capacity, etc.); lowness (of economic or social position)
	薄弱	bwó--	22	SV/N: weak; weakness
	災	dzāi	23	N: disaster
7	捐官	jywān--	24	VO: to purchase office
	任官		NM5	V: to appoint to office
8	風氣			N: custom, practice, habit (86:7)
	盛行	shèng--		V/SV/N: (to be) prevalent or popular; popularity (of tunes, etc.)
	惡	è	12	SV/N: evil
10	絕		NM6	V: to cease

	土匪			N: bandit
11	來不及		S3	RV: to be unable to get something done on time
12	租稅	(--shwèi)(VII:33)		N: rents and taxes
	明目張膽	-----dǎn	25	EX: brazen(ly)
83:5	治安			N: order, peace (83:5,9)
	良好			SV/N: good, excellent; excellence
	安定			V/SV/N: to settle (as a family, system, etc.); peaceful, secure, stable; peace, stability
6	便利			SV/N: convenient; convenience
	公道			SV/N: equitable, just, reasonable; just settlement
	救濟			V/N: to administer relief; relief
7	高深			SV/N: (here) high caliber
	適應			SV/N: to be suitable to; adaptation
8	司法			V/N: to execute law; judicial powers
	設備			N: equipment
10	解除	———		V: to strip of, to relieve of
	軍備			N: arms, military equipment, armament
11	列國		NM7	N: The (Allied) Powers
	恭迎	gūng--	26	V: to welcome respectfully
	國際聯盟			N: League of Nations
	她			PN: feminine form for 他
	長期理事			N: permanent seat (technical League of Nations term)
	名額	--é	27	N: quota; position
84:1	纔			A: alternate form for 才

2 取			V:	to select, choose
演進			V/N:	to evolve, develop; evolution (84:4,5,6,11; 85:5,6,10; 86:1; 90:3,8)
4 瓜熟蒂(自)落	gwā--dì--	28	EX:	the natural course of events;(lit.) (when the melon is ripe it breaks off of its own accord)
5 胎	tāi	29	N:	foetus, embryo
人工			N:	manpower (used as adjective: artificial) (85:12; 86:3,5; 87:2)
6 連續性			N:	continuity
			連續	A: continuously
7 無數			Adj:	innumerable
中古			N:	Middle Ages, mediaeval
8 弗浪西斯派	fúlàng--sz--	30,3	N:	Franciscan
威克立夫			N:	Wyclif
9 赫司	hè--		N:	Huss
急進			SV/N:	radical; rapid (as of development) rapidity (85:9)
君主	(jyūn--)	(VII:3)	N:	monarch, monarchy
權力			N:	power
10 埋	mái	31	V:	to bury
路得			N:	Luther (84:10)
火線			N:	fuse
爆發	bàu--	32	V/N:	to break out; breakout, explosion (as a social movement)
85:1 顯出			V:	to show, reveal, exhibit
痕跡	hénjī	19,33	N:	trace
2 物理			N:	physics

3 積聚   --jyù   34   V/N: to pile up, accumulate; piling up,
                                         accumulation

蒸汽機   jēng----   35   N: steam engine

4 動力   N: motive power

呈現   chéng--   36   V: to manifest

7 莫斯科   (mwò)sž--(VII:12),3   N: Moscow

追溯   jwēisù   37   V: to trace back

8 暴動   bàu--   38   N: riot, uprising

敍   syù   39   V: to describe

9 差異   --yì   40   N: difference; differential

10 持續性   N: continuity

呈露   chénglù   36,41   V: to show, reveal

中斷   V/N: to break off or be broken off in
                                          the middle; interruption; break (as
                                          in electric wire, negotiations, etc.)

含   hán   42   V: to contain

12 無意   A: unintentionally

                        無意中   A: unintentionally (85:12)

                        有意   A: with the purpose of (86:6)

                        故意   A: deliberately

演變   V/N: (to) change, evolve; development,
                                          evolution

遲慢   (chŕ--)   (VII:22) SV: slow, delayed

縮短   swō--   43   V/N: to shorten; shortening

86:1 功用   N: usefulness, function

陳腐   NM8   SV: rotten; outdated

2 優於   S2   V: to be superior to ..., excel

3 暴力   bàu--   38   N: violence (89:5,11; 90:3)

4	立法			V/N: to legislate; legislation
	替代			V/CV: to take the place of, replace (87:3,4, etc.) (usually 代替)
5	上…軌道	--gwěi--	44	PT: to get on the right track
	濫用	làn--	45	V/N: (to make) excessive use of
7	局勢			N: situation
8	安寧	NM9		SV/N: peaceful; (at) peace
	皆	jyē	46	A: all, in all cases
10	圖	NM10		V: to plan, scheme
11	打平			RV: to vanquish; to put down disturbance or rebellion and restore peace
	招兵			VO: to raise troops
	購械			V: to purchase arms
	設計			V/N: to make or draw up plans; plan, specifications
12	孔夫子	kǔng----	47	N: Confucius
	正名			V/N: to rectify names; the rectification of names
87:1	憑藉	píngjyè	48,49	CV/N: to rely on; dependence
	提防			V/N: (to take) precautions
	消除			V/N: to eliminate, stamp out, get rid of; elimination
	自居（於）			V: to be proud or boast of being involved in
2	興利除弊	-----bì	50	EX: to encourage the good and get rid of the evil
3	罪惡	--è	12	N: crime, sin
	假	(jyǎ)	NM11	V/CV: to borrow (literary form of 借)
	汝	rǔ		PN: you, your (literary form of 你)

4	盲目	máng--	51	SV/A: blind(ly) (90:3, etc.)
	算不得			V: cannot be counted as; unworthy to be considered as (positive form: 算得)
7	抓住	jwā--	52	RV: to grab, grasp firmly
	變戲法			VO/N: to play tricks, work magic; sleight of hand, tricks
9	孤陋寡聞	----gwǎ--	53	EX: to be limited in knowledge and experience
10	著作	(jù--)	(VII:NM17)	N: writings
11	登着	dēng--	54	V: to print, carry (in newspapers, etc.)
	天津	--jīn	55	N: Tientsin
12	演說			V/N: (to make a) speech, oration
	軍閥	--fá	56	N: warlord
88:1	把持			V/N: to monopolize; to be in absolute control of; (to use undue influence to) control; monopoly
	包辦			V: to monopolize, to take over sole control of (as some enterprise, job, etc.)
	佔有性			N: monopoly (in sense of usurped power)
	祠堂	tsź--		N: ancestral hall
	同鄉會			N: provincial guild
	同學會			N: alumni group
3	意見書			N: memorandum
6	說夢話			VO: to talk nonsense
	辯護士			N: defender (note the use of 士 as "the gentleman who ...")
8	領地			N: fief
9	襲用	(syí--)	(VII:9)	V: to imitate; to take over (in sense of preserving an inherited tradition)

10	停滯	--jr̀	57	V/N: to become blocked, stagnant, impeded; stopping, cessation (88:12)
	過剩	--shèng	58	V/N: (to be) surplus (88:12)
	產物			N: product
11	判決	pàn--	59	V/N: to judge, to adjudicate, to rule that, (to) sentence
	捉	jwō	60	V: to capture, to seize upon
	替死鬼			N: scapegoat
89:1	止			A: here equals 只
2	顯微鏡	--wéijìng	21,61	N: microscope
3	嬾惰	--dwò	62	SV: lazy and indolent (嬾 alternate form of 懶) (90:3)
	聽其自然	(tìng)-----		EX: let nature take its course; let it work itself out; laissez faire
	仔細	dž--	63	SV: careful and detailed; careful about detail
5	懸空	sywán--	64	V: to be unfounded; to suspend in mid-air
	捏造	nyē--	65	V/N: to fabricate, prevaricate; fabrication
6	寧可 (不) … 而不…	níng-----	S4,NM9	PT: prefer (not) to ... than to ...
7	浪費	làng--	30	V/SV/N: (to) waste; wasteful; extravagance
	精力			N: energy
	煽動	shān--	66	V/N: to incite; instigation (as to riot) (91:1)
	盲動	máng--	51	V/N: to act blindly; blindly impulsive act (90:9,11; 91:1)
	劣根性	lyè----	67	N: evil nature, bad stock
8	屠殺	tú--	68	V/N: to slay; slaughter (90:7)

根苗	--myáu	69	N:	sprout; root and sprout
逍遙自在	syāuyáu----		EX:	to be in a blissful state of freedom from care
氣燄	--yàn	70	N:	mood, temper, spirit
兇	syūng	71	SV:	very fierce
90:1 一點一滴	------dī		EX:	drop by drop
收…全功			PT:	to reap all the benefit of
3 口號			N:	slogan (90:6)
標語			N:	motto, slogan, catch phrase (90:6)
5 迂緩	yūhwǎn		SV:	slow and dilatory
6 快捷	--jyé		SV:	quick, immediate (90:7)
貼	tyē	72	V:	to paste up, stick on (as on a wall)
對打			V:	to fight or hit back and forth at each other
8 人家			PN:	other people (in this meaning the first syllable is stressed, the second unstressed and toneless, cf. 81:9)
10 手段			N:	method, means, trick by which one gets something done
分別			V/N:	to distinguish; distinction
舉例			VO:	to give an example
人力車夫			N:	rickshaw coolie (abbr. as 車夫 91:1)
生計			N:	livelihood
12 車廠			N:	(old term for) rickshaw yard or shop
車行	--(háng)		N:	(old term for) rickshaw company
從…入手		S5	PT:	to start from or with ...
實收			V/N:	actually to receive; actual gross

91:1 辦工運			V:	to engage in organizing labor (rare)
工會			N:	labor union
2 預算			V/N:	(to) budget
3 舊曆年	--lì--	73	N:	lunar calendar New Year
懸想	sywǎn--	64	V/N:	to think in the abstract about; fantasy
4 脫卸	--syè	74	V:	to throw off, unload, get rid of
罪過		(VII:NM7)	N:	crime
洋鬼子			N:	foreign devil (a term sometimes used to refer to foreigners in China)
5 立說			V:	to set up or establish a theory
6 創議			V/N:	to set forth a platform or program; initial proposal, initiation, proposal
7 何等			A:	what a ... (literary form of 多麼)
重大			SV:	great, heavy (91:8)
出風頭			VO:	to show off
發牢騷	----sāu	75	VO:	to complain, grumble
一言(可以)興／喪邦	----- sàngbāng	76,77	EX:	a word can make/break the state
8 兢兢業業	jīng-----		EX:	wary and fearful
責任心			N:	sense of responsibility
竭力	jyé--	78	V/A:	(to put forth) all one's strength; energetically
排除			V/N:	to get rid of, expel, eliminate; expelling, elimination
9 虛懷	syū--	79	V:	to accept humbly
採納	(--nà)	(VII:35)	V/N:	to adopt, accept; adoption, acceptance
暗示			V/N:	to hint, be subtle; hint
10 提醒			V:	to remind, to be reminded of

CHARACTERS TO BE LEARNED

1. 探 tàn   V: to search out, explore

   探路   V: to explore the way or road (79:2)

   探險 VO/N: to explore; exploration

        探險家   N: explorer

        探險隊   N: exploration team (implication of
                     some danger involved)

   探問/聽 V/N: to inquire; inquiry

   探親   V/N: to visit or visits with relatives, especially
               parents

   探望   V/N: (to) visit

   探求   V/N: (to seek or) search into

   探病   VO: to inquire after or visit a sick person

   試探   V/N: to test, try out or explore (as a method
               or experiment); try

2. 頗 pwŏ   A: quite; somewhat, rather (precedes SV) (79:8; 103:8;
                     104:7)
   頗久/好/美/劣/多
   rather long (of time)/good/beautiful/evil/
   many or a lot

3. 斯 sż   (1) SP/N: this, these (in literary or formal writing)
   生於斯死於斯 ex: to be born and die in this place (or in one
                   place) (138:12)

   斯人斯事   EX: such an act by such a man

   斯人斯疾   EX: (lit.) How could such a person contract such an
                 illness? (fig.) to have a failing or defect

       (2) Used in transliteration

   莫斯科   N: Moscow (85:7)

   馬克斯   N: Marx (113:10; 114:3)

   俄羅斯   N: Russia (usually used for pre-Soviet period)

羅斯福　　N: Roosevelt

4. 剷 chǎn　　V: to root up or out; to shovel, cut, pare down; to level off

剷除 V/N: to eliminate, get rid of, uproot, eradicate; elimination of (80:2,3; 81:2; 86:1, etc.)

剷去　V: to get rid of, obliterate

剷草　VO: to weed

剷地　VO: to level off a plot of land

5. 仇 chóu　　N: hatred

仇敵　N: enemy (80:4,10; 82:9, etc.)

仇恨 V/N: to hate; hatred

和...有仇 PT: to hate someone (for something)

仇人　N: personal enemy; hated opponent or rival

仇視 V/N: (to hate or regard with) enmity (applied to people, nations, race, etc.)

6. 疾 jí　　(1) BF: illness, disease

疾病　N: disease (38:7; 80:6; 82:11)

疾苦　N: distress (100:4; 170:3)

積勞成疾 EX: Overwork causes illness.

(2) BF: urgently; hastily

疾行／走　V: to walk hastily

疾速　A: very rapidly

7. 昧 mèi　　BF: obscure, dark

愚昧 SV/N: ignorant; ignorance (80:7; 82:3,5; 89:10)

昧着良心　VO: to go against conscience, to be ungrateful

暗昧　SV: obscure

8. 貪 tān　　V/SV: to covet or desire (80:8)

貪多   V: to be greedy

貪睡/名/吃 SV: greedy for sleep/fame/food

貪財 SV: avaricious

貪便宜 VO: to be greedy for petty advantage (便 read pyan)

貪官 N: corrupt officials

貪圖 V: to scheme for or be greedy for (abstract things like fame)

貪圖名利 EX: to seek after fame and advantage

貪心不足 EX: to be insatiably greedy

貪小失大 EX: to scheme for the petty advantage and thereby to lose the big

9. 污 wū
(汙)   BF: unclean, dirty, filthy

貪污 V/N: to be corrupt; corruption (80:8; 82:7,8,12; 89:10, etc.)

貪污無能 EX: avaricious and incapable

貪官污吏 N: corrupt officials

污泥 N: mud

同流合污 EX: to become spoiled or corrupt by association with bad elements

污點 N: blemish; stain, stigma

污辱 V/N: to profane; (to) insult

10. 富 fù   (1) SV: wealthy, rich (94:2, 138:10)

富麗堂皇 EX: fabulous and beautiful (of architecture, decoration, etc.) (2:10)

富農 N: rich peasant (34:6)

富人 N: rich people, rich person (80:11)

富商 N: rich merchant (172:9)

富貴 N: wealth and honor (used as adjective: rich and privileged) (163:12)

財富 N: wealth; valuables

富強 SV: strong and prosperous (of states)

國富民強 EX: (to be) a prosperous country

富國強兵 EX: to enrich a country and strengthen its military forces

(2) Used in transliteration

阿富汗 N: Afghanistan (92:10)

11. 崩 bēng (1) BF: fall into ruin

崩壞 V: to collapse; to disintegrate (80:11; 88:7)

崩了 V: to break away, collapse (as dam, cliff, etc.)

山崩 N: landslide

山崩了。
There has been a landslide.

雪崩 N: snowslide; avalanche

(2) V: to die, pass away (of an emperor)

帝崩 EX: the emperor dies

駕崩 V/N: to die; death (of an emperor)

12. 惡 è SV/N: evil, depravity (100:2; 112:5)

惡例 N: evil example (59:5)

惡魔 N: bad demon (81:1; 89:10) (魔 mwó devil)

惡習慣 N: evil habits (82:8)

罪惡 N: crime (87:3; 120:3)

罪大惡極 EX: an extremely serious offense or crime (121:8)

作惡 V: to commit evil

無惡不作 EX: to stop at nothing; to
practice all types of wickedness

惡霸   N: ruffian; gangster type

惡霸地主   N: wicked (cruel) landlord

惡勢力   N: evil influence or power

險惡 SV: dangerous

萬惡 Adj: extremely evil

惡感   N: bad impression

惡作劇 V/N: to make fun of, play tricks; practical jokes,
trick

惡意   N: malice

惡有惡報 EX: evil has an evil recompense

13. 肺 fèi   N: lungs (81:6,10)

肺病   N: pulmonary tuberculosis or pneumonia

沒心沒肺 EX: heartless, inhuman (of a person)

14. 核 hé   (1) N: stone of fruits; lump

肺結核   N: pulmonary tuberculosis (81:6,10)

核心   N: center, kernel, essence (as of a problem);
axis (110:5)

核心問題／組織 N: central problem/
headquarters organization

核子   N: neutron

核子武器 N: nuclear weapons

核子物理學 N: nuclear physics

(2) V: to investigate, consider the facts; to estimate

核算 V/N: (to) double-check a calculation

考核 V/N: to check; to inspect, to examine and evaluate;
examination and evaluation

核對 V/N: to check two lists or accounts, etc. against each other; proofreading

核准 V/N: (to grant) approval or permission (after due consideration)

審核 V/N: to review and take action upon (as budgets, applications, etc.); review, examination

15. 衰 shwāi   BF: weak; decline, decay, fade

衰弱 SV/N: weak; weakness (81:7; 97:2)

衰亡 V/N: (to) collapse; (to) decline, to be destroyed; destruction (81:8)

衰落 V/N: (to) decline (of states, empires, families) (116:11; 117:11; 118:6, etc.)

衰朽 V/SV: to decay, be decadent; to dry up, wither (151:3)

衰敗 V/N: (to) decline or decay (of states, empires, families, etc.) (167:5)

衰老 SV/N: old and decrepit, withering (lit. and fig.)

衰運   N: declining fortunes

16. 瘧 nywè   BF: fever, malaria

瘧疾   N: malaria (81:7,8,9,10)

(yàu)   瘧子   N: malaria

發瘧子   VO: to have malaria

17. 俱 jyū   (1) A: entirely, all without exception (174:8)
   (jyù)
與生俱來   EX: innate, inborn (81:10)

與年俱進   EX: to increase year by year (117:1)

俱全／有   V: to be complete; to have everything at hand (also 具全／有)

一應俱全   EX: all essentials are on hand

俱備   V: all complete; all ready (also 具備)

萬事俱備   EX: everything is ready

(2) Used in transliteration

俱樂部   N: club (where people enjoy themselves)

18. 苟 gǒu   BF: illicit, careless, improper

苟簡   SV: insignificant (76:12)

苟延生命   EX: to keep alive with difficulty (81:11)

苟且偷生   EX: to keep alive in a fool's paradise; to live
in improper ease

苟且了事   EX: to settle a matter carelessly

苟且之事   N: illicit affair

苟安 V/N: (to steal) improper ease or leisure

苟全／存 V/N: (to maintain one's) life under hostile
powers or in difficult situations

19. 痕 hén   BF: scar, trace (81:12)

傷痕   N: scar from wounds

20. 超 chāu   BF: exceed, step over, surpass

超過   V: to exceed, step over (82:1; 107:7)

出／入超   N: favorable/unfavorable balance of trade (117:1)

超階級   VO: to transcend class; to be above or beyond
class (128:6; 129:4)

超度   V: to conduct souls to heaven (Buddh.) (142:6)

超出   V: to exceed (143:11)

超越   V: to excel, surpass, exceed

高超   SV: lofty, rarefied (used of thought, learning,
etc.)

超然   SV: lofty (of attitudes); transcendent

21. 微 wéi
(wēi)   BF: tiny, minute, slight

略微   A: slightly, slight (3:6)

低微 SV/N: low (of social origin, productive capacity, etc.); lowness; meanness (of economic or social status) (82:5)

衰微 V/N: (to) decline (of cities, governments, etc.) (117:12)

微小 SV: tiny, slight (126:12)

微乎其微 EX: to a very slight degree (lit. smaller than small) (136:9)

微賤 SV: humble, base, low (170:3)

微不足道 EX: too small to be worthy of mention

微風 N: breezes, slight wind

微笑 N: to smile; slight smile

微弱 SV: slight; weak

22. 薄 bwó (báu) SV: thin, slight, insubstantial; mean (opp. of 厚)

薄弱 SV: fragile or weak (82:5)

微薄 SV/N: very small, little, slight; slightness (as of incomes, etc.) (106:5)

荒薄 SV/N: barren, desolate; desolateness (171:9)

刻薄 SV: mean, unsympathetic; harsh; harshness

輕薄 SV/N: flirtatious, frivolous; flirtatiousness

薄餅 N: very thin pancakes used to wrap Peking duck and other delicacies (something like the Mexican tortilla) (張)

(bwò) 薄荷 N: peppermint

23. 災 (灾) dzāi N: calamity, misfortune (82:5) (場)

兵災 N: scourge of the military (i.e. devastation wrought by troops billeted or in combat) (118:10)

災荒 N: famine

災荒四起 ex: there is widespread famine

水災   N: flood

天災   N: natural disaster

　　　　天災人禍   EX: natural and man-made disasters

火災   N: calamitous fire

災難   N: disaster

災民   N: refugees

災害   N: calamity, misery, misfortunes

救災   VO: to relieve famine

24. 捐 jywān   (1)   V: to contribute or subscribe to

捐官   VO: to purchase an office or rank (82:7)

捐錢   VO: to contribute money or subscribe to

捐助 V/N: to assist, aid; aid, donation

(2)   N: tax, excise (筆)

捐稅   N: taxes

稅捐處   N: tax and revenue office or bureau

25. 膽 dǎn   N: gall; (fig.) bravery

明目張膽   EX: brazenly, openly (82:12)

膽子   N: courage, daring, bravery (103:7)

　　　他的膽子大。
　　　He is very bold.

大膽(的)   A: boldly (112:2)

膽量   N: daring, bravery, courage

　　　他有膽量。
　　　He is brave.

苦膽   N: gall

26. 恭 gūng   BF: respect; respectfully

恭迎   V: to welcome respectfully (83:11)

恭喜　V: to congratulate

恭喜發財　EX: "Congratulations and may you prosper!" (traditional New Year's greeting)

恭賀　V: to congratulate

恭敬 V/SV: to respect; respectful

恭順 SV: submissive, yielding, agreeable

27. 額 é　(1) BF: amount, quota

名額　N: quota; position (83:11)

數額　N: fixed number

定額　N: quota; fixed number

額外　A: beyond the stated number; in addition

缺額　N: incomplete complement; vacancy

超額 V/A: to exceed a quota; in excess of a prescribed quota

(2) BF: forehead

額頭　N: forehead

額角　N: temples (as forehead)

額骨　N: frontal bone

額手相慶　EX: (lit. to raise the hand to the brow in mutual congratulation); to exchange congratulations on some felicitous public event (such as a national political or military victory)

28. 瓜 gwā　N: melon (84:4) Rad. 97

西瓜　N: watermelon

木瓜　N: papaya

黃瓜　N: cucumber

南瓜　N: pumpkin

瓜子(兒)　N: watermelon seeds

多瓜　N: winter melon (used in a famous Chinese soup)

瓜分 V/N: to divide or cut up into portions; division or carving up of

笨瓜　N: stupid fool

29. 胎 tāi　　　N: foetus, embryo (84:5)

脫胎換骨　EX: (lit. to evolve from the foetus and change the bones); to undergo a thorough change and thus to differ from the model (129:2)

懷胎 VO: to be pregnant

墮/打胎 VO: to undergo an abortion

輪胎　N: tire

30. 浪 làng　(1) BF: waste or spill over

浪費 V/SV/N: (to) waste; extravagant; extravagance (89:7)

流浪 V/N: to drift from place to place (often in exile); to roam about (from necessity); exile (142:8)

流浪漢　N: drifter

流浪街頭　EX: to roam or wander about in streets

浪人　N: ruffians, rascals; ronin (158:3)

浪子　N: prodigal son

(2)　N: wave

聲浪　N: sound wave; cry (145:2)

波浪　N: wave

浪頭　N: wave

風浪　N: wind and waves

興風作浪　EX: to create a great fuss about something

乘風破浪　EX: (lit. to ride the wind and break the waves); (fig.) to aspire to great things

31. 埋 mái　　V: to bury or hide in the ground (84:10)

　　埋伏 V/N: (to) ambush

　　　埋伏兵馬　VO: to dispose forces in ambush

　　　打埋伏　VO: to conceal, disguise (as one's purpose, intentions, etc.)

　　收埋　V: to claim and bury (a body)

　　活埋　V: to bury alive

　　埋頭苦幹 EX: to bury oneself in hard work; to work hard

32. 爆 bàu　　V: to explode

　　爆發 V/N: (lit. or fig.) to erupt, break out, burst forth, explode; eruption, explosion, outbreak (as of war, sudden disorder or riot) (84:10; 127:9)

　　爆炸 V/N: to explode; explosion

　　爆竹／仗　N: firecrackers

33. 跡 jī
　(迹蹟)　　BF: trace, step or footstep (8:1)

　　痕跡　N: trace of; scar (85:1)

　　發跡　V: to make a name; rise to distinction (i.e. to leave a trace or mark) (137:1)

　　迹(蹟)象　N: trace, mark (150:10)

　　古蹟　N: ruins, site of an old ruin, town, etc.

　　事蹟　N: story, one's record or biography

　　足跡　N: footprint, traces

　　奇蹟　N: miracle

　　遺蹟　N: historical traces, vestiges

34. 聚 jyù　　V: to gather, collect together, assemble; amass

積聚 V/N: to pile up, accumulate; piling up, accumulation (85:3)

聚集 V/N: to concentrate or assemble together; concentration (137:8)

聚居   V: to live concentrated in one area (33:1; 137:10)

聚居社區   N: community (137:9)

聚衆   V: to assemble a mass or group (166:1; 172:4)

聚精會神   EX: to concentrate intently with all one's faculties

聚會 V/N: (to form a) gathering

35. 蒸 jēng   V: to steam

蒸汽   N: steam

蒸汽機   N: steam engine (85:3) (部)

蒸發 V/N: to evaporate; evaporation

蒸蒸日上   EX: to flourish more and more day after day

蒸包子 VO/N: (to) steam dumplings

36. 呈 chéng   BF: reveal, manifest, petition

呈現   V: to manifest or be manifested or disclosed; to reveal, to appear (85:4)

簽呈   N: official request or petition

37. 追 jwēi   (1)   V: to follow, pursue

追趕   V: to pursue, chase, follow after (1:10; 158:5)

追隨   V/N: (to) follow, to go with; pursuit of (149:6)

追逐   V/N: (to) chase, pursue; pursuit

追捕   V: to pursue and arrest

追討   V: to dun or press for repayment of debts

(2) BF: trace out or back; seek out or for

追述 V/N: to recount; to explain; explanation, recounting (109:T)

追說　V: to trace, explain, recount (109:3)

追究 V/N: to pursue, hound, go after, to investigate; inquisition; investigation (122:3)

追求 V/N: to go into thoroughly; to seek; pursue (as girl friends); pursuit (127:9; 140:10)

追問 V/N: to inquire with persistence into; inquiry

追尋　V: to examine a matter with thoroughness, to go after

追想 V/N: to think back, recall; reflection

追悔　V: to feel remorse, regret

追加 V/N: to add to or supplement; addition, supplement

　　追加條件　N: additional clauses or conditions

　　追加費　N: additional expenses

　　追加預算　V/N: (to bring forward) additional budget items or estimates

38. 暴 bàu　　SV: violent, brutal, tyrannical

暴動 V/N: (to) riot; insurrection (85:8; 86:9; 90:7, etc.)

暴力　N: violence, brutal force (86:3; 89:5,11; 90:3)

荒時暴月　EX: (in) times of famine and disaster (105:12)

粗暴　SV: crude, coarse (156:9)

暴行　N: atrocities, violence; violent acts

暴政　N: tyranny

暴亂　N: riot, revolt

暴燥 SV/N: hot tempered; hot temper

暴風雨　N: storm

暴徒　N: desperado

抗暴   V: to resist tyranny

    抗暴運動   N: movement to resist tyranny

暴君   N: tyrant

除暴   V: to eradicate evil

39. 敍 syù   BF: state, discuss, narrate; trace, describe (85:8)
(叙)

   敍述 V/N: to describe, state, trace out; narration, statement (99:5)

   敍說 V/N: to state; statement

   敍事 VO: to recount or narrate facts

     敍事詩   N: narrative poem （首）

   敍舊   V: to discuss or chat about old times

敍家常 VO: to discuss or chat about family events

40. 異 yì   BF: different (111:4; 140:11; 171:1)

   差異   N: difference; discrepancy (85:9)

   異常   A: extraordinary; exceptional; abnormal (152:7; 170:4)

   異民族   N: different or foreign tribes or peoples (173:11; 175:3)

   優異 SV/N: outstanding; distinguished; distinction

   異域   N: foreign regions

排除異已 EX: to get rid of those who oppose you

毫無異議 EX: without the slightest objection

   異教   N: heresy

     異教徒   N: heretics

異口同聲 EX: many voices raised in one cry

   異心   N: hostility, indifference

41. 露 lù   (1) V: to disclose, to expose

呈露　　V: to show, reveal (85:10)

暴露 V/SV: to reveal, to disclose, expose; to be revealing (as of women's clothes) (暴 also read pù)

　　　　暴露無遺　EX: to reveal or disclose completely (149:9)

露營　V/N: to camp out; bivouac

露天　　N: outside (of a building) (used as adjective); in the open, under an open sky

　　　　露天食堂　N: open-air dining hall or eating place

揭露　　V: to reveal, uncover (as of secret, etc.)

(lòu)　　露出來　RV: to show, expose, disclose, reveal

顯露 V/N: to reveal (as talent/spot, etc.), disclose;. revelation, disclosure

透露 V/N: to reveal, disclose, leak (as news); revelation, disclose (as a secret)

露骨　SV: uncovered or undisguised; brutally frank; broad (as of a joke)

(lù)　　(2) BF: dew

露水　　N: dew

42. 含 hán　　　V: to hold in the mouth; to contain

含有　　V: to contain, possess, include (abstract in usage) (88:1; 114:8)

包含　　V: to contain, include (104:12)

含義　　N: implication; connotation

含糊／混　SV: vague, unclear, obscure (of meaning)

含蓄 SV/N: subtle; suggestive; very indirect; implication; indirection (in speech)

43. 縮 swō　　　V: to shrink, draw in or back, reduce in size

縮短 V/N: to shorten, curtail; shortening, reduction, curtailing (85:12)

縮小 V/N: to become or make smaller; shrinkage (lit. and fig.) (134:9)

退縮　V: to draw back, retract (152:11)

收縮 V/N: to shrink; shrinkage (as of materials)

　　　收縮量　N: shrinkage (as of woolens)

緊縮 V/N: to trim, tighten, reduce; tightening; reduction (of budgets, etc.)

縮寫 V/N: to abbreviate; abbreviation

縮減　V: to reduce

縮水　V: to shrink in water or washing

44. 軌 gwěi　　　BF: track, path, groove; rule, law

軌道　N: path or road (fig. implies the right or proper road) (86:5)

　　　上軌道　VO: to get on the right track (abstract)

　　　經濟改革以後政治就上了軌道。
　　　Politics have gotten on the right track since the economic reform.

正軌　N: normal way, proper road or track (fig.) (109:7)

鐵軌　N: railroad track (條)

出軌　V: to run off the track (lit.)

行爲不軌　EX: improper in conduct

越軌 V/N: to go off the track (lit. and fig.)

45. 濫 làn　　　BF: overflow, go to excess

濫用 V/N: to use extravagantly (with implication of) (to) misuse or abuse (86:5)

　　　濫用職權　VO: to misuse authority

濫殺　V: to massacre (171:12)

濫交朋友　VO: to make friends indiscriminately

46. 皆 jyē　A: all, in all cases entirely (functions like 都)
(86:8; 117:8)

連戰皆勝／敗　V: to be victorious/defeated in every battle

皆大歡喜　EX: everybody's happy

47. 孔 kǔng　(1)　N: opening, hole

毛孔　N: pores of the skin

面孔　N: face (one's face and facial expression)

(2) Surname

孔(夫)子　N: Confucius (86:12; 140:10,11; 171:3)

孔廟　N: Confucian temple

48. 憑 píng　CV: to rely on, to base oneself on

你憑什麼說我？
What right have you to criticize me?

口說無憑　EX: oral promise is no proof (139:9)

憑良心說　V: to speak in all conscience

憑據／證　N: evidence, proof (usually in written form)

文憑　N: diploma

憑空　AV: to be unfounded; without evidence or reason

我不能憑空向人借錢。
I can't borrow money from people without a reason.

任／聽憑　V: to allow X to do as he desires

任憑他們去辦好了，反正有人會收拾他們。
Let them do as they please. They'll get their comeuppance anyway.

49. 藉 jyè　BF: by means of; taking advantage of; to avail oneself of (99:3; 109:6; 122:8)

憑藉CV/N: to rely on; dependence (57:6; 87:1)

憑藉武力侵略其他國家是違反聯合國憲章的。
To commit armed aggression against another
state is in violation of the U.N. Charter.

藉機會 VO: to take the opportunity of (99:3)

藉口／詞CV/N: (to take as) pretext

他藉口有病不來上課。
He gave illness as his excuse for not coming
to class.

他以下雨爲藉口，不來上課。
The pretext he gave for not coming to class
was that it was raining.

藉故 AV: to make an excuse

藉以 EX: thereby (vestige of a literary construction
meaning 用來 and can best be constructed as
藉此來 or用它來）

旅行很有意思，並可藉以增加見識。
Travel is very interesting and can thereby
broaden one's experience.

50. 弊 bì   BF: distressed; fraud, corruption

興利除弊 EX: to encourage good and get rid of evil (87:2)

舞弊 V/N: (to engage in) corrupt practices (121:12)

流弊   N: corrupt practices (141:3)

弊病／端 N: evil practices

作弊 VO: to practice fraud; to cheat (as on exams)

51. 盲 máng   BF: blind

盲目SV/A: blind(ly); not physical blindness, but
inability to see the truth in a situation
(87:4; 90:3)

盲動 V/N: to act blindly or without thinking; blindly
impulsive action (89:7; 90:9,10,11; 91:1,3)

盲從 V/N: to follow blindly; blind acceptance (148:3)

文盲　N: an illiterate

色盲 V/N: to be color blind; color blindness

52. 抓 jwā　　　V: to snatch, grab, seize

抓住　RV: to grab hold of (87:7)

亂抓一把　ex: to pick up a handful at random (fig. of ideas, etc.) (174:6)

抓賊／特務　VO: to catch a thief/an enemy agent

53. 寡 gwǎ　　　BF: few, lonely, little

孤陋寡聞　EX: to be limited in knowledge and experience (87:9)

寡不敵衆　EX: the few are no match for the many

寡人　PN: I, the ruler (classical formula by which the ruler referred to himself as the Solitary One)

寡情　SV: hard to do any favors, ungrateful, hardhearted

寡情寡義　V: to be treacherous, ungrateful

寡婦　N: widow

守寡　VO: to remain a widow (for chastity's sake)

54. 登 dēng　(1)　V: to mount, to ascend

登陸　V: to land (on shore)

登陸艇　N: landing craft

登岸　V: to land or climb ashore

登臺　VO: to mount the platform; to come on the stage

登車　V: to get on the train (or other vehicle)

一步登天　EX: to ascend to great eminence with one jump

(2)　V: to record, to publish (87:11)

登記 V/N: to register, to make a record of; registration (not used for academic registration but for registration with the police, etc.) (126:8)

你已經登記了麼？
Have you registered yet?

登載 V/N: to publish or print (in a newspaper);
appearance or publication in a paper (156:3)

登報 VO: to appear or print in a paper

登廣告 VO: to publish an advertisement

55. 津 jīn   (1) BF: ford, stream

天津   N: Tientsin (87:11; 119:3)

(2) BF: saliva; moisten; overflow

津津有味 EX: intensely interesting (of a book, etc.)

56. 閥 fá   BF: left-hand entrance in a triple gate; (thus)
classification according to rank

軍閥   N: warlord (14:10, 87:12; 102:2; 103:10, etc.)

財閥   N: tycoon; zaibatsu

57. 滯 jr   BF: obstruct, hinder, congeal, stop

停滯 V/N: to stop; stopping or cessation of (88:10,12;
119:8)

停滯不前／進 EX: to stagnate; to stop and
not advance (96:5)

滯留 V/N: (to) stay, (to) sojourn

滯銷 V/N: to sell slowly or be unsaleable; slow sale of

58. 剩 shèng   V: to remain, be left over
(賸)

過剩 V/N: to be in excess; surplus; excess (as
production) (47:7; 88:10,12; 118:9; 136:11)

剩餘 V/N: to be left over; surplus (103:5)

剩餘物資   N: surplus goods

剩餘價值   N: surplus value

剩下   V: to remain, be left over (107:2)

殘剩 Adj: remnant (171:11)

剩貨／飯　N: remaining or surplus goods/food, etc.

59. 判 pàn　　　V: to judge, decide

判決 V/N: to judge, decide, sentence; judgment, decision, sentence (88:11)

批判 V/N: to evaluate critically; critical evaluation (127:7,11; 148:4)

判罪　VO: to sentence (legal); to declare guilty

談判 V/N: to negotiate; negotiations

和平談判　N: peace negotiations

審判 V/N: to try a case, to adjudge; adjudication

裁判 V/N: to try, judge; judgment, trial; referee

判例　　N: legal precedents

判斷 V/N: to judge, judgment

判斷力　N: powers of judgment

判定 V/N: to decide; judgment

60. 捉 jwō　　　V: to seize, arrest, catch, capture (2:2; 88:11; 164:2)

捕捉　　V: to capture

捉賊　　VO: to capture a thief

活捉　　V: to capture alive

捉拿　　V: to arrest, to seize

61. 鏡 jìng　　BF: mirror

顯微鏡　　N: microscope (89:2) （架）

鏡子　　N: mirror （面）

照鏡子　　VO: to look in a mirror

放大鏡　　N: magnifying glass

望遠鏡　　N: telescope （架）

眼鏡　　N: eye glasses （副）

62. 惰 dwò   BF: indolent, careless

　　　　　　　懶惰 SV: lazy and indolent (嬾惰 is not common)
　　　　　　　　　(89:3; 90:3)

　　　　　　　惰性 N: laziness, inertia

63. 仔 dž   BF: minute, small

　　　　　　　仔細 SV: very careful of detail; meticulous (89:3)

64. 懸 sywán   V: (lit. and fig.) to suspend or dangle in mid-air
　　　　　　　　　without support (142:8)

　　　　　　　懸空 V: to hang or be suspended in mid-air; to be
　　　　　　　　　unfounded (89:5)

　　　　　　　懸想 V/N: to think in the abstract, (thus) to dream
　　　　　　　　　about; to long for; fantasy (91:3)

　　　　　　　懸隔 V: to be separated from or far apart

　　　　　　　　　天地懸隔 EX: the distance between heaven
　　　　　　　　　　　and earth (129:11)

　　　　　　　懸案 N: unresolved or pending case or question

　　　　　　　懸掛 V: to hang up, suspend

　　　　　　　懸而未決 EX: to be pending or undecided (as of decisions,
　　　　　　　　　legal cases, etc.)

　　　　　　　懸念 V/N: to think anxiously about; to be in suspense
　　　　　　　　　about; remembering, missing (of people)

65. 揑 nyē   (1) V: to pinch or knead with the fingers as dough
　 (捏)
　　　　　　　揑住 RV: to pinch firmly (as with fingers)

　　　　　　　揑一把 V: to take a pinch

　　　　　　　　　揑一把冷汗 VO: to be frightened or scared;
　　　　　　　　　　　to break out into cold
　　　　　　　　　　　perspiration

　　　　　　(2) BF: trump up or fabricate

　　　　　　　揑造 V: to fabricate, trump up (89:5)

66. 煽 shān   V: to incite, fan (as a revolt)

煽動 V/N: to stir up, to incite (as emotions, riot); inciting (89:7; 91:1)

67. 劣 lyè   BF: degraded; evil, bad

劣根性   N: evil nature, bad stock (89:7)

劣績   N: bad record (121:12)

劣等   N: low grade

優劣   N: fitness; rank order; quality

惡劣   SV: evil, wicked

劣勢   N: unfavorable position or situation

處於劣勢   EX: to be in an unfavorable position or situation

68. 屠 tú   BF: kill, slaughter

屠殺 V/N: (to) slaughter, massacre (89:8; 157:10)

屠夫   N: butcher (172:7)

屠城   VO: to slaughter the inhabitants of a captured city

69. 苗 myáu   N: sprouts, shoots of plants

根苗   N: sprout; sprout from the root (89:8)

花生苗   N: peanut sprouts (129:8, 10)

火苗   N: flame

70. 燄 yàn
(焰)   BF: flame, blaze

氣燄   N: mood, temper, emotional anger (89:8)

氣燄萬丈   EX: puffed up and overbearing

火燄   N: blaze of a fire; flame (153:4)

71. 兇 syūng
(凶)   SV: fierce, cruel (89:8)

行兇   V: to commit murder

兇手   N: assassin, murderer

幫兇   N: accomplice

兇惡／暴   SV: cruel, evil

兇燄   N: arrogance, haughtiness; evil potential (of wicked person or enemy)

72. 貼 tyē   V: to stick or paste on (as a wall, etc.) (90:6)

貼標語   VO: to paste up posters or slogans

伏貼 V/SV: (to be) obedient, submissive, compliant

伏伏貼貼   A: compliantly, submissively

體貼 SV/N: solicitous; solicitude for others

她真是一個好太太，非常體貼她丈夫。
She is really a good wife and very solicitous of her husband.

津貼   V/N: (to give a) subsidy, allowance

73. 曆 lì   BF: calendar

曆書   N: calendar (something like an almanac) (7:3)

舊曆年   N: Chinese New Year (91:3)

陰曆   N: lunar calendar (133:1)

陰曆年   N: lunar New Year

陽曆   N: solar calendar

陽曆年   N: New Year's Day (January 1)

日曆   N: calendar

曆法   N: method of calendrical reckoning

74. 卸 syè   V: to unload, get rid of

脫卸   V: to throw off, unload, get rid of (91:4)

卸責   V: to lay down the responsibility; to put the blame on others

卸任   V: to resign or put down the burdens of office

卸貨   VO: to unload goods

75. 騷 sāu   BF: annoy, stir up

　　　　　　牢騷   N: complaint (91:7)

　　　　　　　　發牢騷   VO: to complain, grumble

　　　　　　騷擾 V/N: to harass, disturb (as with lightning raids,
　　　　　　　　　　etc.); harassment (170:8)

76. 喪 sàng   (1) BF: lose (by death)

　　　　　　喪失 V/N: to lose; loss (of something important as
　　　　　　　　　　usefulness, reputation, etc.) (38:7; 174:1,10)

　　　　　　　　喪失自由   EX: to lose freedom or liberty

　　　　　　喪氣   SV: melancholy; dejected

　　　　　　喪命   VO: to lose one's life

　　　　喪權辱國   EX: humiliating loss of national power and
　　　　　　　　　prestige

　　　　　　喪良心   VO: to have no conscience; to be depraved

　　(sāng) (2) BF: funeral

　　　　　　喪事   N: funeral

　　　　　　送喪   V: to escort a funeral

　　　　　　喪禮   N: funeral rites

　　　　　　喪服   N: mourning robes

　　　　　　守喪   VO: to observe mourning rites

77. 邦 bāng   N: state, country (91:8)

　　　　　　盟邦   N: ally; alliance; allied nation (98:10)

　　　　　　聯邦   N: union, federation

　　　　　　　　蘇維埃社會主義共和國聯邦 N: Union of Soviet
　　　　　　　　　　　　　　　　　　　　　Socialist
　　　　　　　　　　　　　　　　　　　　　Republics

　　　　　　　　聯邦共和國   N: federated republic

　　　　　　　　聯邦調查局   N: Federal Bureau of Investigation

友邦　N: friendly nations

邦交　N: international relations

禮敎之邦　N: country of traditional propriety and culture

78. 竭 jyé　　BF: exhaust, to the utmost; put forth a great effort

竭力 V/A: to use every effort; exhaustively (91:8; 146:8; 163:3)

日竭一日 EX: to get more and more difficult; to decrease day by day (117:9)

竭盡 V/A: to the utmost, to exhaust (as strength)

竭誠　A: sincerely, in all sincerity

79. 虛 syū　　(1) SV: empty, hollow, unreal

虛無 Adj: empty, unreal (142:8)

虛無主義　N: nihilism

虛僞 SV: hypocritical (171:12)

虛榮 SV: vain; vanity

虛榮心　N: vanity; vainglorious desire for vanity and wealth

虛假 SV: false, hypocritical

虛名　N: unfounded reputation

虛報 V/N: (to make a) false report

虛妄 SV: vain, dissolute

虛字　N: "empty word"; particle (as in wen-yen)

虛幻　N: illusion (used as adjective: illusory)

虛弱 SV: weak (of body), decrepit

虛想　N: fancy, imagination

虛構　V: to trump up

空虛 SV: empty (in the abstract sense)

虛線　N: dotted line (used in math, etc.)

(2) BF: humble

虛懷 V/A: to be humble; humbly (91:9)

虛心 SV/A: humble; humbly

　　虛心求教　ex: to seek enlightenment or
　　　　　　　　　instruction with humility

　　虛心接受　ex: to accept with humility

心虛　SV: afraid lest something be found out

　　作賊心虛　EX: (lit. thieves live in fear)
　　　　　　　　　to fear discovery of a secret
　　　　　　　　　fault or past wrong doing

NEW MEANINGS

1. 偏
　　　BF: perversely

　　偏愛 AV: to make a stubborn point of... (81:1)
　　　　　　(cf. definition of 偏愛 in IA:39)

　　偏要 AV: to insist perversely on ...
　　　　別人告訴他那兒很危險，可是他偏要去。
　　　　People told him it was dangerous to go there
　　　　but he perversely insisted on going.

　　偏偏　A: unfortunately; as luck would have it; "of all
　　　　　　times"
　　　　他偏偏要現在來。
　　　　He would come now of all times.

2. 莊
　　　BF: village (often as final element in village names)

　　村莊　N: village (81:9)

　李/石家莊　N: Li/Shih-chiachuang (the Li/Shih family
　　　　　　　village)

3. 害
　　　BF: sick with; suffer from (81:9)

　　害病　VO: to be sick, suffer from a disease

4. 丁   BF: individual person, individual

    人丁   N: people, population (in a family) (81:9)

    零丁   SV: disconsolate, alone

        孤苦零丁   EX: all alone

    壯丁   N: an able-bodied man

    兵丁   N: soldiers

    園丁   N: gardeners

    添丁   VO: to have a son

5. 任   V/N: to employ, appoint; term of office

    任官   VO: to appoint an official (82:7)

    任命／用 V/N: to employ, appoint; employment, appointment
                (as of officials)

        任命單   N: list of appointees

    接任   V: to take over an office from

    繼任   V: to succeed to the office of

    上／下任 V/N: to take/leave office; the previous/next term
                of office; predecessor/successor

  首／前／現／新／後任總統   N: first/former/present/new/next president

6. 絕   V: to break off, stop, cease

    絕滅   V: to extinguish (of a family, race, species,
                etc.) (81:9)

    絕望 V/N: (to) despair (107:2)

    絕交   V: to break off (friendly/diplomatic) relations

7. 列   BF: series; file of

    列國   N: the various nations (83:11)

    列強   N: the (Great) Powers (116:2,8,9, etc.)

    行列   N: ranks (as of a parade, army) (行 read háng)

列車　N: (railroad) train of cars

8. 陳　　　　BF: stale, old, a long time

陳腐　SV: spoiled by keeping; rotten; outdated (86:1)

陳貨　N: old stock (as inventory)

出清陳貨　EX: to clear out old stock

陳舊　SV: stale, old-fashioned

陳糧／米　N: stale grain

9. 寧
（甯寗寍寕）
(1) BF: peaceful

安寧 SV/N: quiet and peaceful; peace, rest (86:8; 89:7)

寧靜　SV: quiet

康寧　N: health and peace, good health

心神不寧　EX: uneasy, not peaceful in mind; apprehensive

(2)　A: ... rather ... than to ...

寧可（不）…也不　PT: to prefer (not) to ... than to ... (89:6)
(see X Structure 4 below)

寧願／肯　A: to prefer to; would rather

寧爲玉碎，不爲瓦全　EX: (lit. better to be a jade broken than a
tile intact); rather die for a noble cause
than continue to live a shameful or
inglorious life

10. 圖　　　　V: to scheme, plan for or to (86:10)

圖財　V: to scheme for wealth

圖謀　V: to scheme, plot

圖報　V: to hope to repay (as a kindness) (does not
apply to money)

惟利是圖　EX: to care only for profit

有利可圖　EX: an advantageous situation

別有所圖　EX: to have ulterior motives or intentions

希圖　　V: to hope for or to

意圖 V/N: to attempt, intend; attempt, intention

11. 假 jyǎ   BF: borrow or avail oneself of (87:3; 157:3)

假借　　V: to borrow; to use metaphors

假道　　VO: to go by way of or via

假公濟私　EX: to pretend to work for the public while
stealthily attending to one's selfish aims
(濟 to profit, to aid)

假手於人　EX: to do something through a third agent

STRUCTURE NOTES

1. 與 + O + 俱 + Verb

In this construction 與 is a CV and 俱 an adverb with the force of "always," "in every case." The 與 + O + 俱 unit functions as an adverbial modifier on the following verb. When 與 is followed by nouns such as 年，月，日，etc., the construction is similar to the colloquial 每 + N + 都 + (在) + V as in:

物價每年都(在)漲。

Prices are rising each year.

俱 may also mean 同時 in the construction 與生俱來 .

2. A 甚／優／etc. 於 B

$$ N(P)_1 + SV + 於 + N(P)_2 $$

我們不得不承認瘧疾的可怕甚於肺結核，甚於花柳，甚於鴉片。

We cannot but admit that malaria is more dreadful than tuberculosis, syphilis or opium. (81:10)

自覺的革命都優於不自覺的演進。

Self-conscious revolution is always superior to undirected evolution. (86:2)

Notes:

1. A and B are nouns or nominalized expressions.

2. The SV is monosyllabic.

3. 得／不及   RE: (not) to be in time

A. 來得／不及   RV: (not) to be in/on time (to ...) (used both as an auxiliary verb and a main verb.)

時間太晚了，我們已經來不及了。
It's too late. We are already late.

他就要走，我們來不及送他了。
He's just about to leave. We won't be in time to say goodbye.

Notes:

1.

$$S + \begin{bmatrix} VP_1 \\ V + O_1 \end{bmatrix} + 還來不及 ，\begin{Bmatrix} 何況 \\ 更談不到 \\ 不用說 \\ 那能／有 \end{Bmatrix} + \begin{bmatrix} VP_2 \\ O_2 \end{bmatrix}$$

他囘家還來不及，何況去接你！

He doesn't even have time to go home let alone go pick
you up!

a.   The above construction is a variation of 沒有 ... 更談
不到 ... IB Structure 4.

b.   Note that in the first clause of the above pattern
$S + \begin{bmatrix} VP_1 \\ V+O_1 \end{bmatrix}$ functions as the subject while 還來不及
functions as the predicate.

2.

$$S_1 + 都／還 + 來不及 + V + \begin{Bmatrix} 何況 \\ 更談不到 \\ 不用說 \end{Bmatrix} + S_2$$

他都來不及去何況你！

He doesn't even have the time to go, so how could you!

a.   Note that in the above pattern when 來不及 is used
as an AV, the juxtaposition is between S_1 and S_2.

B.   等得／不及   RV: to be (un)able to wait (used only as a main
verb)

4. $S + \begin{Bmatrix} 寧可 \\ 寧可不 \end{Bmatrix} + A + \begin{Bmatrix} 也要 \\ 也不(要) \end{Bmatrix} + B$ PT: would prefer B even if it
means A (where A + B are
both VP)

$$\left.\begin{matrix} S + VP_1 \text{ (2nd preference)} \\ S + VP_2 \text{ (1st preference)} \end{matrix}\right\} \longrightarrow \boxed{S + 寧可 + VP_1 + 也要 + VP_2}$$

我可以受苦。
我 要 結 婚。 } ⟶ 我寧可受苦，也要結婚。

I want to marry even if it means that I may suffer for this.

$$\boxed{S + 寧可 + VP_1 + 也不(要) + VP_2}$$

我可以受苦。
我不要結婚。 } ⟶ 我寧可受苦，也不要結婚。

I don't want to marry even if it means that I may suffer for this.

$$\boxed{S + 寧可不 + VP_1 + 也要 + VP_2}$$

我可以不出國。
我 要 結 婚 。 } ⟶ 我寧可不出國也要結婚。

I want to marry even if it means that I may not go abroad.

$$\boxed{S + 寧可不 + VP_1 + 也不(要) + VP_2}$$

我可以不出國。
我不要結婚 。 } ⟶ 我寧可不出國也不要結婚。

I don't want to marry even if it means that I may not go abroad.

Notes:

1. The construction is used to emphasize a preference by stating the price one would be willing to pay to attain it.

2. The preference of the speaker is contained in the second clause.

5. 從... 入手   PT: to begin from/by ...

(1) 從 is a CV followed by an N or VP as its object.

(2) 入手 and its variants such as 着想 , 開始 function as main verbs here.

學中文應從發音入手。

In studying Chinese, one should begin with pronunciation.

有人主張普及教育應從編輯課本，增設學校入手。

Some people contend that spreading education should begin with the compilation of textbooks and such steps as the addition of schools.

E X E R C I S E S

I. Correlative Structures

A．...還/都來不及，那能/何況/更談不到/etc...

1．自從他生意失敗以來，他連謀生還來不及，那能談到捐錢給別人？

2．他連苟且偷生還來不及，更談不到衣錦還鄉了。

3．目前國內經濟情形混亂，物價直線上升想要穩定物價都來不及，那能進一步推行墾荒計劃？

B．寧可...也...

1．我寧可失掉這份職業，也不能忍受這種侮辱。

2．寧可脫離聯邦而陷於孤立，也要爲眞理奮鬥到底。

3．寧可破壞了兩國的邦交，也不能與外國訂立這種喪權辱國的條約。

4．他寧可辭職，甘心忍受卸任後的空虛生活，也要堅持他的主張，絕不屈服於任何壓力。

II. Miscellaneous

A．與生俱來；與年俱進；與日俱增

1．別人都說他那種貪吃懶做的劣根性是與生俱來的，可是我却認爲那是後天環境所造成的。

2．有病不治而聽其自然，換句話說就是找死。因爲處在科學知識與日俱增的時代，治病眞是易如反掌的事，有甚麼可顧慮的呢？

3．新省長就任後，原想大加改革，使全省的政治，經濟都能上軌道。但是由於他用人不當，結果不但沒有達到興利除弊的目的，官吏舞弊的情形，反而與日俱增了。

B．甚於，優於，etc. (A SV於 B)

1．這次地震所造成的災害甚於去年的暴風雨，估計損失達四百萬元之多，無家可歸的人有兩千左右。

2．軍閥爭奪地盤，兵匪擾亂百姓，這種禍亂甚於天災。政府倘不設法制止，遺禍之深眞是不堪想像。

3. 假如你想研究民國初年錢莊在舊式經濟制度上所起的作用，最好根據以往 (past) 的實際調查和統計數字，因為依據事實是遠勝於憑空想像的。

C. 從...入手

1. 大夫說治他的病必須先從改造環境謀求心理正常入手才對，否則是徒勞無功的。

2. 會議決定要編製一本名人錄。我私下裡想，以這種有限的預算，根本不可能。但是，命令總歸是命令，你說應從那兒入手？

3. 想劇除官吏濫用職權的弊病，必須從嚴格劃分職責入手。

D. 在於

1. 總統說：生活的目的在於促進人類共同的生活，生命的意義在於創造宇宙繼起的生命。

2. 實施耕者有其田的要旨在於使農村秩序穩定；同時顧到地主與農民雙方的利益以免發生無謂的 (pointless) 糾紛；以和平的方法達到繁榮農村經濟的目的。

3. 社會主義經濟的唯一目的在於滿足人民的物質和文化的需要。

E. 況且

1. 大家群起指責他措置失當，況且人證、物證俱在而連他自己也承認是他的過失。但是假如我們往深裡探究一下，他的確是代人受過的。

2. 這個計劃，限於人力財力，很難實行，況且其中有很多憑空懸想不切實際的地方。

3. 那位老先生身體衰弱，況且有肺病，如何能擔負起一家人的生活！

F. 嘗，未嘗不，何嘗 (不)

1. 為了逃避匪禍，他們不惜離鄉背井，流浪外地。但為了自身少受痛苦起見，暫時忍耐回鄉以期與骨肉團圓，也未嘗不是一個好辦法。

2. 阿里山的風景雖然人人說好，可是我却也未嘗去過，以後一定要想辦法去玩玩。

3. 這一次的和談完全是第三方面的壓力所致，其實他們雙方何嘗願意妥協呢？

4. 在從前帝王掌權的中國社會裡，政府常常採用愚民政策。如果我們能顧及當時的社會環境就能明白採取這種政策未嘗不是沒有理由的。

5. 我何嘗不想跟他和平相處，可是他老是對我敵視，我有甚麼辦法呢？

G. 上（...）軌道

1. 毛澤東的共黨政權到了現在還沒上經濟軌道，再過十年也未必上得了。原因是共產主義的經濟理論不太健全所致。

2. 擇善而從是上太平治事軌道的方法之一。

3. 有些不明瞭南美情形的人總覺得南美洲各國的元首競選的目的不是想把他們的國家帶上天下太平物富民安的軌道，而是為了一己之私（自己）。

H. 一點一滴的；一步一步的

1. 傳統思想的形成是由於千千萬萬的人，在生於斯死於斯的環境裡，一步一步的奮鬥，一點一滴的積累，經過無數的年頭才形成的。

2. 對於這件事我看還是一步一步的去做，不要輕舉妄動，免得自討沒趣。

3. 他的學識之所以能與年俱進，是他一步一步努力的結果。世界上沒有任何一件事是可以不勞而獲的。

III. Variations on Familiar Patterns

A. 如果...何必...

1. 如果你真的不喜歡他的為人，何必在他面前巴結他呢？

2. 如果貪官污吏不嚴厲懲治，我們何必大談政治維新呢？

3. 在今天的會議桌上有一個人站起來質問主席說：「如果事情不叫我們知道，那又何必叫我們來開會呢？」

B. ...不過...而／但...却...

1. 生活補助金（subsidy）不過是政府對於失業者暫時的保護措施，而他却想永遠依靠這種補助金來維持生活了。

2. 發牢騷不過是一種消極無能的表現，而他却以為這樣就可以解決問題，恐怕行不通吧。

I. Correlative Structures

   A.   ...都／還來不及，那能／何況／更談不到／

      1. There is no time to study ordinary weapons, to say
          nothing of nuclear ones.

      2. He is too busy currying favor with them. How would
          he dare offend them?

   B.   寧可 ... 也 ...

      1. The attitude most Ming loyalists took was that they
          would rather die in strange places than work for the
          Manchus.

      2. He would rather stick firmly to his prejudices than
          accept criticism from others.

      3. The political opinions of Japanese politicians have
          been completely revealed in that for the sake of
          the future they would rather offend certain nations
          with whom they presently have diplomatic relations
          than not trade with the Communists bloc.

      4. He would rather fabricate facts to hide his
          deficiencies than seek the advice of others.

II. Miscellaneous

   A.   與生俱來，與年俱進，與日俱增

      1. Knowledge grows with the years and is not achieved
          all at once.

      2. The old view was that stuttering (口吃) was an
          inborn defect, but now we know that this is not
          true, and that stuttering is due to psychological
          factors.

      3. Because the number of schools is daily increasing,
          soon it will be possible to accommodate all those
          who want to go to school.

   B.   甚／優於 /etc. (A SV 於 B)

      1. Such crimes as inciting the masses and disturbing
          the peace are worse than false registration with the
          police (虛報戶口). How can he be sentenced for
          just a couple of years?

2. The intellectual poison that comes from superstitious belief in the dogmas of the ancients is really worse than superstitious belief in spirits, because the latter (後者) is limited to the one area of religion while the former (前者) influences many areas.

3. Some people contend that in industrially underdeveloped nations, protective tariffs are better than free trade.

C. 從...入手

1. If one wants to enjoy a good reputation as a scholar, he must begin by studying his subject earnestly.

2. If you want to be an official, you must begin by studying law. Although this may sound laughable, I ask you if it isn't true.

3. The Catholic Pope plans to re-establish friendly relations with the Eastern Orthodox Church (東正教). Therefore he began by visiting the Holy Land as a first step towards his goal.

D. 在於

1. The aim of the First Five Year Plan is to develop heavy industry, a necessary first step toward the modernization of national defense.

2. The job of the Committee to Promote the National Language is to train teachers of the national language, to edit and publish newspapers and books with the notations in the standard pronunciation, and generally to promote education in the national language.

3. The greatest value of science lies in training people to be orderly and systematic in their thinking.

E. 況且

1. Under present conditions, their going on like this is a waste of effort. How much the more so when people don't appreciate what he is doing!

2. His income was originally very inadequate, and how much the more so now when he is in a situation where his living expenses are inevitably higher!

F. 上 ... 軌道

1. To get a society on the right track politically
    one has to start from education.

2. To get a backward people on the right track towards
    modernization is not a thing which can be
    accomplished in a short period of time.

3. They agreed that generally speaking when politics
    were in good shape the economy would also be in
    good shape.

G. 一點一滴的 ; 一步一步的

1. Most experience is accumulated step by step. It can
    rarely be found in books.

2. Do not belittle this little bit of strength. In
    time it can pierce an iron wall.

3. Beginning today I want to resolve to move very
    realistically step by step to improve my knowledge
    of history.

III. Variations on a Familiar Pattern

如果 ... 何必 ...

1. If he were not unhappy about what happened at the
    last meeting, why would he always mention it?

2. If there were no question about his character, why
    would he have to act like this?

3. If there weren't some trouble over the copyright on
    his book, why would he be fighting a legal battle
    with his publisher?

IV. Review Sentences

Use:

只有 ... 才 ...   只要 ... 就 ...   只是 ... 而已

沒有 ... 而能 ...   那有 ... 就可以 ...   至於

懸而未決   結果   未嘗

1. How can one call oneself a specialist after a few days'
    study? If one could become a specialist without special
    training, there would be specialists everywhere.

2. As a result all he did was to make himself a few more
    enemies. Whether or not his chief goal can be attained
    is still an unresolved question.

3. He has never believed in any religion or "ism." Why
    do you now accuse him of political crimes and keep
    him under surveillance?

4. (a) So long as one does not lose his self-confidence,
    does not waste energy or time, and is able to keep going
    forward, nothing can keep him from reaching his goal.

    (b) Only if one does not lose his self-confidence, does
    not waste energy or time, and is able to keep going
    forward step by step can he reach his goal.

5. He insists I did it deliberately, and has never been
    friendly to me. This is a great misunderstanding.
    How did I know he was connected with this? Otherwise
    I would never have undertaken it.

我們爲了不引起爭論起見，對於這種說法，至少在目前這個階段，無
需提及。

庸醫固然值得我們警惕，但是他們只對少數人有害，不致危害全國，
然而國家元首若是庸人則其爲害就無窮了。

到我衰老無用之時即是你們滅亡之日，這是何等重大的問題，而你們
還在這兒苟且偷生實在令人傷心。

The paragraphs below are the opening pages of a long, December 1939 treatise by Mao, which is divided into two main sections. The first deals with Chinese society in its ancient, feudal, and modern colonial or semi-colonial state. The second, "The Chinese Revolution," discusses the nature, objectives, and future of revolutionary movements of the past century.

Mao Tse-tung, <u>Selected Works of Mao Tse-tung</u> (Mao Tse-tung hsuan-chi), Peking, 1955, Vol. II, pp. 615-619.

<u>92:5</u> 相等			V:	to be equal
6 肥田	féi--	1	N:	fertile fields
沃地	wò--	2	N:	rich land
縱橫	dzūng--	3 S1	V/N:	to transverse; to cross both horizontally and vertically; length and breadth
森林	sēn--	4	N:	forest
貯藏	jǔ--		V:	to store, contain
7 豐富	fēng--	5	SV:	abundant, rich (93:10)
舟楫	jōují		N:	navigation (communication by water)
灌溉	(gwàngài)	(VII: 47,48)	V/N:	to irrigate; irrigation
8 生息			V:	to live and propagate
9 接壤	--ràng		V:	to border on, be contiguous with (92:10,12)
10 阿富汗	----hàn	(VII:25)	N:	Afghanistan
不丹	--dān	6	N:	Bhutan
尼泊爾	nípwoěr	7	N:	Nepal
緬甸	myǎndyàn	8,9	N:	Burma
11 菲律賓	fēi--bīn	10	N:	Philippines
給予	--yǔ	11 S2	V:	to provide

93:4	藏人	(dzàng--)(VII:NM8)		N:	Tibetans
	維吾爾	--wŭěr	12,7	N:	Uighur
	苗人		NM1	N:	Miao people
	彝人	yí--		N:	Yi people
	僮人	jwàng--		N:	Chuang (or T'ung) tribe (in SW China)
	仲家人	jùng----		N:	Chung-chia people
7	若干			N:	a certain amount: (also: numerous)
8	公社			N:	commune
	崩潰	--kwèi	13	V/N:	(to) collapse
	奴隸	núlì	14,15	N:	slave (94:11; 96:2)
9	開化			V/SV:	to civilize; civilized
	素稱	(VII:NM19)		V:	to have been long known for
94:1	將近			V/A:	to be approaching; nearly, almost
	可考			V:	to be verifiable
	以 ... 著稱		S3	PT:	to be known for ...
2	刻苦耐勞	----nài--	16	EX:	to be long-suffering and hard-working
	酷愛	kù--	17	V:	to love dearly
3	黑暗			SV/N:	black, dark; darkness (lit. and fig.)
4	起義			V/N:	to rise up in revolt; uprising (94:5)
	貴族			N:	nobility (95:3,5,6,7,8)
5	由於 ... 才能 ...		S4	PT:	only by/through/because of ...
	更換	(VII:NM3)		V/N:	(to) change
7	英雄	--syúng	18	N:	hero
10	悠久	yōu--	19	SV:	long (of history)
11	陷	syàn	20	V:	to fall into (as a pit, trap, calamity)

12	遲緩	--hwǎn	21	SV:	slow, retarded (of time, motion)
95:2	自給自足	(--jǐ----)		EX:	self-sufficient
3	享用			V:	to enjoy the use of (95:7)
	交換			V/N:	(to) exchange (95:4)
6	皇室	--shr̀	22	N:	royal court (95:7,8)
	將			CV:	把 (as pretransitive CV)
	收穫	--hwò	23	N:	harvest, crop
	一成		NM2	N:	one-tenth
7	奉獻	--syàn	24	V/N:	to offer up, present; contribution; donation
	農奴	--nú	14	N:	serf
8	靠...過活			PT:	to live on or by means of (i.e. to live off, to meet one's expenses from ...)
	強迫			V/N:	to compel; coercion (95:8,9)
	繳納	jyǎu--	25	V:	to pay (as taxes)
	貢稅	gùng--	26	N:	taxes
9	官吏	(--lì)	(VII:21)	N:	official
10	諸侯	--hóu	27	N:	feudal lord
11	割據稱雄	-----syúng	18	ex:	to set up oneself as a ruler over territory one has seized
12	保留			V/N:	to preserve, keep, retain; preserving of (as customs, etc.)
	至高無上			EX:	the highest, supreme (lit. the highest without anything higher)
96:1	官職			N:	official posts, offices
	刑	syíng	28	N:	punishment; (here) law, legal matters
	錢			N:	(here) finances
	穀	gǔ	29	N:	grain; (here) granaries

紳士   shēn--   30   N: the "gentry"; gentleman

3 束縛   shùfú   V/N: to restrain, control; to bind;
                                        restraint, restriction, bonds

隨意   V/A: to be casual; casually

4 殘酷   --kù   17   SV/N: cruel; cruelty

CHARACTERS TO BE LEARNED

1. 肥 féi   SV: fat, fertile, rich

   肥田   N: fertile field (92:6)

   肥料   N: fertilizer (105:12)

   賣國自肥   ex: to profit from being a traitor (153:4)

   肥肉   N: fat meat (塊)

   肥美   SV: fertile (land)

   肥大   SV: big (as clothing)

2. 沃 wò   BF: fertilize, enrich

   沃地   N: rich land (92:6)

   肥沃   SV: rich and fertile

3. 縱 dzūng   (1) BF: perpendicular, vertical

   縱橫 V/N: to transverse, to cross both perpendicularly
              and horizontally; length and breadth (92:6)

   縱／橫面   N: vertical/horizontal plane

   縱斷面   N: vertical section

   (dzùng) (2) BF: loosen, let go

   放縱   SV: impulsive, unconventional; indulgent

   (3) CJ: even though, although

   縱然／使／令…也…   PT: even if/though (see XI Structure 1)

4. 森 sēn   (1) BF: forest

        森林 N: forests (92:6)

      (2) BF: dignified

        森嚴 SV: stern faced (applied to organizations or people with fear-inspiring power and authority)

      (3) BF: dark, gloomy

        陰森 SV: dark, gloomy

5. 豐 fēng   BF: abundant, fruitful

        豐富 SV: plentiful or abundant (as of supplies, experience, etc.) (92:7)

           他的經驗很豐富。
           He has lots of (rich) experience.

        豐收 N: good harvest (次)

      豐功偉業 EX: numerous achievements and great accomplishments

        豐滿 SV: pleasingly plump (complimentary term applied to women)

        豐年 N: good year (i.e. abundant harvest)

      豐衣足食 EX: well off (lit. with ample clothes and food)

6. 丹 dān   (1) N: cinnabar, red

        丹紅 N: red color

      (2) Used in transliteration

        不丹 N: Bhutan (92:10)

7. 爾 ěr   (1) PN: you, your (literary) (92:10)

      (2) BF: so; --like; like that

        偶爾 A: accidentally; by chance; unexpectedly (lit. sudden-like)

      (3) Used in transliteration

        威爾遜 N: Wilson (遜 sywùn) (60:11)

尼泊爾   N: Nepal (尼 ní) (92:10)

8. 緬 myǎn   BF: Burma

9. 甸 dyàn   BF: Burma

緬甸   N: Burma (92:10; 98:10)

10. 賓 bīn   (1) BF: guest
（賓）

貴/外/來賓   N: honorable/foreign/guests

賓客   N: guest

相敬如賓   EX: (often applied to married couples who) respect each other as a host respects his guests (accolade for great mutual respect and politeness)

賓至如歸   EX: (a place or situation where) guests feel as comfortable as in their own homes

(2) Used in transliteration and in names of persons

菲律賓   N: Philippine Islands (菲 read fēi) (92:11)

11. 予 yǔ   V: to give, to grant (literary) (120:10; 121:5,12; 122:3)

予以   V: to give, provide with (49:11; 120:6; 122:1; 154:3)

如果你再犯校規，學校將予以開除。

If you persist in breaking the school rules, the school will expel you.

給予   V: to give or supply; to grant (here used as a CV but normally used as a regular verb taking direct and indirect objects.) (92:11)

12. 吾 wú   (1) PN: I, me, my (literary and newspaper style)

吾等 PN: we, us

吾人 PN: we, our

吾子/友   N: my son/friend

(2) Used in transliteration

維吾爾人   N: Uighur (93:4)

13. 潰 kwèi   BF: breach in the dykes

崩潰 V/N: (to) collapse (as of dynasties, governments)
(93:8; 171:5)

經濟／精神／軍事崩潰 V/N: economic/nervous/
military collapse

潰敗 V/N: to be defeated; defeat, collapse (as troops
in battle)

潰不成軍 EX: to be smashed (of an army)

擊潰 V: to smash or rout (the enemy)

潰散 V: to dissolve, disintegrate, disperse

潰爛 V: to burst (as an abcess, etc.), rot

14. 奴 nú   BF: slave (93:8)

農奴 N: agricultural slave; serf (95:7)

奴役 V/N: to enslave; enslavement, slavery (106:10)

奴才 N: (a willing) slave (also used as abusive term)

洋奴 N: "foreign slave" (used of people considered
too eagerly subservient to the West
politically, culturally, or economically)

亡國奴 N: citizen of a state that has been destroyed
or defeated

（被）奴化 V: to (be enslaved or) enslave; enslavement

奴化教育 N: "servile" education (i.e.
education designed to serve the
interests of a dictator,
foreign power or clique)

守財奴 N: miser

15. 隸 lì   (1) BF: belong to; attached to

奴隸 N: (an unwilling) slave (63:5; 74:10; 93:8)

隸籍 V: to be enrolled as a member; to be on the
books of (110:11)

(2) BF: style of characters intermediate between ancient seal and regular modern characters

隷書　N: the li style of characters

16. 耐 nài　　　　BF: patience, endurance; withstand (164:11)

耐勞 SV/V: able to endure or bear (as hardship, etc.) (94:2)

吃苦耐勞　EX: painstaking and hard working

耐人研究　ex: to bear investigating (164:11)

耐人尋味　ex: intensely interesting

耐用　SV: durable

能耐　N: ability

耐心　N: patience (in practical situations)

耐久　SV: long lasting; durable

(不)耐煩　SV: to be (im)patient with

耐性　N: patience (natural faculty)

耐得/不住　RV: (un)bearable, can(not) bear

忍耐 V/N: to be patient and long suffering; patience

17. 酷 kù　　　(1) BF: cruel, ruthless, tyrannical

殘酷 SV/N: cruel; cruelty (96:4)

冷酷 SV/N: coldly cruel; ruthless; heartlessness

(2) BF: very

酷愛　V: to be very fond of, devoted to (94:2)

酷熱　V: to be extremely hot

18. 雄 syúng　　　BF: male; virile, strong, brave

英雄　N: hero (94:7; 127:9; 161:11; 162:5)

稱雄　V: to consider oneself important or powerful; to be the ruling power of ... (95:11)

雄雞　N: cock, rooster

雄壯　SV: very handsome, strong, well-formed, grand
　　　　　　(of scenery, nature or song)

雄才大略　EX: great talent and excellent strategy

雄辯　N: vigorous debate or argument

事實勝於雄辯。
Facts always triumph (over pure argument).

雄心　N: great ambition

19. 悠 yōu　BF: distant, far-reaching

悠久　SV: long (of history, relationships, etc.)
　　　　　(94:10)

悠長　SV: long (in period of time) (140:4)

悠遠　SV: distant

悠閒　SV: easy-going; relaxed; leisurely

20. 陷 syàn　V: to fall in, sink into (94:11)

陷於/入　V: to fall into or under (as rule, heel, etc.)
　　　　　　(116:4; 127:8; 150:1)

攻陷　V: to attack and capture

陷害　V: to harm or betray another; to involve another
　　　　　in trouble

陷落　V: (to) fall, to have fallen (as into enemy
　　　　　hands)

21. 緩 hwǎn　BF: slow, tardy, delay; ease

遲緩　SV: slow, delayed, tardy (of time, motion, etc.;
　　　　　does not refer to mental development) (94:12)

從緩　V: to delay, proceed in a leisurely manner (154:1)

和緩　SV: moderate (as of steps or measures) (154:10)

緩和　V: to ease, alleviate, relax (of a situation)
　　　　　(172:1)

緩慢　SV: slow, easy-going, dilatory

緩衝 V/N: (to act as) buffer

緩衝國   N: buffer state

緩兵之計   N: strategy of delaying the enemy approach
while devising means to deal with the
situation

22. 室 shr̀   (1) BF: family

皇室   N: royal family (95:6)

家室   N: household, family

宗室   N: Imperial House; imperial clansmen; descendants
in male line from founder of the dynasty

(2) BF: rooms that have a special function

住室   N: living accommodations; rooms (173:8)

教室   N: classroom

會客室   N: reception room, etc.

23. 穫 hwò   BF: cut grain, reap

收穫   N: harvest (lit. and fig.) (95:6) (次)

24. 獻 syàn   BF: offer up, present

奉獻 V/N: to offer up, to present; contribution;
donation (as tribute) (95:7)

文獻   N: documents; collection of documents

供獻 V/N: (to) supply; to offer; offering

獻給   V: to give or present to

獻身   V: to devote or dedicate oneself to

獻技   V: to show off one's skill or ability

獻計   VO: to offer a strategy

25. 繳 jyǎu   V: to hand over or deliver to; to turn in

繳納   V: to pay (as taxes) (95:8)

繳稅　VO: to pay taxes

繳款／費　VO: to pay obligations (dues, etc.)

繳清　V: to pay up in full; to be paid in full

繳獲　V: to capture

繳還／回　V: to pay back

26. 貢 gùng　　　N: tribute; gifts (from a vassal)

貢獻 V/N: to contribute; contribution (8:5; 99:12; 146:9)

貢稅　N: taxes (95:8)

進貢 VO/N: (to pay) tribute

27. 侯 hóu　　　N: marquis (5:12)

諸侯　N: feudal lord (95:10)

28. 刑 syíng　　　N: punishment (96:1)

刑具　N: torture instruments (127:5)

酷刑　N: torture (171:1)

處死刑　VO: to sentence to death (171:3)

處極刑　VO: to sentence to death

刑罰　N: corporal punishment

徒刑　N: sentence (i.e. legal sentence)

五年徒刑　N: five-year sentence

無期徒刑　N: life imprisonment

緩刑 V/N: to reprieve; delay in carrying out of a legal sentence; deferred execution of a sentence

29. 穀 gǔ　　　BF: grain, cereal (96:1)

穀子　N: grain, millet

五穀　N: main food grains

30. 紳 shēn   BF: "gentry"

        紳士   N: member of the "gentry"; gentleman (96:1)

        劣紳   N: oppressive gentry (104:1)

        紳商   N: "gentry" and merchants

        鄉紳   N: "local gentry"

NEW MEANINGS

1. 苗   N: minority group in Southwest China

        苗人   N: Miao people (93:4)

2. 成   N: one-tenth part of (95:6)

        一／二／四成   N: 10/20/40%, etc.

                我的自行車雖然用了一年多可是看起來還九成新呢。

                Although I have used my bicycle for over a year, it looks ninety per cent new.

STRUCTURE NOTES

1.　縱然 ... 也...　　　　　PT: even if ...

S_1 + VP_1 (concession)) → { 縱(然)/etc. + S_1 } + VP_1 + S_2 + 也/亦 + VP_2
S_2 + VP_2 (statement)) → { S_1 + 縱(然)/etc. }

東西越來越便宜。) → 縱然東西越來越便宜，人們也不一定會買。
人們不一定會買。)

Even though things get increasingly cheaper, people will not
necessarily buy.

Notes:

　1.　縱使／令，即使，就是，etc. can be substituted for 縱(然).

　2.　縱然 ... 也 ... is a variation of the 就是 ... 也 ... pattern.

　3.　縱然 sometimes substitutes for 雖然 in the 雖然 ... 但是 ...
　　　（也／還／可是）... series.

　　雖／縱然目前中國工業生產已經較前增加，但是還不能稱為一個工業國家。
　　Although at present China's industrial production has already
　　increased in comparison with the past, she still cannot be
　　considered an industrial country.

2.　給予　　　V: to give, provide with

予 and 給予 are literary versions of 給 and like 給 must be followed
by an object.　They occur in the 給 ...以 pattern. (see V Structure 5)

3.　以...著稱　　　PT: to be known for ...

S + 以 + { VP / Clause } + 著稱

中國以礦產豐富著稱。　　　　　　（以 + S + V）
China is known for its rich mineral deposits.

中國人以吃苦耐勞著稱。　　　　　　（以 + V + O）
Chinese are known for their patient endurance of hardship.

<u>Notes:</u>

1. 以 functions here as a CV of reason (cf. V Structure 4 point 2) (lit. the Chinese because of patient endurance of hardship are known)

2. 著稱 is the main verb after 以 + VP/clause.

3. 聞名 /出名, etc., can be substituted for 著稱 .

4.   ... 是由於 ... 才 ... (的)   PT: only because of/by/through

   a.   ... 是由於 ... 才... 的 is an emphatic expression derived from S + 由於 + O + VP. (cf. III Structure 3 point 4, I Structure 11) to which two emphatic elements have been added.

     (1) ... 是 ... 的 is an emphatic expression.

     (2) 才 is an emphatic adverb.

$$S_1 + VP_1 \text{ (result)} \atop S_2 + VP_2 \text{ (cause)} \Bigr\} \longrightarrow \boxed{S_1 + 由於 + S_2 \text{ (+的)} + VP_2 + VP_1}$$

我的事業獲得成功。
朋友幫助。   } ⟶ 我的事業由於朋友(的)幫助獲得成功。

My project succeeded. } ⟶ My project succeeded because friends
Friends helped.   helped.

   b. The addition of the emphatic expression S + 是 + VP + 的 emphasizes the cause of success.

我的事業是由於朋友(的)幫助獲得成功的。

   c. The addition of the emphatic adverb 才 emphasizes an already emphatic pattern.

我的事業是由於朋友(的)幫助才獲得成功的。

My project succeeded only because friends helped.

      *   *   *   *   *

<u>Note for Review</u>

   1. Variations of 不但 :

     不但 ... 同時 ... (94:2)

不但 ⋯ 而且 ⋯ 又 ⋯ 並 ⋯ (95:2; 95:8)

2. 而 (cf. III Structure 1)

    a.   Contrastive use of 而 (94:6; 95:3)

    b.   Additive use of 而 (94:10)

    c.   ⋯ 而 ⋯ 則 ⋯ (95:5)

E X E R C I S E S

I.   Correlative Structures

A. 縱使／然／令 ... 也／亦／還etc...

1. 縱使一個人的壽命可以延長，能夠長生不老，也不可能學盡萬事萬物而成爲一個眞正的博學多才者。

2. 倘若關起門來計劃，那就是閉門造車。縱然計劃非常完善，也難免有許多不合事實的地方而不能付諸實施。

B. 縱然／縱使 ... 但是／可是／etc...

1. 縱然是肥田，但如不加以耕種，收穫就不會豐富。

2. 縱使他很出風頭，可是並不受人歡迎。

3. 縱然他已衰老，但是仍然心身健全，富有勇氣與信心。

II. Miscellaneous

A. 以 ... 著稱

1. 近東的國家以生產石油著稱，世界各地石油的供給多半都取給於此。

2. 這個以產米著稱的國家竟然發生糧荒的現象，那要不是因爲天災恐怕就是有甚麼人禍吧。

3. 雖然中國以歷史悠久，土地廣大，人口衆多著稱於世，但是倘若人民不刻苦耐勞，從事耕種開發，那麼縱使地廣人多，又有甚麼好處？

B. 給予

1. 每當你失望、痛苦的時候，孩子們總會給予你無窮的希望與歡樂。

2. 總統對災民備極關懷，並給予他們無限的鼓舞與安慰。

I. Correlative Stuctures

A. 縱使／縱然 ... 也／還 /etc.

    1. In a society where politics are not yet on the right track, even if you had great talent you probably would have no place to use it.

    2. No matter what the goal may be, so long as one has plans, methods, and patience, even though he may meet many difficulties, he won't be defeated.

    3. Even if the Marine Corps could land there for a sneak attack upon the enemy, the war would not necessarily be won.

B. 縱然／縱使 ... 但是／可是 /etc.

    1. Despite the fact that he is a robber, he is always very pleasant to the people he is about to rob.

    2. Although his theories are obsolete, many people still approve of his ideas.

    3. Granted that he makes things sound well when he talks, but when it comes to getting things done, he has no achievements to speak of.

II. Miscellaneous

A. 以 ... 著稱

    1. France is one of the advanced democratic countries of the world. Its people are famous for their passionate love of liberty.

    2. Chingtechen in Kiangsi is famous for producing porcelain. Most people who go there buy the well-known products of the region as souvenirs.

    3. Switzerland, famous throughout the world for manufacturing watches, is located between Germany and Italy. It is a neutral state which for the past hundred years has not been affected by war.

B. 給予

    1. China's Sinkiang province has abundant oil deposits which provide the people of the area with a source of wealth. Peking has a rich library to provide the people of the capital with the sources of knowledge.

2.   The more aid you give, the more criticism you reap.

III. Review Sentences

Use:

...之一	既然	甚至	不過...而已
與年俱增	加以	由於	給...以
在於	由於...所致	只消...即可	

1.   Tea is one of the daily necessities of the Uighur people.

2.   The crux of the problem lies in the fact that there is
     no way to make up the annually increasing deficit.
     Of course reducing the scale of the organization can
     improve the situation temporarily, but it is only a
     short-range step.

3.   The Chinese Communists claim that the fighting spirit
     and organizational strength of the Chinese working class
     was much stronger after going through the May Thirtieth
     Strike Movement.

4.   As I see it, since his fields are so fertile and his
     technique so good, it will be only a few years before
     he can enjoy an abundant harvest which will serve as a
     model for the people of the region.

5.   A famous Chinese writer once analyzed the distinction
     between 奴隸 and 奴才 . The former, because of their
     social origin or other limitations imposed by society,
     submitted to their masters only superficially but in
     their hearts they had not yielded. The latter were
     different. The 奴才 were willing to serve their masters
     for the sake of their own immediate petty advantage
     (小便宜) and even beat or cursed their fellow slaves.

6.   Since its founding, the state has consistently used this
     method to develop the civilian economy. Although it is
     not scientific, each year there is an abundant harvest
     and increased industrial production.

7.   The Nepalese government has already gotten on the right
     political track. At present the future depends entirely
     on what measures the government adopts.

8. This outbreak has occurred only because the Court and major officials never adopted the suggestions of the peasants and ordinary people.

9. That this task could be successfully concluded was due entirely to everyone's wholehearted support (奉獻).

10. 所謂「知足常樂」不過是一種不進取的藉口而已，但你却把它當做生活的原則，豈不可笑？

11. 巴黎歌劇院在一八六一年開工到一八七四年才建成。耗資千萬，一切設備均極講究，堪稱世界上最華麗的戲院之一。

Write Sentences Using:

1. ...也好...也好

2. 寧可...也...

3. 到...地步

4. 豈

5. 以致於

In this excerpt from his work <u>Soviet Russia in China</u>, Chiang outlines the national and international policies of his government in the postwar period. On the international front he calls for support for the United Nations, peaceful coexistence with Russia and details his policies towards individual Asiatic nations. On the domestic front, he calls for constitutional government, unity and economic development.

Chiang Kai-shek, <u>Soviet Russia in China</u> (Su-e tsai Chung-kuo) Taipei, 1957, pp. 133-137.

<u>97:2</u>	束縛	shùfú	1,2	V/N:	to control, restrain; to bind; restrictions, restraint; bonds
	北伐	--fā	3	N:	Northern Expedition (1927)
3	致力於		(VII:NM5)	VO:	to expend energy on, work hard at
	外患	--hwàn	4	N:	external calamities (98:6)
	內憂	--yōu	5	N:	internal misfortune, distress, catastrophe
	接踵而來	--jǔng----		EX:	to follow in rapid succession or heel upon heel
	終竟			A:	in the end, finally
4	支出			V/N:	to pay out; to cost; outgo, expense
	計		NM1	V/A:	to amount to; altogether, total
	法幣	--bì	6	N:	(term **for**) legal tender of the Sino-Japanese War period
5	結束	--shù	1	V/N:	to terminate; termination, conclusion (97:10,11; 99:8)
	渴望			V:	to long for
9	雖...。亦...			PT:	literary variation of 雖然 ... 也 ...
	權益			N:	rights and interests

	所		S1	A: review note on 所 as relative adverb
10	萬國			N: all nations of the world
	...者		S2	P: one who ... (88:2)
	私利			N: private or selfish interest
11	抱定	(bàu--)	(VII:18)	V: to hold firm
98:2	發起國			N: sponsoring state
	維護			V/N: to protect, guard; protection, maintenance
3	忠實	jūng--	7	SV: loyal, honest, sincere
4	報復		NM2	V: to take revenge on
	和約			N: peace treaty
5	強權			N: power (in the sense of a strong state)
8	韓國	hán--	8	N: Korea
9	泰國	tài--	9	N: Thailand
	正常			SV: normal
	友好			SV/N: friendly; friendship
10	恪守	kē-- (chywè)--		V: to observe faithfully
	信義			N: moral commitment
12	派遣	--chyǎn	10	V/N: (to) dispatch
	北緯	--wěi		N: northern latitude
	投降	tóu--	11	V/N: (to) surrender
99:1	一俟	--sz̀	12,S3	CJ: as soon as
3	忽視	(VII: NM6)		V/N: to overlook; (to) neglect
6	期間			N: period (of time) (100:4)
	制頒	--bān	13	V: to draw up and promulgate

7	外衞			N: supporters, satellite
	中止			V: to stop in the middle
8	訓政			N: tutelage government
9	私人			N: private individual
10	政見			N: political opinions
	常規			N: fixed procedure
	取決於			V: to be resolved in, by or at
	議場			N: "the conference table"
	政爭			N: abbrev. of 政治鬥爭
11	水準			N: standard (of living, achievement, etc.)
12	提供			V: to offer, to make available to
	福祉	--jr̆		N: happiness
100:1	申明	shēn--	14	V: to state clearly; to expound clearly
3	締造	dì--	15	V: build, create, construct
	永久			A: permanent, long-lasting
	四鄰親睦	-----mù		ex: to have friendly relations with neighbors on all sides (隣 is alternate form of 鄰)
	四境安定			ex: to have peace on all sides
	戰局			N: war situation
4	被難	--nàn		V: to be suffering, be hard-pressed
	同胞	--bāu	16	N: compatriot
	撫恤	--syù		V/N: to comfort and pension; pension (to war survivors, etc.)
	安輯閭閻	----lyúyán		EX: to bring peace to the people (lit. the villages)
	醫治			V/N: to cure, ameliorate; treatment (of disease)

5 犧牲   syīshēng   17,18   V/N: (to) sacrifice

  時際   N: time, moment

  開創   V/N: inaugurate; inauguration

7 只有...纔能...   PT: same as 只有 ... 才 ...
                                        (see IV Structure 8)

  臻   jēn   V: to reach, to arrive at

  充沛   --pèi   SV: abundant, full (literary)

8 期求   NM3   V: to seek, to long for

  祈嚮   chìsyàng   19,20   V: to hope fervently for (literary)

CHARACTERS TO BE LEARNED

1. 束 shù   (1) BF: bind, keep in order; restrain

       結束 V/N: to conclude; to bring to a close; conclusion
                (30:4; 97:5,10; 99:8)

       約束 V/N: to restrain; restraint (154:3)

       裝束   N: style of dress; attire

       管束 V/N: to restrain, (to) control; restraint

     束手無策 EX: to be helpless; to have no policy for dealing
                with a situation

    (2) M: bundle of (flowers)

    一束花 (兒)   N: a bundle of flowers

2. 縛 fú   V: to tie, to bind

       束縛 V/N: (lit. to bind with a strap or rope) to
                restrain or control, restrict; restriction,
                control, restraint (96:3; 97:2; 135:5, etc.)

不平等條約不僅束縛了中國經濟的發展也影
響了政治的措施。

The unequal treaties not only restricted
China's economic development but have also
influenced its political steps.

中國不進步的原因，一部分是受孔子思想的束縛。

Part of the reason for China's lack of progress is the hold of Confucianism.

3. 伐 fá
(fá)

(1) V: to attack or make war against (implies punishing an unworthy or inferior opponent)

北伐 N: The Northern Expedition (1926-1927) (97:2)

黨同伐異 EX: to make comrades of those who agree with you and to punish those who differ

討伐 V/N: (to send a) punitive expedition (against)

征伐 V/N: to make war; punitive expedition

侵伐 V/N: to invade; aggression

(fá) (2) V: to cut down

伐樹／木 VO: to fell trees

4. 患 hwàn

(1) BF: misfortune; calamity (118:10)

外患 N: foreign or external disaster; disaster from abroad (97:3; 98:6; 171:8, etc.)

邊患 N: border troubles (with nomads, etc.) (171:5)

禍患 N: disaster, calamity

患難之交 EX: friendship that endures adversity

水患 N: flood

後患 N: disastrous aftermath

後患無窮 EX: The shadows of disaster persist without end.

(2) BF: suffer from

患病 VO: to be sick

病患（者） N: the sick

5. 憂 yōu

BF: grief, melancholy; concerned over

內憂外患 EX: internal distress and external calamity (97:3; 171:8)

憂慮 V/N: (to) worry, anxiety

擔憂 SV/V: worry

憂國憂民　ex: to worry about the state and the people

後顧之憂　EX: fear for the rear (military figure used figuratively)

憂患　N: dire straits, calamity, disaster

6. 幣 bì　　BF: currency, coin

法幣　N: legal tender (of the Sino-Japanese War period) (97:4) (圓 : 元)

紙幣　N: paper money (116:3; 117:4,5) (圓 / 元)

錢/貨幣　N: currency

幣制　N: currency system

幣制改革　N: currency reform

造幣廠　N: mint (as Treasury)

7. 忠 jūng　　BF: loyal, faithful (168:11; 170:10,11; 171:2; 172:3,5, etc.)

效忠　V: to be loyal to (one's leader or country) (36:4)

忠實　SV: loyal or faithful (98:3; 114:3)

忠誠　SV: faithful and sincere

忠臣　N: loyal minister or official

忠心 SV/N: loyal to; faithful to; loyalty

忠心保國　EX: loyally to defend the country

盡忠　V: to be very loyal to

盡忠報國　EX: extremely loyal to one's country

忠勇　SV: loyal and brave (to country)

忠義 SV/N: loyal and upright; loyalty

忠良　N: faithful and excellent persons

8. 韓 hán　(1)　N: (one name for) Korea

韓國　N: Korea (this is the term for Korea used in Taiwan) (98:8)

(2) Surname

9. 泰 tài　(1) BF: liberal; prosperous; exalted

國泰民安　EX: the state is prosperous and the people at peace

舒泰　SV: healthy, comfortable

泰然　SV: calm and composed; dignified; with dignity

泰山　N: Taishan (famous Chinese mountain)

安泰　SV: peaceful, healthy (of life)

(2) Used in transliteration

泰國　N: Thailand (98:9)

10. 遣 chyǎn　BF: dispatch, depute or send

派遣 V/N: (to) dispatch (of troops) (98:12)

先遣 Adj: vanguard (174:10)

先遣部隊　N: advance guard

遣散 V/N: to disperse, discharge (from the army, office, etc.)

消遣 V/N: to pass or kill time; pastime

調遣 V/N: (to) transfer

遣使／兵　VO: to send an envoy/soldier

遣送 V/N: to send away

遣送回國　ex: to send someone back to his native country

差遣 V/N: to send, to be sent (差 chāi)

11. 投 tóu   (1) V: to throw in or at; to cast (as a vote); to present
                    or hand over to, to go in the direction of

            投資 VO/N: to invest; investment (of funds) (117:7)

            投入   V: to throw into (as troops into a battle,
                       materials into production, etc.) (149:4)

            投票 VO: to vote

            投案 V: to appear in court

        (2) BF: surrender; submit to; join

            投降 V/N: (to) surrender (98:12; 174:9)

            投機 V/SV: to take advantage of an opportunity; to
                       speculate; opportunistic (117:7)

                投機份子   N: opportunist

            投誠 V: to return to allegiance to (i.e. give up
                     rebellion or resistance) (122:3)

            投軍 V: to enlist in or join the army (172:8)

            投敵 V: to go over to the enemy, defect (172:10)

            投考 V: to report or appear for an examination

12. 俟 sź   BF: wait

            一俟 CJ: as soon as (99:1)

        俟下月／明年 CV: wait until next month/year

            俟候 V: to wait

            俟命 VO: to wait for orders or instructions

            俟時 VO: to wait till; to wait for an opportunity

        俟機而行／動 EX: to await an opportunity to take action

13. 頒 bān   (1) BF: promulgate, make known, proclaim

            制頒 V: to draw up and promulgate (99:6)

            頒佈 V/N: to promulgate, proclaim; promulgation

頒發 V/N: to issue orders; promulgation

頒行 V/N: to promulgate and carry out; promulgation

頒定   V: to issue orders; to promulgate

大頒   V: to proclaim on a great scale

(2) BF: striped or variegated

頒白   V: to be gray-haired

他的頭髮已經頒白。
His hair is gray.

14. 申 shēn   (1) BF: state, report, extend

申明 V/N: to announce, make known; announcement (100:1)

申報 V/N: (to) report (to a superior)

申請 V/N: to petition; to apply; application

申請書   N: petition, application

申訴 V/N: (to) appeal, (to) petition

申述 V/N: to state, narrate; statement

(2) Surname

15. 締 dì   BF: connection; closely joined

締造 V/N: build, establish, construct; establishment, construction (as peace) (100:3)

取締 V/N: to suppress, repress, (to) control; restraint (151:2)

締結   V: to conclude (as a treaty)

締結條約   VO: to conclude a treaty

16. 胞 bāu (pāu)   BF: womb, breathren

同胞   N: fellow countrymen, compatriot (100:4; 157:5)

胞兄/弟   N: brothers by the same mother

細胞   N: cell (biol.)

17. 犧 syī   BF: sacrifice; victims for sacrifice

18. 牲 shēng   BF: animals; sacrificial animals

     犧牲 V/N: (to) sacrifice (100:5; 115:5; 157:2; 175:1)

       犧牲精神 N: spirit of self-sacrifice

     牲口   N: farm animals (頭)

19. 祈 chí   BF: pray; request (100:8; 112:6,7)

     祈求 V/N: to beg or implore; pray

     祈望 V/N: to hope, to expect that; expectation, hope

20. 嚮 syàng   BF: incline towards; facing

     祈嚮 V: to hope for (literary) (100:8)

     嚮導 N: guide (also name of famous early Communist magazine) (101:4)

     嚮往 V: to incline to; to desire

NEW MEANINGS

1. 計   V/A: to amount to; total, altogether (often used instead of 一共 in summarizing large numbers) (97:4)

    總/共計 V/N: (to come to a) total of

    計...人 PT: number of persons ... estimated at ...

2. 報   BF: revenge

    報復 V/N: (to take) revenge (98:4)

    報仇 VO: to take revenge

       君子報仇十年不晚。
       Ten years late is not too late for a gentleman to take his revenge.

       立志報仇殺盡敵人。
       He vowed to take revenge and wipe out the enemy.

    報答 V/N: to repay (as kindness)

3. 期　　　V: hope, anticipate (literary) (100:8; 113:11)

　　期求　V: to seek (in sense of) to long for (100:8)

　　期望 V/N: to hope, anticipate; anticipation, expectation

　　以期　ex: in the hope that ... (see II Structure 4)

STRUCTURE NOTES

1. 所

   A. When 所 is not used in a noun it functions as an adverb preceding a transitive verb.

   B. However, in translation 所...的 or 所 can usually be equated to "that which ... ," "him who ... ," or "what ... ."

   > 人民所渴望的是復員，國家所需要的是建設。
   > What the people thirst for is recovery, and what the State needs is building up. (97:5)

   所 in this use is a residue of literary Chinese. It is a structure or function word with no referential meaning. Thus in colloquial Chinese this 所 may be omitted in the example above. Less frequently the 的 in 所...的 may be omitted.

   > 五十年國民所期求(的)，八年抗戰所祈嚮(的)就在這最大最後的成功。
   > What the people hoped for for fifty years, and what the eight years of the War of Resistance prayed for was this biggest and final success. (100:8)

   C. 所 frequently co-occurs with coverbs of agent 為，由 . (see VI Structure 10)

2. 者   P: (nominalizer equal to) he/those who ... ; that which ...

   A. 者 nominalizes certain verbs

       革命者   N: revolutionist

       作 者   N: author

       記 者   N: reporter

   B. 者 nominalizes VP's or clauses

   a. CV + O + V + 者

       為和平 (而) 鬥爭者   Those who struggle for peace

   b. $V + \begin{cases} S + VP \\ V + O \end{cases} + 者$

贊成 { 學生自由參加 / 舉行大選 } 者

Those who approve free participation by students
Those who approve holding elections

爲萬國互助者當然成功；爲個人或一民族之私利者自當消滅於無形。

Those who work for international cooperation will of
course succeed. Those who work for the private gain of
one individual or race naturally will disappear without
a trace. (97:10,11)

C.   的(人) is a colloquial form of 者 which usually occurs following
a verb phrase or clause.

Note:

1.   爲, which usually functions as a CV, is here used as a full
verb in the sense of "to work for," "to be in favor of." (wéi)

3.   一俟 ... (後/以後 /etc.) ... 即/ 就 /etc. ...   PT: as soon as ...

$$S_1 + VP_1 \atop S_2 + VP_2 \Big\} \longrightarrow \left[\begin{matrix} 一俟 + S_1 + VP_1 + (後) + S_2 \\ S_2 + 一俟 + S_1 + VP_1 + (後) \end{matrix} \right\} + 即 + VP_2 \right]$$

行政院核定。
電力減價可實施。 }→{ 一俟行政院核定後電力減價案即可實施。
電力減價案，一俟行政院核定後，即可實施。}

As soon as the Executive Yuan approves, the bill for the reduction in electricity rates can become effective.

Note:

1. Compare with:

$$S_1 + VP_1 \atop S_2 + VP_2 \Big\} \longrightarrow \left[S_1 + 一 (經) + VP_1 + S_2 + \Big\{ {就 \atop 即} \Big\} + VP_2 \right]$$

a.   行政院一批准，電力減價案即可實施。

b.   我遠征軍在緬甸戰場的任務一經完成立即撤囘本國。
As soon as the mission of our expeditionary force in
Burma was finished, it immediately returned home.
(98:11)

If $S_1 = S_2$, S_2 may be omitted.

✳   ✳   ✳   ✳   ✳

Note for Review

1. 爲

    a. CV of purpose 爲 ... 而 ... (97:2,9; 98:4; 100:4)

    b. CV of agent (99:7)

    c. as a full verb

        (1) = to 作 (特爲敍述) (98:2; 99:5)

        (2) = 是 (100:6)

2. 只要 ... 必 ... (97:6) (cf. I A Structure 2)

3. 雖 ... 亦 ... (97:9)

E X E R C I S E S

I. Correlative Structures

A. 一俟...就/立即/etc.

1. 一俟各項籌備工作妥當我們的公司就可以正式成立了。

2. 我們現在暫時不能採取行動，一俟各方面都預備好了，他們會立即通知我們大家同時進行。

3. 一俟擴大編制的方案通過之後，我立即給你想辦法安排一個職位，你回去等消息吧。

II. Review Sentences

1. 作為一個軍人必須抱定為國犧牲的精神才可以衛國守土，而不致於臨陣投敵了。

2. 根據學校當局所頒佈的有關申請津貼的新辦法，津貼的給予與否主要的是取決於學業成績及所研究科目對社會的重要性如何。

3. 永樂大典是中國的著名叢書之一，包括經史子集等兩萬多卷，但因為歷次戰爭中，屢經散失，其中有很多為英德日各國所奪取。

4. 許多偉大的作家運用文字和他們的想像，寫出不朽的創作，這些創作乃是有關人類生活最真實最生動的記載。

5. 當學潮發生之際，政府既未設法阻止於前，又無力鎮壓於後，以致於學潮愈來愈擴大，終至全國各地罷課遊行的事情層出不窮。

6. 即使在科學發達的今日，仍然有些人在各種舊觀念，舊思想和舊傳統束縛下，信古人的教條和「專家」的學說，而不敢有所作為。

7. 解放奴隸的戰爭持續了兩年之久，結果南軍為北軍所敗。

I. <u>Correlative Structures</u>

A. 一俟 ... 就/即/etc.

 1. He has already been granted entrance to an American university and so as soon as he graduates, he can go.

 2. The new company law has many improvements, and as soon as it passes the Legislative Yuan it can be promulgated and go into effect.

II. <u>Review Sentences</u>

<u>Use</u>:

只有 ... 才	爲 ... 所	依 ... 而進行	基於 ... 而來
當 ... 之際	... 之一	由於 ... 所致	在 ... 之下
是由於 ... 而來的	尤其是	爲 ... 而 ...	告失敗
加強	只要 ... 就 ...	跟 ... 而 ...	

1. The regulations of this alumni association (校友會) are very simple. As long as you pay your dues on time, you can enjoy the privileges of membership.

2. The use of particles as punctuation is a characteristic of the Chinese classical language.

3. The reason the guerilla uprising this time failed was that there was a difference of opinion among the leaders. Furthermore the fact they were under the leadership of an inexperienced general was also a cause of defeat.

4. That one can succeed only with hard work is a statement born of real experience.

5. Although the selection and application of a particular military strategy depends on the particular situation, military factors are sometimes not the only basis for decision.

6. In general such methods are used to strengthen the patriotic feeling between compatriots.

7. That politics have been in great confusion in China in the past century is rooted in its long series of internal catastrophes and external calamities.

8. If you will only examine it carefully once more, you can reduce the errors.

9. At first they allied themselves with those with whom they agreed in order to attack those who opposed them. Thus they gradually cleaned up their own ranks and so were able to go on a step further to achieve the goals of the Northern Expedition.

10. In an attempt to balance national income and expenditure, they revised the budget and raised taxes.

11. Mongolians and Tibetans are very similar in their habits of eating and living and so forth. This comes largely from the fact that they believe in similar religions.

12. Those two brothers fought over the inheritance and then took the matter to court. The judge's decision was that two-thirds of the inheritance should go to the older brother.

13. While some monarchists were opposing reform, K'ang Yu-wei and Liang Ch'i-ch'ao proposed constitutional reform to the Ch'ing court.

14. With the encouragement of the government, the peasants told of the evil crimes of the landlords in exploiting the peasants year after year. They demanded that the government mete out serious punishment to the landlords.

15. Only by eliminating speculators, increasing cash reserves and stabilizing the currency can the present economic crisis be mitigated.

Write Sentences Using:

1. 凡 . . .

2. 一日 . . . 一日

3. 就 . . . 來說

4. 即是 . . . 亦 . . .

5. 重

6. 告一段落

7. 甚至於 . . . （也／都） . . .

8. 以致於

9. 豈

10. 固然 . . . 但是 . . .

This March 1926 article analyzing the various classes in Chinese
society in terms of their economic base and their revolutionary role
remained the fundamental Communist statement on the problem until
it was superseded in August 1950 by the Central Committee's "Decisions
on the Differentiation of Class Status".

Mao Tse-tung, Selected Works of Mao Tse-tung (Mao Tse-tung hsuan-chi),
Peking, 1953, Vol. 1, pp. 3-11.

101:3	首要		N:	prime importance
4	成效			成績和效果
	未有A而不...	S1	PT:	never a case where ...
9	買辦		N:	compradore (101:11; 103:11; 108:2)
10	附庸	NM1	N:	appendage, dependency
11	不相容		V:	to be incompatible with; not to have interests or considerations that coincide
12	右派		N:	right wing (104:9,10) (左派 102:7; 104:10; 中派 104:9)
102:1	中產階級		N:	middle class (102:4; 102:12; 103:6,8; 108:4)
	矛盾	máudwùn 1,2	SV/N:	contradictory; contradiction (102:6)
2	打擊		V/N:	(to) attack, strike
3	勇猛	--měng 3	SV:	resolute, fearless
	欲	yù 4	V:	to wish, desire
4	威脅	--syé 5	V/N:	to threaten; threat
5	戴季陶	dài--táu 6	N:	Tai Chi-t'ao
	信徒	NM2	N:	believer, disciple
	晨報	chén-- 7	N:	Morning Post
6	惶遽	hwángjyù	SV:	scared, fearful

	狀態			N: mien, bearing, state
8	行得／不通			RV: to be (im)possible to carry out; (not) to be viable
9	豎起	shù--	8	RV: to raise or erect (like a pole)
	第三國際			N: Third International
10	旗幟	--jr̄	9	N: banner, flag
	分化			V/N: (to) split
12	餘地			N: room to manoeuvre in (fig.)
103:2	學生界		NM3	N: student circles (see 知識界 108:3)
	教員		NM4	N: teacher
	小員司			N: clerk
	事務員		NM4	N: clerk
3	律師	--shr̄	10	N: lawyer
4	經營			V: to manage (as a business) (105:4)
5	腦力			N: mental exertion
6	趙公元帥	jàu---- shwài	11,12	N: God of Wealth (often just Duke Chao) (103:10)
	勤	chín	13	SV: diligent, careful, meticulous
7	小財東			N: petty capitalist
	垂	chwéi		V: to drool
	涎水	syán--		N: saliva
9	右翼	--yì	14	N: right-wing (108:4) (左翼 104:8; 108:4)
12	加倍			V/A: to double; greatly increased
104:1	司令			N: commander
	土豪劣紳	--hàu----	15	EX: local rascals and oppressive gentry
2	爲富不仁	-----rén	16	EX: rich and unmerciful

2	來頭			N: backing (i.e. support, background)
3	貿然	màu--		A: recklessly, rashly
	中立			V: to be neutral, neutralize
		中立派 N: neutralists		
4	殷實		NM5	SV: well off, well-to-do
5	結賬	--jàng	17	VO: to do or draw up accounts, pay up or settle accounts
	每逢…一次 就…一次		S2	PT: whenever ...
	咳	hài		IE: exclamation of dismay
	虧		(VII:NM15)	V: to be short or in debt (of money)
6	負債	---jài	18	VO: to incur debts
	漸次			A: time after time, progressively
	凄涼	chī--	19	SV: desolate, dreary
	瞻念	jān--	20	V: to be concerned about
	不寒而慄	--hán--lì		EX: (lit. to tremble for reasons other than cold); afraid or frightened without cause; trembling with fear
8	平時			N/MA: ordinary times; ordinarily
9	高漲	--jǎng	21	V: to rise (as water)
	曙光	shǔ--		N: dawn, hope, prospect
10	裹挾	gwǒsyé	22,23	V: to envelop, encompass, embrace
	附合			V: to go along with, submit to
11	五卅運動	--sà----		N: May Thirtieth Movement
	斷定		NM6	V/N: to determine or settle; judgment, conclusion
12	貧農			N: poor peasant (105:1,2,3,6,8,11; 106:4, etc.)
105:1	店員		NM4	N: shop clerk

小販	--fàn	24	N: small peddler (106:6)
3 細別			N: fine distinctions
4 小商			N: small merchant or business
5 以資		NM7,S3	PT: in order to ...
彌補	mí--		V: to supplement; to make up the deficit
青黃不接			EX: period of hardship between seasons (lit. interval between the consumption of last year's crop and the new harvest)
高利		(VII:NM18)	N: high interest (rate)
借債	--jài	18	VO: to borrow
糴糧	dí--		V: to buy grain
較（之）		S4	CV: to compare (it with ...)
無求於人		S5	ex: to ask nothing of anyone
6 景遇			N: situation, circumstances
7 不及			V: to be inferior to; to be less than; not to come up to; (literary equivalent of 不如) (105:11; 107:4)
8 佃農	dyàn--	25	N: tenant farmer
充足			SV: sufficient, ample (105:12)
9 資金			N: capital (105:12; 107:6)
雜糧			N: various food grains
撈	lāu		V: to trap or catch (as fish)
蝦	syā	26	N: shrimp
飼	sż	27	V: to rear (as animals)
10 豕	shř		N: pig, hog
艱難竭蹶	------jywé		EX: in difficulty; in a difficult situation

	聊以卒歲	lyáu-- dzu--	28,29,S6	EX:	merely to live out this year
11	…較…爲優		S4	PT:	to be superior to
12	歉收	chyàn--	30	V:	to have a bad harvest
	幾			N:	(here) a lot
106:1	乞哀告憐	chĭai----	31,32	EX:	to beg for sympathy
	斗	dǒu	33	N/M:	peck
	升	shēng	NM8	N/M:	pint
	敷衍	fūyǎn	34,35	V:	temporize; to deal with a matter superficially or to delay in dealing with
	債務	jāi--	18	N:	debt
	負重				(here) verb + object
3	係		NM9	V:	to be (= 是)
	被迫			V:	to be forced to
4	負擔			N:	burden
	相稱	--chèn	NM10	V/SV:	to be in balance; balanced
	恐慌			SV/N:	(in) panic
	大致			A:	in general
	商店			N:	store
5	雇員		NM4	N:	employee
	薪資	syīn--	36	N:	salary
	物價			N:	commodity prices
	薪給	syīnjǐ	36	N:	salary
	此輩	--bèi	37	N:	this group (of people)
	叫苦不迭	------dyé		ex:	to recite one's troubles without stopping; to cry out in anguish
6	不相上下			EX:	to be no different from

	肩挑	jyāntyāu	38,39	V: to carry on the shoulder (using a pole with the burden hung at both ends)
	叫賣			V: to call one's wares
	街畔	--pàn		N: roadside
	攤售	tānshòu	40,41	V: to display and sell in a stall
7	吃着	--(jwó)	NM11	N: food and clothes
9	紡織	fǎng--	42	V/N: to weave; weaving; textiles
11	開灤	--lwán		N: K'ailuan (name of a mining company in North China)
	焦作	jyāu--		N: Chiao Tso (mining company)
107:3	碼頭	mǎ--	43	N: wharf
	搬運夫		NM12	N: transport coolie or porter
4	清道夫		NM13,NM12	N: street sweeper
	糞夫	fèn--	NM12	N: night-soil collector
	別無長物			EX: without other resource or assets
	相似			SV: to be alike
5	指…而言		S7	PT: to refer to, have reference to
	長工			N: long-term worker
	月工			N: worker hired by the month
6	零工			N: temporary worker
	營工度日		NM14	ex: to sell their labor to make a living
10	閩	mǐn	44	N: Fukien (Chinese provinces and certain cities are often referred to by the one-character terms listed here and below)
	粵	ywè	45	N: Kwangtung
	三合會			N: Triad Society

湘	syāng	46	N: Hunan
鄂	è	47	N: Hupeh
黔	chyán	48	N: Kweichow
蜀	shǔ	49	N: Szechwan
哥老會			N: Elder Brother Society
皖	wǎn	50	N: Anhwei
豫	yù	51	N: Honan
魯	lǔ	52	N: Shantung

	11	大刀會			N: Big Knife Society
		直隸			N: Chihli (now known as 河北省)
		東三省			N: Three Eastern Provinces (Manchuria)
		在理會			N: name of a secret society
		青幫		NM15	N: the "Green Gang" (secret society)
	12	批		NM16	M: group, batch
		引導			V: to lead
108:1		得法		S8	V: to be skillful or successful
	2	勾結	gōu--	53	V: to connive with; to plot together with
	5	時常			A: often
		陣綫		NM17	N: battle line

CHARACTERS TO BE LEARNED

1. 矛 máu   N: lance or spear   Rad. 110

2. 盾 dwùn   N: shield

　　　　　　矛盾 SV/N: contradictory; contradiction (102:1; 127:6,8, etc.)

　　　　　　　　自相矛盾 EX: self-contradictory

盾牌　N: shield (153:4)

後盾　N: support, backing (for movement, party, political figure)

銀盾　N: silver trophy

3. 猛 měng　　SV: fierce, ferocious; violent

勇猛　SV: courageous, daring, brave (102:3)

猛獸　N: ferocious beast

兇猛　SV: fierce

猛攻　V/N: to attack fiercely; fierce attack

4. 欲 yù　　V: to desire, long for, wish (102:3)

爲所欲爲　EX: to do as one pleases with no regard for others (112:3)

私欲　N: selfish desires or aims

欲望　N: aspirations; desires; expectation; wishes

欲速不達　EX: too much haste won't achieve one's goal

隨心所欲　EX: to follow one's own desires

5. 脅 syé
（脅）
　　(1) BF: take by force; coerce

威脅　V/N: to threaten, menace; threat, menace (102:4; 144:1)

脅迫　V: to coerce, to force

脅從　V: to have been coerced into following or taking part (in something evil)

(2) BF: ribs

脅下　N: region under the armpits

兩脅　N: sides of the chest under the armpits

6. 戴 dài　　(1) Surname (102:5)

(2) BF: uphold, honor

感戴　V: to support out of gratitude; to be grateful to and to honor

推戴 V/N: to commend and uphold; support

愛戴 V/N: (to) love and honor

擁戴　V: to support and honor

(3)　V: to wear, to put on

戴手套／錶 VO: to wear gloves/watch (also of things put on the body as spectacles, etc.)

戴方帽子 VO: to graduate from college; to have an advanced degree (lit. to wear a square hat)

戴高帽子 VO: to flatter (lit. to put on a top hat)

張冠李戴 EX: discrepancy between name and reality (lit. Li wears Chang's hat)

不共戴天 EX: to swear not to live together under the same sky with (specifically refers to murderer of the speaker's father)

7. 晨 chén　　　BF: morning, dawn

晨報　N: The Morning Post (Peking newspaper of the 1920's) (102:5)

早晨　N: (early) morning

晨光　N: daybreak; daylight

晨星　N: morning star (顆)

8. 豎 shù　(1)　V: to erect

豎起來　RV: to raise up (like a flag); to place something upright which has been lying flat (102:9)

豎立　V: to raise or establish

毛髮豎立　EX: with hair standing on end

(2) BF: lengthwise, vertical

豎着寫／排印　ex: to write/print in vertical columns

橫豎　A: in any case; under all circumstances

(3) N: vertical stroke (in writing Chinese characters)

9. 幟 jr̆   BF: pennant, flag

旗幟 N: banner (102:10,11; 150:6)

標幟 N: mark, label or sign

10. 師 shr̄   (1) BF: teacher, instructor

經師 N: classics teacher (6:6)

教師 N: teacher (28:6)

律師 N: lawyer (103:3; 111:6)

老師 N: teacher (colloq.) (135:2)

傳教師 N: missionary (142:6)

醫師 N: medical doctor

祖師 N: patron saint; founder of a sect

師父 N: teacher; master (of apprentices)

師範學校 N: normal school

師母 N: wife of one's teacher

(2) N: division in the Chinese army; troops

會師 V/N: to meet; meeting (of friendly army)(172:3)

師長 N: division commander

出師 VO: to send out troops to

水師 N: navy

11. 趙 jàu   N: Surname (103:6,10)

12. 帥 shwài   BF: leader, commander

元帥 N: generalissimo, marshall (of an army) (103:6,10)

統帥 V/N: to command (of troops); to be the leader of
        a country; commander-in-chief

13. 勤 chín   SV: diligent; industrious (103:6)

勤勞 SV: diligent in labor

勤學/習 V/SV: (to be) diligent in study

勤苦 SV: diligent and long-suffering

勤務 N: duty (limited to military circles)

勤務兵 N: an orderly

出勤 V: to go on duty (military)

勤政愛民 EX: to be diligent in government service and take proper care of the common people

後勤 N: logistics

後勤司令部 N: Quartermaster Headquarters

14. 翼 yì N: wings of a bird; flanks of an army; "wing" of a party

右／左翼 N: right or left wing (103:9; 104:8; 108:4)

小心翼翼 EX: very careful and reverent

兩翼 N: both right and left flanks

15. 豪 hau BF: martial, grand, heroic; gay

土豪 N: village bully; big landowners (derogatory) (104:1)

土豪劣紳 EX: local rascals and oppressive gentry (104:1)

豪門資本 N: capital of people who are extremely wealthy and politically powerful (110:10; 111:5)

富豪 N: the rich (171:6)

豪紳 N: wealthy gentry (172:10)

豪富 N: wealthy person

豪放 SV: straight-forward, open (of attitude), big-hearted; unrestrained

豪華 SV: luxurious, gay, extravagant

自豪 SV: proud of oneself, conceited

16. 仁 rén   N: virtue, benevolence; quality of humanity (104:2)

　　　　　　　仁政　　N: benevolent acts of government (163:12)

　　　　　　　仁義　　N: benevolence and righteousness (173:9)

　　　　　　　仁愛　　N: benevolence and love

　　　　　　　成仁　　V: to die in pursuit of the right, to die
　　　　　　　　　　　　for a cause/country

　　　　　　　　　壯烈成仁　EX: to die a martyr's death

　　　　　　　仁厚　　SV: benevolent and generous

　　　　　大仁大勇　　EX: great benevolence and braveness

17. 賬 jàng   N: account, bill
　　(帳)

　　　　　　　結賬　　VO: to draw up accounts (104:5)

　　　　　　　賬册　　N: account books (121:4) (also 賬本子)

　　　　　　　賬單　　N: bill

　　　　　記/寫賬　　VO: to enter on the account

　　　　　　　算賬　　VO: to do the accounts (both lit. and fig.)

　　　　　　　付賬　　VO: to settle an account

　　　　　　　賬房　　N: accounting office; counting-house, treasurer

18. 債 jài   N: debt

　　　　　　　負債　　VO: to incur a debt (104:6)

　　　　　　　借債　　VO: to borrow money (105:5)

　　　　　　　債務　　N: debt (106:1)

　　　　　　　　　債務人　N: debtor

　　　　　　　償債　　VO: to repay debts (116:9)

　　　　　　　公債　　N: government bonds

　　　　　　　債主　　N: creditor

　　　　　　　國債　　N: national debt

血債　N: blood debt

要／討債　VO: to seek repayment of a debt

債權人　N: creditor

19. 淒 chī　　BF: intense cold

淒涼　SV: desolate (of mood, atmosphere) (104:6; 128:4)

20. 瞻 jān　　BF: look up to

瞻念　V: to be concerned over or about (104:6)

瞻仰　V/N: to look up to with reverence

瞻望　V/N: (fig.) to look ahead (as to the future)

21. 漲 jǎng　　V: to rise (as water); to expand, to rise in price

高漲　V: to rise (high) (104:9)

漲水　v̇: to be in flood

漲潮 VO/N: to rise (of tide), rising tide

漲價　V: to increase in price

暴漲 V/N: to rise suddenly (as water, prices, etc.)

22. 裹 gwǒ　　V: to bind, wrap around (104:10)

包裹　N: parcel (件)

裹脚／足 VO/N: to bind feet (脚 jyǎu N: foot)

裹脚布　N: cloth used to bind feet

裹足不前　EX: to be blocked from forward progress as though your feet were bound

裹上／起來　RV: to wrap up

23. 挾 syé　　(1)　V: to clasp under the arm (104:10; 156:11)

他把書挾在脅下。
He carried his books up under his arms.

(syá)　　挾帶　V: to carry under the arm

挾有   V: to have or cherish (as resentment)

(2) BF: coerce

挾制   V: to intimidate; to oppress

要挾 V/N: (to) demand, extort (要 yāu)

24. 販 fàn   BF: peddle, sell

小販   N: small peddler (105:1; 106:6; 133:3)

販賣   V: to sell, deal or trade in

販子   N: trader

販運   V: to sell and ship (as opium)

25. 佃 dyàn   BF: tenant, rent

佃農   N: tenant farmer (105:8; 129:7,11)

佃戶   N: tenant household (129:6)

26. 蝦 syā   N: shrimp (105:9)

蝦仁   N: (shelled) shrimp

龍蝦   N: lobsters

蝦球   N: shrimp balls

蝦米   N: tiny shrimp (usually dried)

27. 飼 sż   BF: feed (animals) (105:9)

飼養   V: to feed and raise (animals)

飼養業   N: fodder industry

飼料   N: fodder

28. 聊 lyáu   (1) BF: just to; merely, to some degree (105:10)

聊以   ex: merely to

聊以自慰   ex: merely to console oneself

(2) V: to kill time

我跟他聊了半天才走。

I left only after I had shot the breeze
with him for quite a while.

聊天 (兒)   V: to chat or gossip

(3) BF: depend upon

民不聊生   EX: The people have no way to make a living.

無聊   SV: silly; boring, listless; improper

29. 卒 dzú   BF: finish, die

聊以卒歲   EX: merely to live out this year (105:10)

卒業   V: to finish a course of study, to graduate

病卒   V: to die of illness

30. 歉 chyàn   BF: deficient

歉收   V: to have a bad harvest (105:12)

抱歉   SV: apologetic, regretful; sorry that

抱歉話   N: apology (140:1)

道歉   VO: to make a formal apology

31. 乞 chǐ   BF: beg for (as of alms) (106:1)

乞食   VO: to beg for food

乞憐   V: to seek sympathy

乞求   V: to beg for, seek, to implore (for favors, aid, etc.)

乞討   V: to beg for (alms)

乞降   V: to beg to surrender

乞和   V: to beg for a truce

32. 哀 aī   BF: sorrow, wail

乞哀   V: to seek sympathy (106:1)

可哀   SV: miserable, pitiable (166:3)

哀求/告   V: to entreat, importune, implore

哀號   V: to weep noisily (號 háu)

哀哭 V/N: to sob, cry/weep

哀傷 SV: mournful, sad, distressing

哀而不傷 EX: regrettable but not personally distressing; to mourn but not to the point of harmful effect

33. 斗 dǒu   N/M: peck (106:1) Rad. 68

斗膽   N: great courage (lit. gall as large as a peck)

斗室   N: room or quarters as small as a peck

一斗米   M: a peck of rice

烟斗   N: pipe (for smoking)

漏斗   N: funnel

北斗星   N: North Star

34. 敷 fū   (1) V: to apply (as ointment)

敷傷   V: to dress an injury

敷藥 VO: to apply medicine

(2) BF: ample

不敷應用 ex: insufficient for the demand

入不敷出 EX: income is insufficient for expenses

35. 衍 yǎn   BF: overflow

敷衍   V: to delay in dealing with a situation by putting up a show or pretense of doing something about it (106:1); (also) to proliferate, to multiply

敷衍了事 EX: to finish up a matter in a sloppy and unconscientious manner

36. 薪 syīn   BF: wages, salary, pay

薪資　　N: salary (106:5)

薪給　　N: salary (106:5) (給 read jǐ)

薪水　　N: salary

發薪　　VO: to pay a salary

年/月薪　　N: annual/monthly salary

37. 輩　bèi　　N: generation

此輩　　N: this generation (106:5)

下輩　　N: next generation

長輩　　N: older generation

(老)前輩　　N: older generation (polite term)

一輩子　　N: a lifetime

人才輩出　　EX: to produce talents in great abundance

38. 肩　jyān　　N: shoulder (106:6)

並肩　　A: shoulder to shoulder

並肩而行　　ex: to march shoulder to shoulder

並肩作戰　　ex: to fight side by side

肩負　　V: to bear (as if on one's shoulders)

肩負重任　　ex: to bear heavy responsibility

肩章　　N: epaulet

39. 挑　tyāu　　(1) V: to carry (with a pole slung across the shoulders)

肩挑　　V: to carry on the shoulder (106:6)

挑水　　V: to carry water (in two buckets suspended from a pole)

(2) V: to pick out; to choose; to find fault with

挑選　　V: to pick and choose; to select

挑錯　　VO: to find fault with; to criticize

挑眼／毛病   V: to find fault with

挑好日子   VO: to pick out an auspicious day

(tyǎu)   (3)   V: to provoke, stir up

挑戰   V: to challenge (to battle); to provoke a fight

挑戰行爲   N: provocative action

挑事   V: to stir up trouble

40. 攤 tān   (1)   V: to spread out

分攤   V: to divide up money; to share expenses

攤派   V: to assess; to rate proportionately; to apportion

(2)   BF: stall

攤子   N: street stall

地攤兒   N: stall spread on the ground

(3)   M: for flat pile of

一攤書   N: a pile of books

41. 售 shòu   BF: sell, retail

攤售   V: to display and sell (106:6,7)

出售   V: to put up for sale

售票處   N: ticket office

售價   N: selling price

零售   V: to sell retail

零售商   N: retail merchant

銷售   V: to sell

廉售   V: to put on sale

42. 紡 fǎng   V: to spin

紡織 V/N: to weave (as textiles); textiles (106:9)

紡織品　　N: woven goods

紡織工業　N: textile industry

紡織廠　　N: textile factory

紡織機　　N: textile machine

43. 碼 mǎ　　(1) BF: wharf

碼頭　　N: wharf, dock (107:3; 120:11; 121:2)

(2) BF: code, sign

號碼　　N: number (as street or phone number)

四角號碼　N: the Four Corner System for classification of Chinese characters

密碼　　N: code

密碼電報　N: code telegram

起碼　　A: at the least, at a minimum

他起碼有五所房子。
He has at least five houses.

籌碼　　N: counter, chip

(3)　N: English yard; measure

尺碼　　N: sizes (as for clothes, shoes, etc.)

44. 閩 mǐn　　　N: Fukien (107:10)

45. 粵 ywè　　　N: Kwangtung (62:4,7; 107:10)

46. 湘 syāng　　N: Hunan (107:10)

47. 鄂 è　　　　N: Hupeh (107:10)

48. 黔 chyán　　N: Kweichow (107:10)

49. 蜀 shǔ　　　N: Szechwan (107:10)

50. 皖 wǎn　　　N: Anhwei (107:10)

51. 豫 yù　　　　N: Honan (107:10)

52. 魯 lǔ   (1) N: Shantung (107:10)

              (2) BF: stupid, common, vulgar

                   粗魯 SV: coarse, common

              (3) N: Surname

                   魯迅 N: Lu Hsun (165:T)

53. 勾 gōu   V: to hook; inveigle, entice

              勾結 V: to be in league or cahoots with (108:2; 170:11)

              勾引 V: to entice (illegally) (172:10; 174:9)

              勾通 V: to join in a plot with

          一筆勾銷 EX: to wipe out with a stroke of the pen

              勾兒 N: hook

              勾當 N: dealings (something illegal)

              勾留 V: to sojourn, to stay (for a short period)

NEW MEANINGS

1. 庸 yūng   BF: employ, use

              附庸 N: dependency or an appendage of (101:10)

                   附庸國(家) N: dependent state; dependency

2. 徒 tú   BF: follower, discipline

              信徒 N: disciple (convert); believer (102:5)

              教徒 N: religious convert or disciple

              徒弟 N: apprentice

              門徒 N: disciple

              匪徒 N: bandits, brigands

學徒　N: apprentice

暴徒　N: brigands; desperadoes

3. 界　BF: "circles"

自然界　N: natural world (16:7)

學生界　N: student circles (103:2)

知識界　N: intellectual circles (108:3)

各界　N: various circles or sections of society (120:6,8,9)

學術／教育界　N: academic/educational circles

4. 員　BF: one who is a professional at; member of

黨員　N: party member (14:1,7; 16:T; 20:12, etc.)

海員　N: seaman (15:5)

教員　N: teacher (103:1)

事務員　N: clerk (103:1)

店員　N: store clerk (105:1)

雇員　N: employee (106:5)

職員　N: clerk; staff member

工作人員　N: staff member; working personnel

政府人員　N: government personnel

會員　N: member of a certain organization or association

5. 殷　BF: abundant; flourishing; highest degree of

殷實　SV: well-to-do, well off; having property (104:4)

殷勤　SV: diligent, attentive

6. 斷　BF: decide; judge

斷定　V: to decide; to determine, settle (104:11)

果斷　SV: purposeful, determined

這個人作事很果斷。

This man is very decisive in his way of doing things.

判斷 V/N: to determine, judge; judgment

7. 資　BF: aid, assist; depend on, **r**ely on

資助 V/N: to assist, subscribe towards; financial help

資給　V: to assist (as a destitute person)

以資　ex: for the purpose of, so as to, to

送給他三本書以資鼓勵。

Give him three books so as to encourage him.

寄上書三册以資參攷。

Mail you three volumes <u>as</u> (<u>to serve as</u>) reference.

8. 升　N/M: pint (106:1)

9. 係　V: (literary equivalent of)是

10. 稱　V: to weigh or be in balance

(不)相稱　SV: to be (un)balanced or (un)matched (106:4)

稱量　V: to weigh

稱一稱　V: to weigh up

11. 着 jwó　BF: wear, clothing

吃着　N: food and clothing

吃着不窮　EX: inexhaustible supplies of food and clothing

衣着　N: apparel

衣着入時　EX: to be smartly dressed

12. 夫　BF: suffix for "one who ..."

搬運夫　N: transport coolie (lit. one who moves and transports) (107:3)

農夫　N: peasant

13. 清　V: to clean or sweep up

　　清道夫　N: street sweeper (107:4)

　　清算 V/N: to liquidate; liquidation

14. 度　V: to pass or cross over

　　度日　V: to pass the days　(i.e. to make a living) (107:6)

　　　度日如年　EX: (describes) slow passage of time (lit. to live a day is like living a year)

15. 幫　(1)　N: gang, group, clique

　　青幫　N: the "Green Gang" (107:11)

　　幫會　N: gangs, cliques

　　(2)　M: for group or class (of people)

　　一幫人　N: a group of people

16. 批　M: for group or batch (107:12; 151:5)

　　那批人　N: a/that bunch of people

　　有一批難民自中國大陸逃往香港。
　　There was a group of refugees who escaped from the China mainland to Hongkong.

　　大批 N/A: (on a) large scale (155:12)

　　最近中國難民大批地自中國大陸逃往香港。
　　Recently Chinese refugees have been escaping on a great scale to Hongkong from the Chinese mainland.

　　批發　V: wholesale

　　批發買賣　N: wholesale commerce

　　分批　A: in/by batch; in seperate lots

　　一批一批　A: batch by batch, lot by lot

17. 陣　BF: battle; place in battle array; file of soldiers

　　陣綫　N: battle line (108:5)

陣營　N: (lit. and fig.) camp; bloc

陣地　N: battlefield

陣亡　V: to die in battle

STRUCTURE NOTES

1. 未有 ... 而 ... 者/的   PT: there never is a case where ...
                                    without resulting in ...

   Notes:

      1. This is a variation of the 沒有 ... 而 ... 的 pattern in VII
          Structure 10.

      2. No ambiguity arises if the subjects of the two clauses
          (supposition and illogical consequence) are different.

2. 他們每逢年終結賬一次就吃驚一次。

   At the end of every year when they do the accounts they get a shock.

   This can be considered as a combination of two patterns
   (A) 每(逢) ... 就 ...   and   (B) ... 一次就 ... 一次。

   A. 每逢 ... 就 ...

      1. 每逢 can be considered as a CV which takes a noun object.
          Taken as a CV it belongs to that group of moveable CVs
          like (對於 , 爲了,etc.) that can either precede or follow the
          subject.

          $$\left\{ \begin{array}{l} S + 每逢 + O \\ 每逢 + O + S \end{array} \right\} + (就) + VP$$

          每逢禮拜三他就到台北去。
          He goes to Taipei every Wednesday.

      2. 每逢 can be conceived of as a CJ followed by a clause (+的時
          候).

          $$\left. \begin{array}{l} S_1 + VP_1 \\ S_2 + VP_2 \end{array} \right\} \longrightarrow \boxed{每逢 + S_1 + VP_1 + (的時候) + S_2 + 就 + VP_2}$$

          她到台北來。
          我帶她到處去玩。 } → 每逢她到台北來(的時候)我就帶她到處
          去玩。

          Whenever she comes to Taipei, I take her around to
          various places to give her a good time.

Also less frequently:

$$S_2 + 每逢 + S_1 + VP_1 + (的時候) + 就 + VP_2$$

If $S_1 = S_2$, S_2 may be omitted.

3. For 每逢 without 就 see 9:1.

B. ... 一次 ... (就) ... 一次   PT: everytime ...

$$\left.\begin{array}{c} S_1 + VP_1 \\ S_2 + VP_2 \end{array}\right\} \rightarrow \quad S_1 + VP_1 + \left\{\begin{array}{c} 一次 \\ 一回 \\ etc. \end{array}\right\} + S_2 + 就 + VP_2 + \left\{\begin{array}{c} 一次 \\ 一回 \\ etc. \end{array}\right\}$$

$$\left.\begin{array}{c} 我們結賬。 \\ 他們吃驚。 \end{array}\right\} \rightarrow 我們結賬一次，他們就吃驚一次。$$

Everytime we did the accounts, they were stunned.

Notes:

1. If $S_1 = S_2$, S_2 can be omitted.

    他離婚一次就破財一次。
    Everytime he went through a divorce, he suffered financially.

2. Here 一次/回 , etc. function as measure complements
    of occurrence showing the number of times the action
    occurred.

3. If the verb phrase is composed of a verb plus a noun
    object, the measure complement of occurrence may be
    inserted between the verb and the noun object. (compare
    VII Structure 2 where 一天/日 are noun modifiers)

    離一次婚就破一次財。

3. 以資 + Verb   PT: in order to, so as to

a. 以資 consists of two elements, 以 "in order to" and 資 "to
    provide for, to contribute to"   (cf. II Structure 4 以 + V as
    "in order to")

b. 以資 functions as a connecting word of purpose, and must be followed by a Vn (a verb that can also function as a noun), not by V + O.

我們準備開一次舞會以資慶祝。

(action)　　　　　(purpose)

送他三本書以資鼓勵。

Give him three books (so as) to encourage him.

請寄上書三册以資參考。

Please mail three volumes to serve as reference.

4. Comparative formulas

a. <u>A 較之 B SV/V</u>　　　<u>PT: A is more SV/V than B</u>

<u>Notes:</u>

1. 較之 is a literary form of the CV 比 .

2. V is verb with a measure complement or a resultative ending with a SV.

今年糧食價格	較之	去年 (糧食價格)	增加 {一倍之多 / 得 很 多}
S	CV	O	V

The price of grain this year has risen a hundred percent/ a lot as compared with last year.

貧農的無田地較之自耕農的無求於人，自然境遇要苦。

Naturally the lot of poor landless peasants is tougher than that of the independent farmers who till their own land and ask nothing of anyone.

b. <u>A 較(之) B 爲 SV</u>　　　<u>PT: A is more SV than B</u>

<u>Notes:</u>

1. Another literary version of A 比 B SV. 爲 here precedes the SV/V largely for stylistic or euphonic reasons.

商朝銅器較周朝銅器爲優。

The bronze vessels of the Shang are superior to those of the Chou.

2. SV can be monosyllabic or bisyllabic.

c. A SV 於 B (see X Structure II)

Note examples 105:4,5,6,11, etc.   SV is monosyllabic.

d. Cf. also A 比 B SV; B 不如 A SV; A 沒有 B 那麼 SV

5.   不/有/無 ··· 於人/事   PT: to have something/nothing to ...

The above construction is a literary pattern. It may be perhaps
most easily analyzed as a V + O + CV + O construction which in
modern Chinese has been reversed to the CV + O + V + O pattern. In
this pattern 於 is equivalent to 對於 . Thus:

有害於人 ⟶ 對人有害   harmful to people

有助於新中國的建設 ⟶ 對新中國的建設   of benefit to the building
有助   of the new China

有害於公共衞生 ⟶ 對公共衞生有害   harmful to public sanitation

無益於世 ⟶ 對世界沒有益處   of no benefit to the world

The nouns appearing in this construction are generally monosyllabic
abstract nouns.

6.   聊以 + Verb   PT: just (try) to ...

聊 means something like 姑且 .

聊以解嘲 = 姑且用以解說別人的嘲笑。
(I) might as well (try to) use it to turn aside other people's
mockery.

他在公餘常下棋聊以自娛。
He often plays chess after office hours just (trying) to amuse
himself.

7. A (是) 指 B 而言   PT: A refers to/has reference to B

a. Here 而 functions as a connector between 指 and 言.

b. 指 ... 而言

指 and 言 may be construed as verbs in series or by analogy with
爲 ... 而 V specifically as a CV + O + V pattern.

(cf. 111:3) 依 ... 而定   PT: to be determined according to/
                                 in consideration of ...

c.   是指 (着) ... 說的 **is the colloquial equivalent.**

所謂農村無產階級是指長工，月工，零工等雇工而言。
The so-called village proletariat refers to workers hired on a long- or short - term basis, or by the month.

8.   得法   **V: to be skilled at, have the knack of; to be to the point**

得勝   **V: to win**

得志   **V: to realize one's ambition**

得意 **V/SV: to attain prosperity; elated/triumphant**

得當   **SV: appropriate**

得體   **SV: appropriate**

得力 **V/SV: to get the assistance of; capable (of people) of**

得手   **V: to succeed**

得人   **VO: to find the right man (for the job)**

得罪   **V: to offend**

<u>Note also</u>:

不得   **AV: shall not; may not**

閒人不得入內。
Unauthorized persons may not enter.

沒有報名投考者不得申請。
Only those who have registered for the examination may apply.

E X E R C I S E S

I. Correlative Structures

每逢 ... 一次 /etc. 就 ... 一次 /etc.

1. 這家人眞奇怪，每逢他先生發一次薪，他家就打一次架，好像發薪
   與打架是不可分離的兩件事似的。

2. 我想我們得想法子敎訓他了，因爲每逢他得手一次，他的膽子就更
   大一點，我怕長此以往，吃虧的是他自己。

3. 我們每逢查出私貨一次，就發一次通告，以資警告。

II. Structure Words

A. 以資

1. 從前的事雖然不能一筆勾消，但從現在起我們要杜絕敷衍了事，務
   使業務步入正軌，以資補救。

2. 由於政府過去在行政上的缺點太多，所以此次特別提出許多新方案
   ，並採取許多新措施以資改善。

3. 我到美國首都華盛頓去的時候，曾去林肯紀念堂去瞻仰林肯遺容，
   並簽名獻花以資紀念。

B. 較之

1. 這位律師處理恐嚇案件較之佃戶債務糾紛的案件要有經驗的多。

2. 他對於這件事的成就較之歷年來所有成就的總和還要大，的確難得。

3. 他今年的情形較之以往眞是好多了，尤其在言行方面沒有甚麼自相
   矛盾的地方。

C. (是) 指 ... 而言

1. 入不敷出是指收入及支出不平衡而言，跟營養不夠毫無關係。

2. 我所謂的不好的行爲是指無恥的行爲而言。

3. 負債是指欠別人的錢而言，是再清楚也沒有了。

D. 聊以

1. 每次遇到重要事情來臨，我總是緊張萬分，不知如何是好，往往把
   事情弄不好，所以在官場不得意，現在只有到一個小地方來顯顯威
   風，聊以自慰。

2. 在亂世裡人的生命簡直不值錢，死一個人算得了甚麼？所以我看我
   們還是搬到遠遠的鄉下去住，一方面躲避殘忍的現實，一方面聊以
   保全生命。

III.   Miscellaneous

有／無 VERB 於人／事

1. 那個人心裡想：你們富貴人家雖然過着豪華的生活，但我們也不錯
   ，雖然食無魚，出無車，但是無欠於人，豈不心安理得？

2. 乞憐是無恥的行為，男子漢怎能這樣做？何況，我既無求於人也無
   意於是呢！

3. 你雖然說他晚景淒涼，可是我想他安分守己，自得其樂，況且他又
   無求於人，又有什麼淒涼可言呢？

IV.   Review of Comparative Structures

A 比 B SV   A SV 於 B   A （沒）有 B （那麼 or 這麼）SV
A 較 B 為 SV   A 較之 B 更（為）SV   A 不如 B

1. 肩挑小販獲利不多，經濟情形比企業家苦（or 較企業家為苦；苦於
   企業家；較之企業家為苦；沒有企業家那麼好；不如企業家）難怪
   他們在荒年的時候只有向親友乞哀告憐，借債度日了。

2. 所謂「苛政猛於虎」，意思是由於政府不良，對於人民害處比野獸
   還要兇猛。（or 較野獸為兇猛；猛於野獸，較之野獸兇猛）

B. Rewrite the following sentences using 較 … 為；甚於；比

1. 以結果來看，捏造事實比誇大事實更嚴重。你看那個銀行經理不是
   因為被人誣告而被辭退了嗎？

2. 有人說出生在富豪之家優於出生在貧苦之家。我想這恐怕是憤世之
   談吧。

I. Correlative Structures

每逢 . . . 一次就 . . . 一次 /etc.

1. Everytime you borrow money from him, you get stung.

2. Everytime they audit the accounts, we are in the red.
    (虧本)

3. In the first few years, everytime the government issued bonds, prices shot up, but in recent years because things have improved economically, this sort of thing doesn't happen anymore.

II. Structure Words

A. 以資

1. To facilitate capital circulation(週轉), we hope our colleagues will soon pay the bills that were sent out when the books were closed at the end of the year.

2. Pessimism has been spreading in military schools. Last week in the new budget the Ministry of Defense increased their appropriations as encouragement.

3. Local industries have been faced with increasingly stiff foreign competition to the point where the legislature passed a high tariff bill as protection.

B. 較之

1. A law-abiding attitude is more important than the law.

2. Although this profession has many advantages when you compare it to many others, it has one big flaw. It is not free from political pressure.

3. Many more people are seeking to join the Peace Corps to do overseas work this year than in previous years.

C. (是)指 . . . 而言

1. Will someone please explain to me what sort of situation that expression alludes to?

2. He said that in the past few years he has contracted many debts and needs a year's leave to repay them. By debts he referred to literary debts.

3. Marshall or Generalissimo refers only to the highest military rank. The connotation of 統帥 is a bit broader. Politically it refers to the head of the state and militarily it refers to the Commander-in-Chief of the three military services (三軍).

III. Miscellaneous

有/無 VERB 於人/事

1. Would you say that Lao-tze's philosophy is to ask nothing from people and to give nothing to the people?

2. Now of course you don't see his faults but when you have something to ask of him, you will find out that he is very careless.

3. At first I was very puzzled, but the more I thought about it the more I realized he really wanted something from me.

IV. Review of Comparative Structures

A. First translate the following sentences then rewrite the comparative portions using each of the following

B 不如 A   A 較之 B 更(爲) SV

A 比 B SV   A (沒) 有 B (那麼 or 這麼) SV

A 較 B 爲 SV

A SV 於 VB

1. Although our casualties in this battle were <u>not as great as</u> last time, the loss of guns and ammunition was <u>much greater</u>.

2. Although the history of European countries is <u>not as long as</u> that of China, their science is much more developed. (also use 不如 , 不及)

B. use 比 , and 較 ... 爲

1. One of the characteristics of the pre-1949 Chinese economy was that the textile industry was <u>more developed</u> than the steel industry.

2. Although salaries of civil servants and teachers <u>have been increased over</u> last year's levels, prices have not yet been affected.

C. Use 比 ，較 ... 爲 and SV 於

1. The tasks and economic status (待遇) of teachers
    are inferior to (苦) to that of lawyers, but it is
    unquestionably true that their position is more
    elevated (清高).

D. Use 較 ... 爲 ，甚於 and 比

1. Some people say the Communist deprivation of the
    people's liberty is much greater than that of the
    ancient kings or emperors.

V. Review Sentences

Use:

一切 ... 惟有 ... 却 ...   從事於   否則

只不過 ... 罷了   以   敷衍了事

譬如

1. His attitude toward the Provincial Association is not
    really very helpful. I think he is merely going through
    the motions.

2. The rights people enjoy and the obligations they must
    meet ought to be stipulated clearly in the constitution.
    Otherwise the people have nothing to follow.

3. When the hsien magistrate gave up his job, a clear
    accounting was made of all financial matters except that
    no mention was made of the confusion over the bond issue.

4. One of the endeavors the United Nations is engaged in is
    improving the world economic situation. For example,
    it has started professional training to raise labor
    productivity in various countries. Member states can
    also borrow money from the International Bank to increase
    capital circulation.

5. 他們之所以能受人民擁護，是因爲他們的黨已經上了太平政治的軌道。

6. 我從未聽說在入不敷出的情形下，還能維持到今天而不關門，可見這個
    人在經營商業方面的確有才幹。

Write Sentences Using:

1. 縱使 ... 但是 ...

2. 從 ... 入手

3. 未嘗不

4. 寧可 ... 也不 ...

5. 如何

6. 何嘗

7. 一俟 ... 就 ...

8. 以 ... 著稱

In the April 5, 1947, issue of the influential magazine, Observer
(Kuan-ch'a), Chang Tung-sun, a well-known Chinese philosopher, outlines
the views of a group of liberal intellectuals who were proposing a
coalition government of the Kuomintang and Communists as the way to
avoid the tragedy of civil war in China in the late 1940's.

Where is China Headed? (Chung-kuo wang ho-ch'u tsou?), Shanghai, 1949,
pp. 67-71.

109:T	用意			N: intent, intention, purpose (109:3; 115:1,2)
2	創刊號	--kān--	1	N: inaugural number or issue
	作			short for 著作
3	目下			MA: (at) present, current
4	明日黃花			EX: to be past the prime; to have lost timeliness (115:10)
	不失爲			ex: (lit. not to miss being) is
6	橋樑	--lyáng	2	N: bridge (109:7; 115:5)
	藉以		S1	PT: in order to, thereby to
7	強盛	--shèng	3	SV: strong
	于			(alternate form for 於) especially after verbs
8	拉攏	--lǔng	4	V: to cultivate people (for some ulterior purpose)
9	中和			V/N: to neutralize (as in chemistry); (fig.) to counteract; neutralization (109:11)
10	和事老			N: peacemaker
	勸架		NM1	V: to mediate a quarrel
	有見于		S2	PT: in view of the fact that ...
	蓋…則…		NM2,S3	PT: since/in as much as ..., then ...

11	介乎…之間		S4	PT: to be a bridge between, to lie or be between
110:1	演爲			V: to develop into
	料定		NM3	V: to assert definitely, take for certain; to assume
2	煩悶	--mèn	5	SV/N: depressed; bored; depression (i.e. lack of spirit, disappointment)
5	壟斷	lǔng--	6	V/N: to monopolize; monopoly (as of markets)
6	並存			V: to coexist
7	鉗制	chyán--	7	V/N: (to restrain or) control by force (112:9,10)
8	諸		NM4	P: fusion of 之於
	並無是處			ex: entirely incorrect
10	盡			A: exhaustively, exclusively
	分配	--pèi	8	V/N: to divide, distribute; distribution or division of
11	親美		NM5	V/N: (to have) pro-American sentiments (115:4,7)
111:1	類似			SV: similar to
2	盡於斯矣	-----yǐ	9	ex: all included therein
3	依…而定			PT: to be determined by (cf. XIII Structure 7)
4	集團			N: bloc, clique (112:3,11)
6	教授	--shòu	10	N: professor
	會計師	(kwài)----	NM6	N: (certified) public accountant
	民營			Adj: civilian owned; privately owned
	廠家			N: factory owner; factory
7	區分		NM7	V: to divide; to classify
9	方式			N: method, way, means (113:7)

	不得已			EX:	cannot be helped; unavoidable
10	撥開	bwŏ--	11	V:	to push to one side, reject
	還	(hwán)	NM8	V:	to repay; to come back to
	漂亮	pyàu--	12	SV:	attractive
112:1	歸根于	(gwēi----)	(VII:28)	ex:	to be attributed to; to trace back to
3	切要		NM9	AV:	to be urgent, pressing
5	逼迫	bī--	13	V/N:	to force or compel; pressure (112:9)
6	痛罵			V:	to curse bitterly
	祈禱	--dǎu	14	V/N:	to pray; prayer (112:7)
7	改頭換面			EX:	to change the appearance (as disguise)
8	特殊	--shū	15	SV:	special, unusual
9	境況			N:	situation
10	與其…毋寧…	(---- wú--)	(VII:36) S5	PT:	to ... is not as good as to ...
11	無如			A:	but unfortunately
12	糜爛	mí--		V/SV/N:	to crush to pulp; crushing (fig. by oppression)
113:1	瀕於	pín--		V:	to approach close to; to be on the verge of (as death)
	老實			SV:	honest, frank (115:6)
	萬一			MA:	if by any chance
2	無憎無愛	--dzēng----	16	ex:	without hatred or love
	理性			N:	reason
4	適宜	--yí	17	SV:	suitable
5	誠心			SV/N:	sincere; sincerity
6	算數			V:	to count (in the sense of to mean business)
7	信任			V/N:	(to) trust

	口口聲聲			EX: with every breath
9	諱言	hwèi--		V: to conceal (as the fact that ...)
10	馬歇爾	--syē--	18	N: Marshall (114:5)
	強調	--(dyàu)		V: to emphasize
11	子孫			N: descendants; sons and grandsons
12	呆板	dāibǎn	19,20	SV: rigid
114:1	預測	--tsè	21	V/N: to foretell; prediction
2	篤守	dǔ--	22	V: to guard carefully; to hold sincerely (of belief)
	中庸		NM10	N: (judicious) mean
	掀起	syān--	23	V: to raise, (here) to stir up
5	認眞			SV: serious about, earnest
	遺憾	--hàn	24	SV/N: (to) regret
6	姑	gū	25,S6	A: might as well ...
	比喻	--yù	26	N: example; parable
9	杞人憂天	chǐ-----		EX: baseless anxiety; pessimistic fear, etc. (refers to the man of Ch'i who was afraid the sky was about to fall)
10	了事	(lyǎu)--	(VII:NM2)	V: to finish or wind up
11	消弭	--mǐ		V: to remove, dispel
	隱患	yǐn--	27	N: hidden danger or disaster
115:1	總匙	--chŕ	28	N: key (as to a situation)
2	敗於垂成	----chwéi--	29	ex: to fail on the verge of success
3	一番	--fān	30	M: for intentions, ideas, etc.
4	意圖			V/N: (to) plan or scheme to
	消納			V: to wipe out, to weaken
5	覺悟	--wù	31	V/N: to become aware of; awareness

6 損人不利已   EX: to harm others and yet not benefit
                                     oneself

7 物資   N: materiel; goods; supplies

10 劑   jì   32   M: dose (for medicine)

起死囘生   EX: to resurrect, to come alive again

湯   tāng   33   N: soup; liquid mixture

11 慘不忍言   tsǎn----- 34   EX: indescribably sad

CHARACTERS TO BE LEARNED

1. 刊 kān   BF: cut, print, publish, periodical

創刊號   N: inaugural issue (109:2)

刊物   N: publications, magazines, periodicals (150:12)

月刊   N: monthly

發刊   V: to publish a periodical

發刊詞   N: inaugural statement of a
            periodical

刊載   V: to publish, to carry (in the sense of publish)

2. 樑 lyáng   N: ridge pole, beam

橋樑   N: bridge (109:6,7; 115:5; 150:4) (座)

屋樑   N: main beam of a house or room (colloq. 大 樑)

3. 盛 shèng   SV: abundant, flourishing, prosperous

繁盛 SV: flourishing, prosperous (59:1; 118:1; 170:7)

盛行V/SV: to prevail; prevalent, popular, common (82:8)

強盛 SV: strong (109:7)

盛衰   N: the rise and fall of fortune

盛極必衰   EX: That which has reached its pinnacle must perish. (118:11)

盛意/情   N: (your) generous intention, kindness

感謝盛意   ex: to thank you for your good intentions

大盛   SV: powerful

士氣大盛   EX: excellent troop morale

盛極一時   EX: extremely prosperous or popular at one time

太平盛世   EX: period of great peace or prosperity

盛大   SV: prosperous, numerous

興盛   SV: booming, flourishing

盛會   N: great meeting

盛裝   N: formal dress (as evening)

盛名   N: fame

4. 攏 lǔng   BF: grasp, drag; collect together

拉攏   V: to cultivate someone (often for ulterior purposes) (109:8)

靠攏   V: to draw close to, draw to the side of (lit. and fig.)

聚攏   V: to assemble, come together

5. 悶 mèn   (1) SV: melancholy, sorrowful, depressed

煩悶 SV/N: dull, listless, depressed; dispirited; depression (110:2)

苦悶   SV: melancholy and depressed (142:5; 164:3,5)

悶得慌   ex: extremely bored, depressed, sad and melancholy

悶悶不樂   EX: sad and depressed, melancholy

(mēn)   (2) V: to cover; to be stuffy (as of air in a room)

悶飯   VO: to cook rice in a tightly covered pot with little water

(3) SV: oppressive, stuffy, sultry (as of weather)

(很)悶 SV: stuffy (of air in a room)

6. 壟 lǔng   BF: mound of earth

壟斷 V/N: to monopolize (a market) (from: a mound of earth on which a trader stood to watch out for trade); monopoly (110:5)

壟斷資本 N: monopoly capital

壟斷市場 VO: to monopolize the market

7. 鉗 chyán   BF: pincers, tongs

鉗制 V/N: to restrict; (to) suppress; control (110:7; 112:9)

鉗子 N: tweezers, pliers, pincers (把)

火鉗 N: fire tongs (把)

8. 配 pèi   (1) V: to match, pair

調配 V/N: to distribute or transfer; distribution (43:4)

軍隊調配得適當才能夠打勝仗。
Only if the army is well deployed can it fight victoriously.

分配 V/N: to (divide up and) distribute; distribution (110:10; 122:6)

支配 V/N: (to) direct; (to) handle; (to) control; direction (116:9; 117:2; 119:7)

配合 V/N: to match, to blend, to supplement, complement; matching, blending; coordination (157:12; 172:11)

配藥 VO: to mix, prepare medicine

配音 V/N: to do the sound or music track; sound effects; background music

配件 N: parts (as for a car or machine)

配備 N: equipment

(2) V: to be worthy of, worthy to or for; to be fit for

他大學還沒畢業，怎麼配作教育部長？

He hasn't even graduated from college. How is he worthy of being the Minister of Education?

9. 矣 yǐ   P: final particle used in the classical style (1) at the end of a sentence which contains a conditional clause; (2) in a manner close to the perfecting function of the colloquial particle 了 (111:2)

10. 授 shòu   V: to give to, confer on

教授 V/N: to teach; professor (111:6; 151:3)

傳授   V: to teach (of masters passing on knowledge to disciples)

授課   V: to teach

授田 VO: to endow with land, to bestow land

授官   V: to appoint to a position

授意   V: to hint

授與   V: to give, to bestow on

口授 V/N: to pass on orally; oral instruction

11. 撥 bwō   (1) V: to adjust (as of the hands of clocks, etc.) (111:10)

撥快 ex: to set (a clock) faster or ahead

請把鐘撥快一點兒。

Please set the clock up a bit.

撥電話號碼 VO: to dial a telephone number

(2) V: to separate out; distribute

撥款／錢 VO: to transfer money, appropriate funds

(3) BF: winnow, agitate

挑撥   V: to stir up trouble or friction

挑撥是非 EX: to stir up trouble; to create friction

12. 漂 pyāu (1) V: to float, to drift on water (cf. 飄 V: to float in the air)

漂浮 V: to float or drift on water

漂流 V: to drift about

(pyàu) (2) BF: look fresh

漂亮 SV: attractive (111:10)

(pyǎu) (3) V: to bleach

漂白 RV: to bleach

漂布 VO: to bleach cloth, linen

13. 逼 bī V: to force or compel; to press

逼迫 V/N: to force, compel, drive or urge to; pressure (112:5,9)

逼緊 V: to press hard or come close to

逼近 V: to draw close to; to press hard upon (as an army on a city)

逼死 V: to hound to death

逼人 VO: to hound a person

逼走 V: to hound someone away

官逼民反 EX: When officials hound the common people too much, they rebel.

逼眞 SV: lifelike; seemingly very real (not really real)

14. 禱 dǎu BF: pray

祈禱 V/N: to pray; prayer (112:6,7)

早/晚禱 N: morning (or evening) prayer

禱告 V/N: to pray; prayer

15. 殊 shū BF: peculiar, singular

懸殊 N/SV: discrepancy; of great difference, differential (43:7)

衆寡懸殊　　EX: too many versus very few

實力懸殊　　EX: a great discrepancy in the
　　　　　　　　actual strength (of two parties,
　　　　　　　　people, etc.)

特殊　SV: special, unusual (112:8; 131:11; 134:4; 137:11)

特殊地位　　EX: special or unique position
　　　　　　　　(112:8)

特殊化　SV: specialized, make unique,
　　　　　　give special status to

16. 憎 dzēng　　BF: hatred; hate (113:2)

憎惡　V: to dislike, hate

可憎　SV: hateful, detestable, loathesome

17. 宜 yí　　BF: right, proper, suitable

適宜　SV: suitable, appropriate (113:4; 135:1; 161:1)

合宜　SV: proper, fitting

相宜　SV: fitting, suitable, appropriate

便宜 SV/N: cheap; advantage (便 read pyán)

討/貪便宜 VO: to be greedy for petty advantage

18. 歇 syē　　(1) V: to rest (from tiredness)

歇一歇　V: to rest a bit

歇一會兒　V: to rest a while

歇乏　V: to rest

歇業　VO: to close a business

(2) Used in transliteration

馬歇爾　　Marshall (爾 read ěr) (113:10)

19. 呆 dāi　　SV: foolish, doltish, idiotic (113:12)
(獃)

獃子　N: simpleton

書獃子　N: thoroughly impractical, bookish
　　　　　　person

獸頭獸腦　EX: blockhead;　person who looks like an idiot

20. 板 bǎn　　(1) SV: stiff, wooden, obstinate

呆板　SV: rigid, fixed, inflexible (fig.) (113:12)

(老) 古板 SV/N: conservative; old-fashioned (of persons)

死板　SV: stiff, obstinate

板起面孔　EX: to harden one's countenance

(2)　N: board, plank

板子　N: board; bamboo or wooden strip used for beating students or criminals

黑板　N: blackboard

木板　N: plank

地板　N: flooring

天花板　N: ceiling

21. 測 tsè　　BF: fathom, measure, estimate

預測 V/N: to foretell; prediction; forecast (114:1)

猜測 V/N: (to) guess

天有不測風雲　EX: No one can tell what the winds may bring. (fig.)

測候所　N: meteorological observations; meteorological station

測量 V/N: (to) survey

測量員　N: surveyor

測量學　N: surveying (i.e. study or art of)

測量局　N: survey office

推測 V/N: to infer; inference

測驗 V/N: (to) test

智力測驗　N: intelligence test

莫測高深 EX: (lit. you cannot take his measure) to be unable to fathom someone's moods, thoughts, expertise, etc.

22. 篤 dǔ   BF: true; genuine; magnanimous; attach importance to

篤守　V: to hold sincerely or truly (of belief, principle) (114:2)

篤實　SV: sincere, true

篤信　V: to believe truly or sincerely

誠篤　SV: sincere

篤學　V: to study diligently

23. 掀 syān   V: to lift up, open, raise up

掀起　V: to raise or lift up (as shades); to stir up (as revolution or rebellion) (114:2)

掀開　RV: to open up, lift up

24. 憾 hàn   BF: regret

遺憾 V/SV/N: (to) regret; regretful (114:5)

感到遺憾　VO: to (feel) regret

抱憾　V: to regret, deplore

抱憾終身　EX: to regret for the rest of one's life

死而無憾　EX: to die without regrets

憾事　N: regrettable matter

25. 姑 gū   (1) A: for the moment, meanwhile (114:6)

姑且　A: might as well; temporarily, for the time being
你姑且讓他說。
You might as well let him talk.

(2) BF: girl; paternal aunt; unmarried girl

姑娘　N: girl, daughter; young lady

姑姑　N: paternal aunts (also 姑母 / 媽 ; in some areas 姑姑 is reserved for unmarried aunts)

姑父/夫　　N: husband of paternal aunt

(3) BF: lenient, tolerant

姑息　　V: to accept resignedly, give in; to appease

姑息主義　N: appeasement; resigned acceptance

對敵人不能姑息。
We must not appease the enemy.

姑念　　V: to be lenient because of ...

姑念初犯，從輕法辦
Because it is a first offense, it will be
treated leniently.

26. 喻 yù　　BF: parable

比喻　　N: parable, example (114:6)

27. 隱 yǐn　　BF: hide, be concealed

隱患　　N: concealed disaster, hidden trouble (114:11)

隱藏　　V: to hide, conceal (122:3)

隱姓埋名　EX: to conceal one's real name

隱居　　V: to dwell in seclusion

隱士　　N: hermit

隱忍　　V: to bear suffering patiently

隱情/痛　　N: hidden feelings/pains

28. 匙 chŕ　　(1) BF: spoon

匙子　　N: spoon

(2) BF: key

總匙　　N: key (as to a situation), master key (115:1,2)

29. 垂 chwéi　　V: to hang down, let fall (103:7)

垂危　　V: to be in danger or peril (28:1)

敗於垂成　ex: to fail on the verge of success (115:2)

功敗垂成　EX: to fail or be defeated on the verge of success (175:2)

垂頭喪氣　EX: to be greatly depressed or frustrated; crestfallen

垂直　V: to be perpendicular

垂死的掙扎　ex: death throes

30. 番 fān　(1)　M: for acts, deeds, careers; time, turn

一番意義　N: idea or meaning (115:3)

一番好意　N: a "well-meant" act, intentions or feelings

三番兩次　A: repeatedly

(2)　N: foreign; barbarian

西番　N: old term for the inhabitants of the Chinghai and Tibetan regions (170:7)

31. 悟 wù　BF: become aware of; apprehend

覺悟 V/N: to become aware of; awareness of (115:5; 151:5)

省悟　V: to comprehend, become awake or sensitive to (省 read sying)

悔悟　N: regret

執迷不悟　EX: to hold obstinately to a wrong view

32. 劑 ji　(1)　M: for dose (of medicine) (115:10)

一劑藥　N: dose of medicine

藥劑師　N: pharmacist

(2) BF: 調劑　V: to bring in balance, to adjust, regulate (調 read tyáu)

33. 湯 tāng　N: soup (115:10; 135:10)

湯藥　N: liquid medicine

湯圓　N: dumplings (in soup)

湯匙　N: soup spoon (把)

牛肉／清湯　N: beef/clear soup

34. 慘 tsǎn　　SV: sad, cruel, grievous; grieved

慘痛　SV: bitterly painful (fig.) (60:8; 151:8)

慘不忍言　EX: indescribably cruel or tragic

慘劇　N: tragedy (118:12)

慘死　V: to die a cruel death

慘敗　V/N: bitter defeat

損失／災情慘重　EX: catastrophic losses/natural calamity

慘境　N: distressing condition

慘變　N: cruel turn of fate

慘無人道　EX: cruelly inhumane

NEW MEANINGS

1. 架　　BF: quarrel

勸架　VO: to mediate a quarrel or fight (109:10)

打架　VO: to quarrel, fight

2. 蓋　　CJ: since, in as much as (literary) (109:10)

近代學人多無創見，蓋因襲舊說所致。
That modern scholars for the most part do not
have creative views is because they are bound
by tradition.

3. 料　　BF: foresee, guess

料定　V: to assume, take for certain (110:1)

不料　A: "to my surprise!"　unexpectedly (151:9;
157:4; 158:11)

料想　V: to anticipate, expect; foresee

料(想)到　RV: to anticipate, expect; foresee

預料　V: to foresee, anticipate

4. 諸   P: fusion of 之於 where 之 is a direct object (110:7)

     付諸實行 ex: to put into practice （付之於實行）

     按諸原理 ex: to put up against basic laws; based on basic laws or principle

5. 親   BF: pro, sympathetically inclined toward

     親美／日 V: pro-American/Japanese, etc. (110:11)

       親共 V: pro-Communist

       親愛 SV: dear

       親密 SV: close, intimate (as of friendships)

       親熱 SV: very close (as of friends)

       親近 V/SV: to be close (of attitudes)

       親信 N: one's own men (close associates of a person who move with him to his new job)

6. 會 kwài   BF: calculate

       會計 N: accounting; accountant

         會計師 N: (certified) public accountant (111:6)

         會計員 N: accountant

         會計年度 N: fiscal year

7. 區   BF: discriminate, distinguish by, assign to

       區分 V: to divide (111:7)

       區別 V/N: to discriminate, distinguish between; distinction, difference (160:5,9; 161:8)

8. 還 hwǎn (1) V: to restore, recompense, repay (111:10)

       還錢 VO: to repay money

       還清 V: to repay in full; to clear up debts

       歸還 V: to return something to its rightful owner

       退還 V: to return (something) to (someone)

(2)   V: to come back to

  還鄉   VO: to return to one's native place

    告老還鄉   EX: to retire and return home

  往還   V: to go and return; to and fro; to give and take (of social relations or obligations)

9. 切   BF: urgent; pressing

  切要   AV: very important (112:3)

  切切   A: urgently (usually used at the end of an official announcement as 切切此佈) (123:3)

  切記   V: to be sure to remember

  切望   V: to be very hopeful of; earnest, keen

  急切SV/A: hasty

  迫切SV/A: urgent; urgently

    我們迫切需要您的支持。
    We urgently need your support.

  思家心切   EX: to be very homesick

  親切   SV: close, intimate (refers to attitudes)

  懇切   SV: sincere

  密切   SV: close, intimate

  切實   SV: practical, realistic, in accordance with reality

  關切   SV: to concern oneself about; to be concerned about

10. 庸 yūng   BF: harmony, constant, unchanging

  中庸   N: (the golden) mean; The <u>Doctrine of the Mean</u> (114:2)

STRUCTURE NOTES

1.　藉以　　　PT: to use the opportunity to; thereby to

藉以 = 藉此以

他計劃到歐洲各地參觀藉以增長見識。

He plans to visit the various countries of Europe to increase his experience.

Note:

　　1.　藉以，用以，function much like 以便。

2.　有見于 = 有鑒于　　　PT: in view of the fact that

政府有鑒於青年之日趨墮落乃設專門機構研究有效的教育方法。

In view of the increasingly dissolute tendencies of youth, the government has established special organizations to study educational measures that might be effective.

Note:

　　1.　有鑒于 functions much as 由於，因為，etc.

3.　蓋 ... 則 ...　　　PT: inasmuch as ... so ... ; because ... , so ...

Literary variation of:

a.　既然 ... 就 ...

b.　因為
　　由於 } ... 所以 ...

c.　蓋 ... 所致 = 由於 ... 所致

　　(cf. VI Structure 2; XIV NM2)

4.　介乎 AB 之間　　　PT: to lie between A and B

cf. (處) 在 YZ 之間 / 中

5.　與其 X 毋寧 Y　　　PT: to prefer Y to X; choose Y before X; to do Y is better than to do X.

$$S + VP_1 \atop S + VP_2 \Bigr\} \longrightarrow \boxed{S + 與其 + VP_1 + \begin{Bmatrix} 毋寧 \\ 不如 \\ etc. \end{Bmatrix} + VP_2}$$

我偷東西。
我 死。 $\Bigr\} \longrightarrow$ 我與其偷東西不如死。

It would be better for me to die than to steal.

現在戰爭已到最後關頭與其做戰敗的奴隸，苟且偷生，毋寧奮鬥到底與
敵人決一死戰。

Now when the war has already reached its last critical stage,
it would be better to make a life and death stand than to survive
ignominiously as conquered slaves.

與其給失業者以經濟的援助，毋寧替他們介紹職業使他們可以維持生活。

To give economic assistance to the unemployed is not as good as to
find jobs for them so they can earn a living.

Notes:

1. This pattern is a literary version of A 不如 B.

2. 莫若 / 如 , 孰若 / 如 , 寧可 , etc. can be substituted for 不如 .

3. 何 / 豈如 can be substituted for 不如 as a rhetorical inter-
    rogative adverb.

6. 姑且   A: for the time being; might as well just (try) to

成功與否我不敢說，只是姑且試試而已。
Whether it will succeed or not, I dare not say, but we might as
well try.

大問題姑且不論，就是這些小問題我還沒完全解決呢。
For the time being let's not discuss the big problems because
even the small ones I have still not completely solved.

Note:

1. 姑且 can sometimes be reduced to 姑 .

✻   ✻   ✻   ✻   ✻

Note for Review

1.   固然 ... 然而 ...   (111:9)

2.   未嘗不 ... 不過 ...   (112:7)

3.   唯（由）... 方(能) ...   (112:10)

4.   既 ... 則 ...   (113:5)

5.   即 ... 亦 ...   (113:12)

6.   雖 ... 而 ...   (115:1)

7.   倘（使）... 則 ...   (115:11)

8.   A 甚於 B (115:7)

E X E R C I S E S

I. Correlative Structures

A. 蓋...則...

1. 蓋知其不可能而爲之則自當失敗無疑。

2. 蓋此乃衆人所不取則我取之何傷。

3. 蓋有大功大業待立則彼之當選亦宜矣。

B. 與其...毋寧...

1. 關於我們兩個的交情，我認爲與其這樣繼續拖下去而使彼此抱憾終身毋寧一刀兩斷從此各不來往。

2. 在這種情形下，與其敷衍一時，毋寧定一個長久的計劃。

3. 雖然事實是如此，可是我認爲與其坐着等死毋寧冒險一試，也許能找到一條生路。

II. Structure Words

A. 藉以

1. 當時黨員常在各種報紙和雜誌上刊登文章藉以宣傳三民主義的思想。

2. 當局舉行演習的目的是藉以測驗戰鬥能力。

3. 他之所以隱姓埋名是想藉以逃避法律責任。

B. 有見於

1. 有見於壟斷的可怕，所以他們才主張節制資本。

2. 父母們有見於天才兒童常爲盛名所累，所以提倡特種教育。

3. 政府有見於測量局的無能故於今日調換該局局長。

C. 介乎/介於...之間/之中

1. 有人說第三黨是介於左翼與右翼之間，其實採取中間路線的黨派不只這一個而已。

2．那些騎牆派的人物既怕得罪了共產黨又怕得罪了國民黨。他們介於二者之間，頗有左右為難的苦處。

3．介於兩個敵人之間給他們作和事老，除了希望他們能和平相處之外，難道還有別的目的嗎？

D.　依...而定

1．你既然憎惡這個環境當然可以請求調職，至於批准與否那得依情形而定。

2．我認為與其完全依命令而行，毋寧依各人的志願而定，這樣比較能發揮各人的才能。

3．有關各部門一切措施的標準都依照新政府所頒佈的文告而定。

III. Miscellaneous

A.　萬一

1．市場上萬一發生壟斷的現象，那麼我們只有援用新近通過的法律了。

2．萬一他還用挑撥離間的手段來破壞你們兩人的感情，就請你立刻告訴我。

3．我想這是不可能的，但是，萬一他真的覺悟了，就請你姑且准他來吧。

B.　姑且

1．你姑且先開始分配。假如不夠，我再請求撥款以資補充。

2．眼看敵人漸漸逼近我們的第一線，可是我們的援軍卻未到，我想我們姑且撤退吧。

3．姑且先作一條垂直線，如果還不能求得證明，則再從頭做起。

C.　一番

1．他的債務一天多似一天，倘若不加一番清理（or不清理一番）恐怕連他自己也不知道誰是他的債主了。

2．要想出人頭地，有所作為，除非下一番功夫，否則恐怕辦不到吧。

3．雖然我屢次跟他解釋，但他仍不了解我這（一）番好意。

I. <u>Correlative Structures</u>

    A. 蓋 ... 則 ...

        1. Since the people are unsettled in mind, how can
           they resist the enemy?

        2. Since government approval cannot be obtained in time,
           there is no way to go ahead to implement the law.

    B. 與其 ... 毋寧 ...

        1. It was decided that it would be better to use
           wooden planks than cardboard because wood lasts
           longer.

        2. Last night I lay awake all night long thinking and
           came to the sad conclusion that it would be
           better to die than to go on like this.

        3. He is very ill. You would do better to call a
           doctor immediately and not wait for him to wake up.

II. <u>Structure Words</u>

    A. 藉以

        1. This new monthly hopes to improve our understanding
           of the intellectual currents in the various countries
           of the world by printing translations of representa-
           tive works of the new philosophical schools.

        2. We are trying to reduce the danger by adding another
           beam to share the weight of the ceiling.

        3. He tightened his control step by step hoping
           thereby to monopolize the whole company and expand
           his influence even further.

    B. 有見於

        1. In view of the fact that the sale of bleaching powder
           is very good, our factory is now producing it in
           large quantities.

        2. In view of your success last time, I dare say you
           will succeed again this time.

        3. Remembering the accident (車禍) which occurred
           last year because the switching of the cars was not
           properly done, the Railroad Administration has now

launched a special program to promote operating safety.

C. 介乎／於...之間／之中

1. The very nature of joint state-private commerce is that it lies in between the public and private sectors combining elements of both.

2. The proposals of the compromise party lie between the two extremes. Their attitude is neither positive nor negative. As I see it, they do not have any independent opinions of their own.

3. That little country can maintain its independence not because its power is great but because it happens to be located between two strong countries and can take advantage of the contradictions between them to strengthen its own position.

D. 依...而定

1. Whether or not you can be a pharmacist will be determined by your success on the examination.

2. Whether or not the constitution can be put into operation on schedule will be determined by political conditions at the time.

3. Whether or not I buy this will depend on the price.

III. Miscellaneous

A. 萬一

1. He is looking for a lawyer so he can determine how to divide his property in case he should die young.

2. You'd better take an umbrella along. What would you do if it rained?

3. If by any chance things should work out as we figure they might, then I wonder what his next step will be.

B. 姑且

1. Since you are bored and unhappy here, I think you might as well go to Europe for a change of scene.

2. For the moment, I won't publish your name. But if you still don't come to your senses, it may be unpleasant for you.

3. I suggest that we might as well first give him this dose of medicine and then see.

C. 一番

1. Although his graduation thesis is already finished, it has to be revised once more before it can be published.

2. Everytime I see him he scolds me.

IV. <u>Review Sentences</u>

<u>Use</u>:

既不...亦不...   發生／起...作用   較...爲優

豈   只有...而已   不是...就是...

加以   難堪   固然...但是...

以至

1. Of course I want to go and see him but when I am with him, he is either cursing or criticizing people, which I find very hard to take, and so I have not gone very often.

2. The goal of this periodical was stated in its inaugural issue. As I see it, although superficially it is a cultural undertaking, it is in fact a propaganda organ.

3. We hope by publishing more news from all sides to play a role in establishing better understanding all around.

4. In view of the general situation, he has to confess.

5. If he does it like this, he won't get stung and no one will take advantage of him. That's fair, isn't it?

6. I think we would do better to take the first choice than the second.

7. It is an undeniable fact that human behavior and temperament are directly or indirectly influenced by environment.

8．倘使你因地位懸殊，而持反對態度，則我們可從長計議。

<u>Write Sentences Using</u>:

1．不致於

2．跟着...而

3．給（...）以...

4．由於...所致

5．應...才是

6．倘使...則...

7．未嘗...不過

8．唯（由）...方...

9．即...亦...

10．甚於

Even this short excerpt clearly shows the resentment against the Unequal Treaties which permeates this wartime treatise of Generalissimo Chiang. Chiang Kai-shek is also known as Chiang Chung-cheng.

Chiang Kai-shek, China's Destiny (Chung-kuo chih ming-yun), Chungking, 1943, pp. 56-61.

116:2	租界			N:	concession (as foreign concession in China) (116:2; 117:6,7; 118:5, etc.)
	治外法權			N:	extraterritoriality
3	貿易	màu--	1	N:	trade (117:1)
	口岸			N:	port (118:5,10)
4	發行			V/N:	to issue; currency issue
	助長			V:	to promote foster, assist, reinforce
	莫大	(mwò--)	(VII:12)	ex:	enormous, great
8	辛丑	--chǒu		N:	cyclical characters for 1901
	抵押	--yā	2	V/N:	to mortgage; security (as for a loan)
9	稅則	(shwèi--)	(VII:33, NM16)	N:	tax schedule
	致使		S1		equivalent to 以致於使得
10	充斥		NM1	V:	to be increasing; to flood (as goods in a market)
117:1	趨勢	(chyū)--	(VII:8)	N:	trend, tendency
	枯竭	kū--	3	V/SV:	to dry up or wither; withered, dry
	鹽務	yán--	4	N:	salt affairs
	稽核	jī--		V/N:	to control or supervise; supervisor, inspector
	鹽稅	yán(shwèi)4,(VII:33)		N:	salt tax
3	凋敝	dyāubì	5,6	SV:	destitute

4	操縱	tsāu--	7	V/N: to manipulate or have control of; manipulation; monopolistic control
7	利潤	--rwùn	8	N: profit
	賦稅	--(shwèi)NM2,(VII:33)		N: taxation
8	營業			V/N: (to conduct a) business (operation)
	恃	shr̀	9	CV: to rely or presume on (literary) (119:7)
9	疲敝不堪	(pí bì-- kān)	10,6 (VII:31)	ex: desperately weak
	生機			N: vitality
	日竭一日		S2	ex: more exhausted day by day
	游民	yóu--	11	N: 游民 = 遊民
	從此日蹙	-----tsù	S3	ex: daily more urgent
10	重心			N: center (of gravity)
11	稍形	shāu--	12	A: somewhat, slightly
	仰給於	--jǐ--	NM3	V: to depend on for support
12	葡	pú		N: (short for) Portugal
	通商			V: to engage in trade and commerce (118:5)
118:1	相繼			A: in succession; one after the other
	大一統			ex: overall or general unification
	規模			N: model, pattern
3	疏密	shū--	13	N: density, distribution (dispersal over an area)
	周徧		NM4	SV: extensive and encompassing; widespread (as of a road network)
4	成規			N: traditional pattern
	偏枯	--kū	3	SV: paralyzed on one side; partially withered

	訂立			V: to draw; formulate; establish (as an agreement or contract)
5	埠	(bù)	(VII:38)	N: port, treaty port (literary)
	年復一年		S2	A: year after year
	滙萃	hwèitswèi	14	V/N: to gather; to be collected or amassed; gathering together
6	起點			N: starting point; point of origin
	伸張	shēn--	15	V/N: to extend; extension
	溝洫	--syù		N: drains and ditches
	失修			V: to be in disrepair
7	堤防	(dí--)	(VII:39)	N: embankment, dyke
	頹廢	twéi--	16	V: to be in ruins; to be destroyed or decadent
	洊至	jyàn--		V: to come time and again
	邱里	chyōu--		N: village
	墟	syū		N: wasteland; rubble
	轉死於溝壑	------hwò		ex: to die (in ditches) in miserable poverty as a result of a drifting life
	壯者	jwàng--	17	N: strong, able-bodied, healthy persons
10	流寇	--kòu	18	N: roving bandits or robbers
	游資	yóu--	11	N: free or floating capital (118:11)
11	湧	yǔng	19	V: to well or swell up; to float or bubble up
12	錢莊		NM5	N: (former private) bank
	交易所			N: stock exchange
	信託	(--twō)	(VII:27)	N: credit (financial), trust
	標金			N: gold bars

接踵而來	--jǔng----		ex: to follow closely one on the heels of the other
119:1 國防			N: national defense (119:2,9)
3 大抵		NM6	A: in general, on the whole
大連			N: Dairen
4 廈門	syà--	20	N: Amoy
砲艦	--jyàn	21	N: gunboat
封鎖	--swǒ	22	V/N: (to) blockade (119:5,8)
5 幹線		NM7	N: trunk lines
據點			N: base, focal point
7 割裂	--lyè	23	V: to split or divide into
試想			V: to suppose
9 阻塞	--sè	24	V: to block, stop up

CHARACTERS TO BE LEARNED

1. 貿 màu   (1) BF: barter or trade

貿易   N: trade (116:3; 117:1; 170:7)

沿海貿易權 N: right of coastal commerce (116:3)

貿易總值   N: total trade (value)

對外貿易   N: foreign trade

海上貿易   N: maritime trade; overseas trade

中外貿易   N: trade between China and foreign nations

貿易風   N: trade wind

(2) BF: rashly

貿然   A: rashly, recklessly, impulsively (104:3)

你不可以貿然參加這個會議。

You can't just brashly go to this meeting.

2. 押 yā (1) V: to mortgage, to pledge, pawn

抵押 V/N: to mortgage; security; collateral (116:8)

押租 N: deposit on rent

典押 V: to pawn

押款 N: to leave a deposit; money left on deposit; money lent on a mortgage (筆)

(2) BF: detain in custody

押起來 V: to take into custody

看押 V: to detain in custody (看 read kān)

押解/送 V: to send in custody to a certain place

3. 枯 kū BF: dry, decayed, withered

枯竭 V/SV: (to be) exhausted or dried up, withered (117:1)

偏枯 V: to be partially withered (118:4; 162:2)

枯乾 V/SV: to be dried up

枯朽 V: to be rotten

4. 鹽 yán N: salt

鹽務 N: salt administration (117:1)

鹽務局 N: Salt Gabelle

鹽稅 N: salt tax (117:1)

鹽田 N: evaporation pools for obtaining salt from sea water

海鹽 N: salt refined from sea water

粗/細鹽 N: (un)refined salt

鹽水 N: salt water

食鹽 N: table salt

私鹽   N: smuggled salt

鹽場   N: salt field

鹽商   N: salt producer

鹽類   N: salts (chemical)

5. 凋 dyāu   BF: faded, withered

凋零   V: to fall (as scattered leaves)

凋落   V: to fade

凋謝   V: to fade and fall (as flowers)

6. 敝 bì   BF: poor, unworthy, worn out

凋敝 V/SV: destitute (117:3)

敝姓/國   N: "my humble name/country"

7. 操 tsāu   (1) BF: grasp, manage

操縱 V/N: to control, monopolize; monopolistic control of (as a market, source of supplies, etc.) (117:4; 170:9)

操勞 V/SV: (to be) painstaking

操心 VO/SV: to worry; to take pains

別操這個心了。
Don't worry about this.

操在...手裡   ex: to be in the grasp of ...

操作 V/N: (to do) manual labor

操生殺之權   ex: to have the power of life and death (of judges, emperors or people in power)

(2) BF: exercise, drill; conduct

操練 V/N: (to) practice, drill

體操   N: setting-up exercises

作體操   VO: to do physical exercise

早操   N: morning exercise

操場　N: exercise (athletic) field

操行／守　N: deportment (as in school); conduct (personal)

8. 潤 rwùn　　BF: moisten, enrich

利潤　N: profit (financial) (117:7)

潤濕 V/SV: moist (also 濕潤)

肥潤 V/SV: to fatten, enrich; sleek

9. 恃 shr　　CV: to rely on, presume on (literary) (117:8; 119:7)

依／仗恃　V: to rely on, to depend on

恃財　V: to rely on one's wealth

恃勝輕進　EX: to pursue the enemy recklessly after an initial small victory (which may have been a trap)

10. 疲 pi　　BF: tired, weary, exhausted

疲敝　SV: weak, weary, exhausted

疲敝不堪　ex: to be unbearably weak (117:9)

疲乏　SV: exhausted, fatigued

疲於奔命　EX: exhausted from being too much on the go

疲勞 SV/N: exhausted; exhaustion

疲勞審問　N: round the clock interrogation

疲勞轟炸　EX: to bombard repeatedly so as to make people exhausted; tiresome speeches, instructions, etc.

11. 游 yóu　(1)　V: to float, roam, to swim

游資　N: free or floating capital (118:10,11)

游擊　N: guerilla

游擊隊　N: guerilla band

打游擊　VO: to fight a guerilla war; to eat from one place to another (to have no regular eating place) (colloq.)

游擊戰   N: guerilla war （ 場 ）

interchangeable with 遊 in the following usages:

游民   N: vagabond loafer (117:9)

無業游民   N: unemployed vagrants

散兵游勇 EX: irregular or dispersed troops; deserters
(122:2)

游行V/N: to demonstrate; demonstration (152:3,5,9,10)

游行隊伍   N: demonstrating group or column
(157:8,11; 158:7,11)

游戲V/N: to amuse; games, recreation; amusement
(160:11; 161:3,9; 164:9)

游玩V/N: to play or relax; relaxation

游歷   V: to sightsee

游手好閒 EX: an idler who loves to waste time （ 好 hàu）

(2) BF: reaches (of a river)

上／下游   N: upper/lower reaches of a stream

12. 稍 shāu   BF: somewhat, a little (117:11)

稍稍／微   A: slightly, somewhat

稍有 EX: to have or make some minor differences

稍有不合 EX: to be a bit different or
unsuitable

稍有進步 EX: to have made a little progress

稍加   V: to make some additions

稍加小心 EX: to be a little more careful

稍加努力 EX: to put forth a little more
effort

稍久   A: a little longer

13. 疏 shū   (1) BF: sparse

  (疎Xsū)   疏密   N: distribution, density of distribution (118:3)

                疏遠V/SV: to be distant from, estranged (138:10)

                疏散   V: to scatter, disperse, evacuate; dispersal

              (2) BF: careless, remiss, negligent

                生疏V/SV: to be unpracticed; not well acquainted

                疏於   V: to be remiss or careless about

                      疏於防範／練習 VO: to be careless about
                                         precautions against (as
                                         thieves/practice, etc.)

                疏忽V/SV/N: to be careless, neglectful; neglect

              (3) BF: dredge, or clear out

                疏通 V/N: to make matters clear; to try to bring about
                        an understanding; removal of a block to
                        understanding

                疏導V/N: to remove obstructions; removal of obstructions

14. 匯 hwèi   (1) BF: waters converging on one spot

  (滙)   匯合   V: to gather together in one place; to come
                        together (172:5)

              (2) BF: remit; bank draft

                匯票   N: draft; money order

                匯款VO/N: to transmit a sum of money; remittance;
                        draft (筆)

                匯費   N: remittance fee

                外匯   N: foreign exchange

15. 伸 shēn   BF: extend, stretch out

                伸張 V/N: to extend; expand, spread out; dissemination,
                        spread (118:6)

                伸訴 V/N: to present a complaint; legal complaint

引伸 V/N: to infer, to stretch out; inference

伸入　V: to stretch, extend or penetrate into

伸出/開 RV: to stretch out

伸手　VO: to stretch out the hand

伸手不見五指　EX: to be unable to see one's own hand (usually describes dense darkness or fog)

16. 頹 twéi　　BF: destroyed, ruined, decadent

頹廢 SV: destroyed, ruined, decadent; low spirited (118:7)

頹勢　N: decline; declining condition or trend

頹敗　V: to be routed or overthrown

17. 壯 jwàng　　SV: strong, healthy (118:7)

強壯 SV: robust

兵強馬壯　EX: good soldiers and fine horses

壯丁　N: able-bodied man; adult male (subject to conscription)

壯大 SV: strong, flourishing

精壯 SV: well-trained and strong

壯麗 SV: grand

少壯 Adj: young

少壯派　N: "Young Turks" (i.e. radical group)

壯年　N: manhood; prime of life

壯志　N: firmness of purpose; determination; resolution

18. 寇 kòu　　BF: bandit, robber; cruel, tyrannize

流寇　N: roving bandits or robbers (118:10; 172:6)

外寇　N: foreign bandits or robbers

日寇　　N: Japanese bandits (common term during Sino-Japanese War, 1937-1945)

入寇　　V: to invade or encroach upon (territory)

殘寇　　N: remnant bandits or robbers

海寇　　N: pirates

俄寇　　N: (term of opprobrium applied to) Russians

寇邊　　V: to invade the border

19. 湧 yǔng　　V: to bubble up; to flow rapidly
(涌)

風起雲湧　EX: (lit. the wind rises and the clouds well up); very widespread or prevalent (118:11)

湧上來　RV: to surge or bubble forth or up

湧出　V: to surge or gush forth

湧進　V: to burst in upon

20. 廈 syà　　(1) BF: large building
(厦)

大廈　　N: (modern) office building, mansion (as of apartment buildings)

高樓大廈　EX: large tall buildings

(2) Place name

廈門　　N: Amoy (119:4)

21. 艦 jyàn　　BF: warship (144:1)

砲艦　　N: gunboat (119:4) (隻 measure for first five entries)

軍艦　　N: military vessel; warship

主力/戰鬥艦　N: battleship

驅逐艦　　N: destroyer

航空母艦　　N: aircraft carrier

艦長　　N: captain of a warship or fleet

艦隊　　N: fleet (支)

22. 鎖 swǒ   V/N: (to) lock

  封鎖 V/N: (to) lock off; (to) blockade (119:4,5,8)

  鎖起來 RV: to lock up

23. 裂 lyè   V: to split, crack, to rip open

  割裂   V: to split or separate into (119:7)

  破裂 V/N: to break, to tear; (to) crack (149:3)

  決裂 V/N: to grow apart, split off from; split (172:9)

  分裂 V/N: (to) split (fig. as political, social, etc.)

    四分五裂 EX: broken into pieces

  裂開   V: to split open

  崩裂 V/N: (to) cave in (like a landslide); (to) break open (as of a sore); breaking open

    山崩地裂   EX: (lit. the mountain caved in and the ground split open); time of great national catastrophe

  裂痕   N: fissure

24. 塞 sè   (1) V: to stop up or block

  阻塞   V: to close up, block or stop up (119:9)

  塞責   V: to perform duties in a perfunctory manner

    敷衍塞責   EX: to finish up a matter in a sloppy and unconscientious manner and perform duties in a perfunctory way

(sāi)
(sei)   (2) V: to block or stop up

  塞住 RV: to stop up, block up

  塞滿 RV: to stuff full (as a truck)

  塞子   N: cork (to a bottle)

(sài)   (3) BF: pass, northern and eastern frontiers

邊塞　　　N: border passes, frontiers

塞外／北　N: area beyond or north of the passes

NEW MEANINGS

1. 斤　　　BF: extend

　　充斥　V: to be on the increase; to flood (as goods in a market (116:10)

2. 賦　　　BF: levy, exact, give, pay; wealth

　　賦稅　N: taxes; taxation (117:7)

　　財賦　N: wealth, riches (117:12)

　　田賦　N: land taxes

3. 給 jǐ　　BF: supply, provide

　　家給人足　EX: situation in which all are prosperous and well-provided for (of district or country) (114:2)

　　仰給於...　V: to rely on ... for support (117:11)

　　供給 V/N: (to) support (materially) (148:5)

　　　　我供給他上學。
　　　　I pay his school bills.

　　給養　N: provisions

　　發給　V: to issue or grant (as passport, certificate, etc.)

　　配給 V/N: (to) ration

　　自給自足　EX: self-supporting

4. 周　　　BF: all around, everywhere

　　周徧　SV: spread out in all directions; extensive (118:3)

　　周全　V: to help toward the completion of some project

　　周密　SV: complete; thorough (of thought, plans, etc.)

周到 SV: thorough and thoughtful (as arrangements
    for social occasion or entertainment);
    hospitable

他給我們預備的很周到。
He had prepared things beautifully for us.

周知 V: to be widely known

眾所周知 EX: everyone knows

5. 莊 (1) BF: indicating place of business

錢莊 N: (former private) bank (118:12)

茶(葉)莊 N: shop which sells tea

做莊 VO: to be the banker (in a gambling game)

(2) Surname

老莊學說 N: Taoism; thought of Laotze and Chuangtze

6. 抵 BF: generally; on the whole (as a whole)

大抵 MA: in general; on the whole (119:3; 160:10;
    165:4)

7. 幹 BF: trunk of tree or of the body

幹線 N: main line; trunk lines (as of a railway)
    (119:5)

幹部 N: cadre (126:5; 130:9)

枝幹 N: trunk and branches

主幹 N: backbone, mainstay (as of an organization)

STRUCTURE NOTES

1. 致使

A. Translates like 以致於使 (cf. IV Structure 6)

B. Compare 弄得，使得.

他（因爲）事前沒有通知 {致使 / 弄得 / 使得} 大家臨時手忙脚亂。

Because he did not supply information in advance, it meant every one was terribly busy when the time came.

2. 日 VERB 一日

A. PT: to VERB more and more day by day

日甚一日 = 一天比一天厲害
worse and worse/more and more each day

日竭一日 = 一天比一天少
fewer and fewer/more and more exhausted each day

B. 日/年復一日/年 PT: day/year after day/year

日復一日 = 一天又一天

3. 日多/蹙

日多/增 = 一天比一天多 more and more each day

日蹙/少 = 一天比一天少 less and less each day

cf. 日益 IX Structure 1.

Note for review:

1. 即 ... 亦 ... (= 連 ... 亦 ...)(117:2)
2. 凡 ... 無不 ... (117:2)
3. 不獨 ... 並且 ... (117:3)

4. 既 ...亦 ... (118:3)

5. 雖 ...而 ... (118:9)

6. 既 ...於是 ... (118:11)

7. 若 ...則 ... (119:8)

8. 自 ...以至於 ... (117:11)

9. 然而 ...卻 ... (117:4)

10. 乃至於 (116:4)

11. SV 不堪 (117:9)

12. 由 as CV of agent (117:1)

E X E R C I S E S

I. Miscellaneous

A.日／年復一日／年

1. 我年復一年的給他們疏通，其用意無非是想幫他們一點忙，沒有其他目的。

2. 股東會議決定，雖然利潤年復一年的增加，但是絕不增設第二分廠；我認為非常可惜。

B.日竭一日

1. 現在他的精力似乎已到了日竭一日的程度了，你看他那種疲敝不堪的樣子！

C.致使

1. 近來因為散兵游勇日見增加，致使社會秩序日益混亂。

2. 雖然部隊給養日增，可是浪費也日多，致使主管不滿，因而辭職。

3. 最近因為工作繁重所以常常加班到半夜，致使每日睡眠不足。

I.   Miscellaneous

A.   年/日復一年/日

1.   The number of the guerrillas in their country is
     increasing every year. How can they talk of peace?

2.   The value of our trade increases year by year show-
     ing that our economy is on the road to prosperity.

B.   日竭一日

1.   A blockade of that country must be carried out by
     naval vessels. It won't last long because their
     industry is declining daily.

C.   致使

1.   Recently the weather has been very good, but because
     too much snow has accumulated, there is no way to
     get rid of it making transportation difficult for
     the moment.

2.   Although the tariff regulations are good, because
     of improper administration, it has come to the point
     where receipts have actually dropped.

3.   Because a serious new split developed between
     those two parties, the work of trying to bring about
     an understanding between them has proceeded very
     slowly, to the point where the meeting cannot open
     on time.

II.   Review Sentences

Use: 凡是 ...   SV 不堪   不堪 VERB   有見於

      固有   由於 ... 所致   一律   不獨 ... 並且 ...

      加以

1.   The present tariff system is an extraordinarily good
     system. Not only can it increase the government's
     tax receipts, but it can also protect our native
     products.

2.   After a major illness one should be careful not to
     exert himself too much. Otherwise he may get unbearably
     tired.

3. Taking cognizance of the fact that the use of salt steadily expands, the authorities have stipulated that all new inventions relevant to the production of salt will be welcomed and encouraged by the government.

4. Their profit has not reached anticipated levels because of inadequate management.

5. They have abolished the original system of salt taxes but the new one has not yet been promulgated and so cannot be put into effect.

6. If the guerrilla war continues, the losses on both sides will be too terrible to contemplate.

7. 游資之所以能興風作浪，是因爲經濟政策不健全所致。

8. 在過去三百年中錢莊制度成爲中國金融界唯一的交易機關，深爲各方所倚重。

9. 抵押借款也好，信用借款也好，總之，今天得把錢拿來，否則，難關是無法度過的。

10. 我國固有的體操固然早已不存在，然而，新興的體操又何嘗存在呢！

Write Sentence Using:

1. 皆

2. 於是

3. 予以

4. 以資

5. 得志

6. 縱然 ... 還 ...

7. 藉以

8. 姑且

9. 與其 ... 毋寧 ...

10. 無求於人

XVI. EIGHT ARTICLES PROMULGATED BY THE HEADQUARTERS OF THE CHINESE PEOPLE'S
LIBERATION ARMY

In the final stages of the Civil War, the People's Liberation Army
issued the following statement on the political and social role of the
Army in the period of hostilities and transition.

The Present Situation and Our Responsibility (Mu-ch'ien hsing-shih ho
wo-men ti jen-wu) Hongkong, 1949, pp. 199-201.

120:7	總部			N: general headquarters
	約法			N: articles, covenant, code (120:6)
3	業已		NM1	A: already
5	怙惡不悛	hù----chywān		EX: obdurate and irreclaimable (121:8)
6	茲	dz̄	1	A: now, herewith
9	搗亂	dǎu--	2	V: to cause trouble, to make trouble
10	搶刼	--jyé	3	V: to plunder, rob
11	牧業	mù--	4	N: pastoral or herding industry
	倉庫	tsāngkù	5,6	N: storehouse (121:1)
	船舶	--bwó	7	N: ships, boats (121:1)
	牧場	mù--	4	N: cattle ranch
12	照常			A: as usual
121:1	沒收	(mwò)--	NM2	V/N: to confiscate; confiscation
2	郵政			N: postal service
	接管			V: to take over and run (as an enterprise from an enemy, former owner, etc.) (121:3,4,5)
3	股份	gǔ--	8	N: stock (in a company)
	調查屬實			EX: to determine the facts (in a legal case, of ownership, etc.)
	供職			V: to hold an appointment or have a job (121:3,7)

4 照舊   V/A: (to continue) as of old

   圖表   N: drawings (as for machines, houses), charts, tables

   檔案   dǎng--   9   N: files, records (121:11; 122:1)

   聽候   NM3   V: to wait, to await (121:11)

   清點   V/N: (to check) inventory; stocktaking

5 獎   jyǎng   10   V/N: reward

   怠工   dài--   11   V/N: to be slack about or slovenly on the job; slow-down

   准予   V: to be permitted to; to allow (121:12)

   量才錄用   NM4   EX: to employ in accordance with qualifications

6 體育場所   N: exercise grounds or facilities

9 國大   N: abbr. of 國民大會

   參議員   N: senator

   保甲人員   NM5   N: pao-chia personnel

10 不加   V: abbr. of 不加以

   俘虜   fú(lǔ)   12   V/N: (to take) prisoner
                          (VII:6)

   責成   V: to charge (with responsibility)

   職守   N: duty, official responsibility

11 一技之長   EX: good point; something one is good at

12 分別   A: respectively

122:1 交代   V/N: to hand over, to give an accounting of; an accounting of

                          作一個交代 VO: to give an accounting of (event, responsibility)

                          他離職時交代的不清楚。
                          When he left his job he did not turn things over very clearly.

3 報到   V: (here) to report to the authorities;
                                        (usually) to report for duty

   查究   V/N: to investigate; investigation

4 窩藏   wō--   13   V: to conceal, hide away

   處分   (chǔ--)   NM6   V/N: to punish; punishment

5 合理   SV: reasonable

8 農作   Adj: agricultural

11 法令   N: law, order, command

   間諜   (jyàn)dyé   NM7,14   N: spy

12 包庇   --bì   15   V: to protect; to conceal the truth about

123:2 安居樂業   EX: to live peacefully and work happily

   切勿   --wù   16   AV: on no account, by no means

3 謠言   yáu--   17   N: rumor

CHARACTERS TO BE LEARNED

1. 茲   dz̄   BF: now; this, here
   (茲)
              茲   A: now herewith (120:6)

                 茲因   now because of

                 茲有   there is now

                 茲請/擇 /etc.   now invite/choose, etc.

2. 搗   dǎu   V: to pound, ram down; to stir or poke

           搗亂   V: to cause a disturbance; to create trouble; to
                    be a nuisance (120:9)

                 搗亂份子 N: one who gives trouble

           搗鬼   V: to play tricks and thus to make trouble

           搗蛋 V/SV: to cause a disturbance, make trouble (of
                    children, trouble-makers, etc.; less serious
                    than 搗鬼)

搗碎 RV: to beat to pieces; to smash

直搗 V: to strike directly at

直搗黃龍 EX: to attack at the vital heart of the enemy

搗米 VO: to hull rice in a mortar

搗藥 VO: to pound drugs

3. 劫 jyé V: to plunder or rob (forcibly)
(刦刧刼)

搶刼 V: to plunder, rob (120:10)

打劫 V: to plunder

趁火打劫 EX: to rob somebody while his house is burning (the implication is to harm someone who is already in trouble)

劫奪 V: to rob forcibly

洗劫 V: to plunder or rob completely of

劫持 V: to kidnap, to carry someone away by force

4. 牧 mù BF: shepherd

牧業 N: pastoral industry; herding (120:11)

牧場 N: grazing grounds; pasture; ranch (120:11)

游牧 N: herding; nomadic pastoral industry (135:12)

游牧民族 N: nomadic peoples

牧童 N: shepherd (172:7)

牧師 N: pastor (Christian)

5. 倉 tsāng (1) N: granary, bin (120:11; 121:1)

穀倉 N: granary

貨倉 N: warehouse

開倉 V: to open the granaries (specifically in times of famine)

(2) BF: hurried

倉忙／促　SV: in a hurry, hurried

6. 庫 kù　　　N: warehouse; storehouse

倉庫　N: warehouse, depot (120:11; 121:1)

國庫　N: national treasury

書庫　N: place where books are stored; stacks

火藥庫　N: arsenal

7. 舶 bwó　BF: ocean-going junk or ship

船舶　N: ships (120:11; 121:1)

舶來品　N: imported goods

8. 股 gǔ　(1)　N: share (as of stock); portion, division, branch

股分(份)　N: share or stock (in a company) (121:3)

股份有限公司　N: limited company

入股　VO: to invest capital in a company by buying shares

股本　N: share-capital

股票　N: shares or stocks

股東　N: share or stockholder

股息　N: dividend

八股文　N: "eight-legged" (traditional style) essay

股長　N: head of a department (of an organization)

(2)　M: for a puff of air

一股子熱／冷／香氣　N: blast of hot/cold/fragrant air

一股子氣　N: sudden spurt of enthusiasm; all in one breath

9. 檔 dǎng　　BF: files, records

檔案　N: files, records; case (121:4,11; 122:1)

歸檔   V: to return to the files

10. 獎 jyǎng (1) N: prize (121:5)

得獎 VO: to win a prize

獎品   N: prize

獎學金 N: scholarship

獎章   N: decoration, medal

開獎 VO: to hold a drawing for (as a national lottery)

(2) BF: encourage, praise

獎勵 V/N: to encourage with rewards; to reward; encouragement

誇獎 V/N: (to) praise

過獎   V: to praise unduly (polite reply to a compliment)

11. 怠 dai   BF: idle, lazy, remiss, rude

怠工 V/N: to slow down on the job by being lazy, careless; to sabotage work; slow-down (121:5)

怠慢 V/SV: to treat disrespectfully or rudely; lacking in proper courtesy or hospitality (often used as a courteous expression to guests to indicate they have not been treated as well at a party as they should have been)

荒怠   V: to neglect

怠忽   V: to be remiss

怠惰 SV: lazy

倦怠 SV: fatigued and listless

12. 俘 fú   BF: prisoner

俘虜 V/N: to take prisoner; prisoner (121:10)

交換俘虜 VO: to exchange prisoners

俘虜營 N: prisoner camp

被俘   V: to be captured

俘獲　V: to have captured (people or weapons)

13. 窩 wō　N/M: (for) nest, den

窩藏　V: to conceal, to hide away (122:4)

被窩　N: quilt

鳥窩　N: bird's nest

酒窩兒　N: dimple

14. 諜 dyé　BF: spy

諜報　N: intelligence report

諜報員　N: intelligence agent

15. 庇 bì　BF: protect, shelter, screen

包庇 V/N: to conceal the truth about (as criminals, traitors, conversations, etc.); to protect from detection; protection, cover (122:12)

庇護　V: to harbor; (to) shelter

政治庇護　EX: political asylum

16. 勿 wù　A: (negative injunction) do not (also one classical term for 不)

切勿　AV: by no means; on no account (classical for 絕對不要 ...)(123:2)

(請)勿　AV: (please) do not ... (classical for 請不要 ...) (155:8)

(請)勿吸煙／入內／etc.
(Please) don't smoke/enter, etc.

非禮勿視／聽／言／動　EX: do not look at/listen to/speak/act without observing the proprieties

17. 謠 yáu　(1) BF: rumor

謠言　N: rumor (123:3)

造謠　VO: to start a rumor

造謠生事   EX: to create trouble by
starting rumors

謠傳 V/N/ex: to noise about; rumor; it is rumored that

(2) BF: ballad

民/歌謠   N: folk songs

NEW MEANINGS

1. 業   BF: already

   業已   A: already (120:3)

   業經   A: alreády, past

2. 沒 mwò   BF: dead, gone, sunk

   沒收   V: to confiscate (121:1; 126:5,6; 130:2,7, etc.)

   沒落   V: decline (147:2)

   埋沒   V: to bury (as talent)

   覆沒   V: to be utterly defeated or destroyed (applies
         usually to armies)

         全軍覆沒。
         The whole army was wiped out.

3. 候   BF: wait

   聽候   V: to await, wait for (as orders) (121:4,11)

   等候   V: to wait for

   候車室   N: waiting room (station)

   候客室   N: reception room

   候補 Adj: to wait to fill a vacancy; awaiting appointment

      候補黨員   N: candidate for party membership

4. 錄   BF: choose for appointment

   錄用   V: to employ or use (121:12)

量才錄用　EX: to employ according to
　　　　　　　 qualifications (121:5)

錄取　V: to take in through examination

5. 甲　　　BF: term for the pao-chia system (of local security)

保甲人員　N: pao-chia system personnel (either militia
　　　　　　 or urban police for registration or security)
　　　　　　 (121:9)

保甲制度　N: pao-chia system (of local security)

某甲　N: John Doe

6. 處　chǔ　　BF: punish, sentence

處分 V/N: to punish; punishment (122:4)

處罰 V/N: to punish; punishment

處死　V: to sentence to death

處刑 VO: to sentence (for punishment)

處決　V: to execute (the death penalty)

7. 間　jyàn　(1) BF: alienate, spy

間諜　N: spy (122:11)

反間　V: to conduct counter-intelligence

反間計 N: counter-intelligence scheme

離間　V: to alienate

挑撥離間　EX: deliberately to stir up trouble
　　　　　　 or friction between friends or
　　　　　　 friendly parties

(2) BF: space between, interrupt

間道 V/N: to go by a by-path; by-path

間斷 V/N: to interrupt, to discontinue; interruption

間不容髮 EX: (fig.) to hang precariously as by a thread

間隔 V/N: to have a distance or space in between;
　　　　　 distance

疏不間親 EX: inappropriate or unwise for a stranger to
attempt to alienate close friends or parents
and children

* * * * * * *

STRUCTURE NOTES

Note for Review:

1. 凡屬 ... 的 N， 均 ... (121:1)

   凡屬 ... 的 N， 一律 ...   (120:11)

2. 如 ... (則) ...   (120:9)

3. 使 ...不致 ...   (122:8)

4. 予 (以)   (120:6,10; 122:1)

5. 藉以   (122:8)

6. 不得 + V   (122:11)

7. 不加 (121:10)

   加以 (122:8)

8. 者 (after a clause) (120:10)

9. 之 (as direct object) (120:7)

10. 方才 (122:7)

11. 均 = 都 (121:2,4)

12. 否則 (122:12)

13. 為 ... 目的   (122:2)

14. 不 ... 不 ...   (121:9)

E X E R C I S E S

I. Review

A. 分別

1. 迄今爲止，這學期犯校規的學生已經有二十人之多，學校方面已分別予以處分。

2. 要想使政治上軌道非得先清除那些貪官汚吏，依照他們犯罪的輕重分別加以懲治不可。

3. 現在上市的股票太多，不是老資格簡直不能分別他們的性質。

4. 「貢獻」跟「奉獻」的分別在那兒？我還不十分清楚，你可以不可以給我說明一下。

B. 予，准予，予以

1. 爲了獎賞工作勤快者當局訂有獎勵辦法，然對工作不勤快者亦應予以嚴懲才對。

2. 現在當局准予間諜自首（to surrender）。一經調查完畢，如無重大嫌疑卽予以自新的機會。

3. 上次被捕的兩個外國人，經過警察局調查以後已經證實不是間諜而予以釋放了。

4. 稅收人員倘若有營私舞弊的違法行爲則人民可以向政府控告，政府應卽予以查究懲辦。

C. 寧可...也...

1. 目前前線的情況對我們不太有利，雖然我們處在這樣孤立的地位，可是我已決定寧可被俘也不願意投降。

2. 他們寧可冒窩藏間諜的危險，也要救助他，確實難得。

D. 甚至；至於；不致於；以致（於）

1. 有些學者對青年教育不熱心，甚至爲了自己的名望，而壟斷研究資料，把知識當做私有財產。這種自私自利的作風對於培養青年異常不利，應該徹底加以消除才好。

2. 至於是否應該用舶來品，我認爲這是一個需要開會來決定的問題。

3. 倘若銀行準備金很充足，借出的款項又能按期收回，則業務不致於
發生障礙。

4. 當秦始皇掌權的時候，由於造長城，修阿房宮而大興土木
(construction) 以致於國家財政的消耗日增一日，人民的生活
也因之日益困苦了。

E. 凡...｜(都／一律／etc.) ...

1. 凡預先繳費者，准享受本社各種福利。

2. 凡曾犯規者，不能再參加此次比賽。

II.   Miscellaneous Review

1. 我認為與其勉強同意，毋寧坦率說出我們所以不同意的理由，尊意
如何？

2. 新總統當政以來，未嘗不想剷除腐化的官吏，本着他的施政方針，
興利除弊，改革舊制。然而政府中保守分子太多，以致新政策的推
行頗受阻礙。

3. 如果在引渡的手續上有麻煩，何必不另作別圖以資補救呢？

4. 因為各人的性格不同，經驗不同，縱使生活在同一個時代，他們的
人生哲學也不一定會相同。

I. Review

   A. 分別

      1. Many people who have worked for years on ranches
         still cannot distinguish between the two types of
         cattle fever.

      2. The uses of "了" in the vernacular are extremely
         complicated. If they are not separately explained,
         it is very difficult to get a clear conception of
         them.

      3. I do not feel that I have the qualifications to
         discuss the distinctions between a limited stock
         company and an unlimited one.

      4. After the conclusion of the war, the Allies arrested
         war criminals and interrogated them separately.

   B. 加以，不加 (以)

      1. Some people maintain that the government ought to
         ban all periodicals which poison youth.

      2. Recently the craze for gambling has been steadily
         increasing. If the government does not interfere,
         the influence on society will be very detrimental.

   C. 足以，藉以，以資

      1. We have just completed a three-day investigation
         into our old personnel files and shall send the
         results on to you for reference.

      2. The government has appropriated large funds for the
         relief of refugees.

      3. The warehouses which have been recently built along
         the wharves are enough to accommodate the cargoes of
         three ships at the same time. It is hoped thus to
         increase trade.

   D. 凡 ...（都／一律／etc.）...

      1. All those who watch the play but don't buy tickets
         will be fined $200.

      2. All companies or stores which smuggle cosmetics will
         be punished by the closing of their places of
         business.

E. 寧可 ... 也 ...

1. My first aim in participating in this limited stock
    company was to help stimulate the business.
    Although it is still not successful today, it can
    still hold on. Therefore even though I may have
    received no dividends, I will not sell out.

2. Even though it means relinquishing his scholarship,
    he will still oppose the strike to the end.

F. 甚至，至於，不致於，以致 (於)

1. If precautions had been taken against flooding,
    the losses would not have been so alarming.

2. As to the form of folksongs and the way in which
    they are sung, those are technical questions which
    we won't raise here for the moment.

3. After that incident occurred, disturbing elements
    in society took advantage of the opportunity to
    create rumors which greatly agitated people and
    confused society at large.

4. It is said some professors are only concerned about
    their own works and reputation and are not in the
    least interested in teaching and won't even assume
    responsibility for students.

G. 與其 ... 毋寧 ...

1. If you want to decide whether a society is good or
    bad, it's better to get some practical experience
    by living there than to listen to endless debates
    on the matter.

2. Some people claim that it would be better to settle
    the Vietnam War by negotiation rather than by force.

II. Review Sentences

Use:

果然   只要 ... 就 ...   為 ... 着想

受   一切 ... 惟有 ... 却 ...

1. Although the air defense measures of that village are
    not complete, there are many mountain caves around.
    As long as you quickly hide in the caves when enemy

planes come, you are quite safe.

2.   After the victory in the War of Resistance, all
     organizations and factories in the Japanese-occupied
     areas were taken over by the government. It was only
     in various areas of the Northeast that factories were
     taken over by the Communists.

3.   As long as the government can devise means to let the
     peasants live peacefully and work happily without being
     disturbed by bandits, the people will be satisfied.

4.   Long ago there was a rumor that there was widespread
     dissatisfaction among the stockholders. Investigation
     proved that this was indeed the case.

<u>Write Sentences Using</u>:

1. 藉以   9.   ...也好，...也好，總...

2. 方才   10. 在於

3. 業已   11. 不得

4. 茲   12. 如...則...

5. 列入...以內   13. 蓋...所致

6. 年復一年   14. 指...而言

7. ...一次 etc. 就...一次   15. 每逢...就...

8. 只消...即可

In this essay, originally entitled "The Rewards of Participation in Land Reform," one of China's leading philosophers, known to Western students through translations of his full and condensed histories of Chinese philosophy, describes how he participated in land reform and how it affected his thinking. The last few pages of the essay have been omitted.

Fung Yu-lan, et al., How Did My Thinking Change? (Wo-ti ssu-hsiang shih tsen-yang chuan-pien kuo-lai ti?), Peking, 1952, pp. 121-132.

124:T	馮友蘭	féng----	1	N: Fung Yu-lan
2	郊區	jyāu--	2	N: suburbs; countryside around a city (131:11,12)
	土改			N: abbr. for 土地改革 (124:2,6,8, etc.)
	張儀村	--yí--	3	N: Chang-yi Village (127:3)
3	果實			N: rewards; fruits (abstract)
	蘆溝橋	lú----		N: Lukouch'iao (scene of the Marco Polo Bridge incident of 1937) (126:12; 129:8; 130:2; 133:3)
	從新			A: from the beginning; all over again
4	返校	fǎn--	4	VO: to return to the school
6	清華			N: Tsinghua University
	大字報			N: big-character newspaper (a propaganda form used on public bulletin boards)
	動機			N: motive, motivation (125:12)
125:2	意味			N: meaning, significance
4	充實			V/SV: to supplement; to be ample
8	一向			MA: heretofore; hitherto, always in the past
9	牽引	chyān--	5	V: (fig.) to pull along

10 一面倒   ex: "to lean to one side" (phrase used by Mao Tse-tung to describe the policy of relying exclusively on the "people" and the Communist world) (128:3; 131:5)

12 出發   V: to start out (lit. and fig.)

    出發點 N: starting point

126:5 高峯   --fēng   6   N: high point, peak; (here) climax

    6 傳   (chwán)   NM1   V: to fetch and bring; summon

       守衞   V/N: (to stand) guard

    7 評議員   N: appraisers, judges, evaluators

       浩浩蕩蕩   hàuhàu   7,8   ex: (here) menacingly and in great
                   dàngdàng   number

       把守住   RV: to guard closely, hold firmly, control

    8 喝問   NM2   V: to question menacingly or fiercely (126:8)

       動手   V: to start, to make a move to ...

       擺   bǎi   9   V: to spread out

    9 象徵   (--jēng)(VII:NM10) N: symbol

127:3 改朝換帝／代   ex: (lit. to change dynasties and exchange emperors) continuation of an old system under a new name

       宦海升沉   hwàn----   10,11 EX: (lit. rise and fall in the sea of
                   chen   officialdom); vicissitudes of official fortune

       相混   V: to mix up

    4 慚愧   tsánkwèi   12,13 V/SV: (to be) ashamed, regretful

    7 馮至   N: Feng Chih

       歌德   N: Goethe (127:10)

    8 現實   N: reality (127:8)

       恐懼   --jyù   14   V/SV/N: to fear; frightened, fearful; fear

9	明朗	--lǎng	15	SV/N:	to be very clear; "the light" (i.e. in the sense of understanding)
	悲劇	bēi--	16	N:	tragedy
10	和諧	--syé		SV:	agreeable; harmonious
128:1	不拘	--jyū	17,S1	CJ:	no matter
2	搞好	gǎu--	18	RV:	to put into good shape
	拖	twō	19	V:	to drag
5	作祟	--swèi	20	V:	to bedevil; to cause trouble
6	待		(VII:NM22)	V:	to await
9	(不)以(...)爲然		S2	V:	(not) to consider as right
	一轉念間			ex:	effortlessly; in a flash; not requiring a second's thought
11	德意志			N:	Germany
	意識形態			N:	ideology
	生來			MA:	by birth, by nature
129:8	一堆一堆	--dwēi--dwēi	21	ex:	in piles, pile by pile
	耪地	pǎng--		V:	to spade up or loosen dirt (129:9)
9	一棵	--kē	22	M:	for trees, plants
	心疼	--téng	23	V:	to be (emotionally) very distressing
	哎呀	āiyā		EX:	"ai ya"; an exclamation of regret
130:2	穩定	(wěn)--	(VII:7)	V/SV:	stable, calm, secure
4	歡欣	--syīn	24	SV:	happy
5	悲哀	bēi--	15	SV:	sad
	儼然	yǎn--	25	A:	seemingly, just like
6	叫花子			N:	beggar
9	呼來喝去		NM2	EX:	to order about in a harsh manner
	掃	sǎu	26	V:	to sweep

10 翻身   V/N: to be emancipated; emancipation (lit. to turn over the body implying to get a new start in life)

11 大爺   --yé   27   N: (here) Big Boss

   咱們   dzán--   28   PN: we (colloquial)

131:6 整風文獻   N: "Documents on the Rectification Movement"

132:1 應付   (VII:NM11) V: to meet or deal with; to temporize (141:4)

   4 術語   N: technical term

     整頓   --dwùn   NM3,29   V/N: to reorganize; reorganization

     檢閱   --ywè   30   V/N: (to) review (of troops)

   5 狡辯   jyǎu--   31   V/N: to argue speciously or sophistically; ridiculous reasoning (i.e. usually in self-justification)

   6 情緒   --syù   32   N: emotion, feelings, mood

   7 把穩   (--wěn)   (VII:7)   V: to maintain firm grasp on or control of

  11 文件   N: documents

133:3 兼作   (jyān--)   (VII:42)   V: to do more than one thing at a time (as to hold two jobs, etc.)

CHARACTERS TO BE LEARNED

1. 馮 féng   Surname (124:T; 127:7)

2. 郊 jyāu   BF: suburbs

       郊區   N: suburban district (124:2; 131:11,12)

       郊外   N: suburban area

       四郊   N: suburbs

       近郊   N: suburbs

       郊遊   N: outing

3. 儀 yí   (1) BF: ceremony, rites; standard, norm

       儀式　N: ceremony (157:3)

       儀表　N: general appearance (of a person)

       儀禮　N: section from The Book of Rites

    儀仗隊　N: guard of honor

  (2) BF: instruments; apparatus

       儀器　N: demonstrating apparatus and such equipment
               used in schools; scientific instruments, etc.

         天文儀器　N: astronomical instruments

4. 返 fǎn   V: to return to (124:4)

    往返 V/N: to go to and fro, back and forth

    返回　V: to go back to

    退返　V: to return to

    返鄉　V: to return to one's native place

    返還　V: to return to

  返國／家 VO: to return to one's own country/home

5. 牽 chyān   V: to lead along, pull, haul, implicate or involve in

    牽引　V: to lead along, drag (125:9)

    牽走　V: to drag off or away (158:5)

    牽制 V/N: to manipulate, control, hamper, restrict;
            control, manipulation (167:11)

    牽掛 V/N: (to) worry; to miss (someone); anxiety

    牽動　RV: to get involved; to drag

   牽牛花　N: morning glories

    牽强　SV: forced; unnatural (in interpretation, etc.)

       牽强附會　EX: (to make) far-fetched
            (comparisons)

牽連/涉   V: to involve

中共和印度在喜馬拉鴉山附近的戰爭牽涉的問題很多。

The Sino-Indian war in the Himalayan region involves a wide range of problems.

6. 峯 fēng   N: mountain peak

（峰）

　　　　　　高峯   N: high point; climax （ 座 ）(126:5)

　　　　　　山峯   N: mountain peak （ 座 ）

7. 浩 hàu   BF: great, enormous (126:7)

　　　　　　浩大   SV: large, enormous

　　　　　　浩然之氣   EX: natural greatness of a soul; magnanimous

8. 蕩 dàng   (1) BF: vast, large

　　　　　　浩浩蕩蕩   ex: exceedingly great in extent or number (126:7)

　　　　　　(2) BF: dissipated, licentious, reckless

　　　　　　放蕩   SV: heedless, careless, dissolute

　　　　　　遊蕩   V: to be dissipated; to loaf

　　　　　　搖蕩 V/N: to move, to disturb; to be agitated in mind; (to) pitch and toss (as a ship at sea)

　　　　　　(3) BF: squander

　　　　　　傾家蕩產   EX: to exhaust family property; to go bankrupt

9. 擺 bǎi   (1) V: to arrange, spread out (126:8; 167:5)

　　　　　　擺架子 VO: to put on airs

　　　　　　擺脫   V: to get rid of; to shake off (as influences, restraints, etc.)

　　　　　　擺酒席 VO: to spread a big feast

　　　　　　擺攤兒 VO: to set up a stall on the ground; to display and sell wares spread on the ground

　　　　　　擺列   V: to arrange, display, exhibit

　　　　　　擺設 V/N: to decorate (as a room); decoration

擺設品　N: bric-a-brac

小擺設　N: bric-a-brac

(2) V/N: to wave, shake or move; pendulum

擺動　V: to oscillate; to move or swing

擺手　V: to wave the hand

擺渡 V/N: to ferry across

搖搖擺擺　ex: swaggering (from pride); staggering (from drink)

搖頭擺尾　EX: (lit. shaking the head and wagging the tail); well content and pleased

擺佈　V: to throw difficulties in another's way, deal with, arrange; to dispose

10. 宦 hwàn　　BF: official (127:3)

宦官(派)　N: eunuch (party) (170:9; 171:1)

宦途　N: official career (connotes vicissitudes)

官宦之家　EX: official families, highly connected families

11. 沉 chén
(沈)　　(1) V: to sink, perish

宦海升沉　EX: (lit. in the sea of officialdom there is rising and falling); the vicissitudes of official life (127:3)

沉下去　RV: to sink down

沉沒　V: to have perished; to sink (沒 read mwò)

(2) SV: heavy

沉重　SV: heavy; serious; grave

沉痛　SV: extremely painful

死氣沉沉　EX: passive, unresponsive; dull, quiet; gloomy

(3) V: to restrain one's emotion

沈著　SV: calm; self-restrained

沈不／得住氣 EX: (un)able to maintain control of oneself

(4) A: very

沉静 SV: very quiet

(5) Surname (as surname must be written 沈 and pronounced shěn)

12. 慚 tsán   BF: ashamed (127:4)

羞慚 SV: ashamed

13. 愧 kwèi   BF: ashamed

慚愧 V/SV/N: to feel ashamed or regretful; shame; remorse (127:4)

14. 懼 jyù   BF: fear, dread

恐懼 SV/N: (to) fear (127:8)

懼怕   V: to fear

懼內   V: to be henpecked

15. 朗 lǎng   BF: clear, open

明朗 SV/N: bright, clear; understanding, "the light" (127:9)

朗朗上口 EX: to read or recite smoothly

晴朗 V/SV: (to become) bright; clear (day or sky)

開朗 V/SV: (to become) clear (weather, situation); broad (view)

16. 悲 bēi   SV: sad, melancholy

悲劇   N: tragedy (127:9; 164:11)

悲哀 SV/N: sad; sadness (130:5)

悲歡成敗   ex: joys and sorrows, successes and failures (161:12)

悲歡離合   EX: joys and sorrows, union and separation

悲觀   SV: pessimistic

悲觀主義　N: pessimism

悲傷　SV: grieved, melancholy, sad

悲喜交集　EX: intermingled grief and joy

悲痛　SV: grieved, melancholy

17. 拘 jyū　(1) BF: restrain, adhere to; restrict

不拘 V/CJ: no matter; not to be particular or stuffy about; irrespective of (128:1)

不拘禮節　EX: to pay no attention to formalities

不拘小節　EX: not to pay attention to details

不拘形式　EX: not to put much stress on established procedures

拘於　V: to be bound by convention, etc.

拘於禮節　ex: to be bound or restrained by formalities

拘泥於　V: to be bigoted in regard to; to hold strictly to the letter of the law; to be rigidly bound by convention or morality (160:3) (泥 nì)
作八股文，由於拘泥於文體，以致不能儘量發揮意見。
Because in writing eight-legged essays, one is too rigidly bound by form, it is impossible to express one's ideas.

拘束　SV: restrained, rigid (of people)

(2) BF: seize

拘捕　V: to detain forcibly

拘禁　V: to keep in custody; to lock up major criminals termporarily awaiting trial

拘留 V/N: to detain forcibly; detention awaiting trial; initial arrest

拘票　N: warrant for arrest

拘管　V: to keep in custody

18. 搞 gǎu   V: to work on (colloq.); (in Chinese Communist usage:
                        "to work over" someone or to apply pressure on
                        something or someone)

                    我不會搞那種花樣。
                    I couldn't play a trick like that.

          搞好 RV: to put in good shape (128:1)

19. 拖 twō   V: to drag along after

        拖泥帶水 EX: muddled, clumsy, involved (as a style of
                        writing, manner of doing things) (lit. all
                        dripping with mud and water) (134:9)

          拖延   V: to put off; procrastinate

          拖欠   V: to delay on (as payments)

          拖鞋   N: slippers

        拖下水 ex: to drag someone down (as into evil)
                    你怎麼拖他下水呢？
                    Why are you pulling him down with you?

                    千萬別把我拖下水！
                    Don't drag me down with you.

        拖拉機   N: tractor (部)

20. 祟 swèi   BF: evil spirit

          作祟   V: to cause trouble; to mess things up; wreak
                        havoc (128:5)

                    我不知道甚麼東西作祟。
                    I don't know what's messing things up.
                    (what's causing the havoc)

        鬼鬼祟祟 ex: secretive and mysterious; stealthy,
                        conspiratorial

21. 堆 dwēi   (1) V/N to heap, pile up (129:8)

          堆積   V: to pile up or accumulate

          堆起來 RV: to pile up

          人堆   N: a crowd of people

錢／書堆   N: piles of money/books

(2) M: for piles or heaps of things

一堆人／書／錢／東西   N: a group of people/books/money/things

一大堆   N: a great pile (of)

22. 棵 kē   M: for trees and plants (129:10)

一棵樹   N: a tree

一棵花   N: a flower

23. 疼 téng   (1) V: to love, have affection for
　　　　　　　　　　他很疼他的孩子。
　　　　　　　　　　He's very fond of his children.

心疼 V/SV: (to be) distressed or pained at (loss or
　　　　　　misfortune of); to begrudge (as money) (129:9)

(2) BF: pain

頭疼 V/SV: to have/be a headache

24. 欣 syīn   BF: delight, happy

歡欣   SV: happy, delighted (130:4)

欣慰   SV: comforted, pleased; contented

欣然   A: happily, pleasantly

欣然同意   ex: happily agree

欣然接受   ex: happily accept

欣喜   SV: pleased, delighted

25. 儼 yǎn   (1) BF: like; as

儼然   A: like, just as, seemingly (130:5)
　　　　　看見他所住的房子，與他的長工所住的，儼然
　　　　　兩個世界。
　　　　　He and his hired help lived in what seemed
　　　　　like two different worlds. (130:5)

(2) BF: majestic, dignified

儼然   A: dignified, stern

26. 掃 sǎu   (1) V: to sweep (130:9)

掃除 V: to sweep or clean out (168:6)

掃地 VO: to sweep the ground

打掃 V: to sweep

掃蕩 V: to make a clean sweep; to mop up (as enemies)

威信掃地 EX: used to describe those who have fallen from positions of power and authority or prestige

風掃落葉 EX: to blow away as easily as the autumn leaves

掃興 V: to spoil one's fun, to disappoint one's hopes

(sàu) (2) N: broom

掃把 N: broom

27. 爺 yé   BF: old gentleman

大爺 N: boss (colloq.); elder uncle (130:11)

老爺 N: maternal grandfather; term of respect for elderly men

N: (polite term for the) son of an established and well-off family

爺爺 N: paternal grandfather

28. 咱 dzán   BF: we (colloq.)

咱們 N: we; you and I (130:11)

29. 頓 dwùn   (1) BF: put in order; prepare

整頓 V/N: to reorganize; to rearrange; reorganization (of households, groups, etc.) (132:4)

安頓 V: to prepare (as accommodations); to arrange

(2) M: for meal

一頓飯   N: a meal

(3) M: of occurrence

說／打／罵一頓 V: to give a dressing down/beating/cursing to

我把他罵了一頓。

I bawled him out.

(4) BF: suddenly, immediately

頓時　MA: at once, forthwith

頓悟　V: to come to a sudden comprehension of

頓改前非　EX: sudden reform of past faults

30. 閱　ywè

BF: peruse, examine, inspect

檢閱　V: to review (as troops) (132:4; 143:6)

閱兵　V: to review troops

閱歷　N: experience

閱報室　N: periodical or newspaper reading room

評閱　V: to read critically; to rate (as examinations)

31. 狡　jyǎu

BF: wily, tricky

狡辯 V/N: to argue sophistically, speciously (usually connotes in defense of one's interests); (specious self-justification) (132:5)

狡計　N: wily plan

狡賴　V: to prevaricate

狡滑　SV: tricky, cunning, slippery or deceitful

32. 緒　syù

BF: clue, thread; continue

情緒　N: emotions, feelings (132:6; 151:12)

頭緒　N: clues, beginnings, loose ends (of a problem)

有頭緒　VO: to have a clue to or about

就緒　V: to get things in shape (as to establish a way of doing something)

大致就緒　EX: in general things are pretty well in order

心緒　N: mood, emotions

緒言   N: preface, introduction

<u>NEW MEANINGS</u>

1. 傳 chwán   V: to summon (126:6)

    傳他來   order him to come

2. 喝   V: to shout at

    喝問   V: to question loudly (menacingly, fiercely)
           (126:8)

    喝道   V: to shout out/loudly (＝大聲說：)

    喝住   V: to shout at someone to stop

3. 整   BF: set in order

    整軍 VO: to reorganize the army (68:3)

    整頓   V: to reorganize (132:4)

    整理   V: to adjust, put in order

        整理國故   ex: to reassess the national
                   heritage; (movement of the
                   early 1920's led by Hu Shih
                   and others to reexamine the
                   cultural tradition of China)

STRUCTURE NOTES

1. 不拘

    A. 不拘   CJ/CV: regardless of, irrespective of (= 不分 , 不管 ,
                    不問 , etc.)

        1. 中華民國公民不拘男女都享有選舉權。
            Citizens of the Republic of China, regardless of whether they
            be men or women, all have the franchise.

        2. 你應該不拘成敗奮鬥到底才行。

            It is only proper that you should fight on to the end regard-
            less of whether you succeed or fail.

        3. 我不拘任何情形總會幫你忙的。
            I'll always help you regardless of the situation.

        Notes:

            1. 不拘 like 不分 / 問 / 管, etc., functions both like a CV
                and a CJ.

            2. The 不拘 + O unit may either precede or follow the
                subject.

            3. 不拘 + O is frequently followed by adverbs 都 , 總 , etc.

            4. O usually consists of two nouns contrastive in their
                semantic relationship (男女 , 成敗) or nouns modified
                by indefinite specifier 甚麼 , 任何 , etc. (any, whatever,
                etc.)

    B. 不拘 as a verb   V: to disregard, ignore, make little of

        他這個人一向不拘形式。
        He has never paid attention to formalities.

2. (不) 以 ... 爲然   PT: to take ... as (un)natural/(not) right

    A. 不以爲然 = 不以爲這樣是對的 = 不這樣想

近來他抽煙喝酒，越來越厲害，雖然我勸他好幾次，他却不以爲然。

Recently his smoking and drinking have been getting worse and worse. Although I have reasoned with him many times, he doesn't think it right.

B.   不以 ... 爲然 = 不以爲 ... 是對的 = 不贊成 ...

很多人認爲由於科學進步，總有一天人類可以征服自然，但我却不以此說爲然。

Many people think that with the progress of science there will come a day when man can conquer nature. However I don't think this theory is right.

C.   Also 頗以爲然 = 以爲這樣是很對的 = 很贊成 .

＊   ＊   ＊   ＊   ＊

Note for Review:

1.   不 ... 不 ... (124:10)

不如此不足以 ...   (130:10)

2.   不 (爲) ... 而 (爲) ... (130:4)

3.   愈 (是) ... 愈 ...   (133:7)

4.   每 ... (一個) 就 ... (一層)   (133:5)

5.   只要 ... 總是 ... (128:1)

6.   即使 ... 只要 ... 就 ...   (128:9)

7.   實在是 ... 而不僅只是 ... (variation of 是 ... 而不是 ...) (129:2)

8.   一 ... 就 ...   (129:8)

9.   既然 (是) ... 當然 (是) ... (128:12; 129:12)

既然 ... 就 ...   (130:11)

10.   無論 ... 何 ... 必需 ...   (131:7)

11.   一方面 ... 一方面 ...   (131:11)

12.   如果 ... 就 ...   (129:9)

13.   所 ... 者   (127:3)

14.   是否   (133:2)

E X E R C I S E S

I. Structure Words

A. 不拘

1. as VERB

a. 他是政府的高級官員，理應非常講究儀表，但向來是不拘
小節的。

b. 不拘禮節的人，不見得就沒有受過高等的教育。

c. 雖然我不願意捐錢，可是拘於情面，只好答應他了。

2. as CV/CJ

a. 不拘那個人，只要是偵查（ spy on ）我國軍事機密的間諜即
須加以逮捕。

b. 不拘錢數多少，只要有獎學金，我總是樂於接受的。

c. 不拘在什麼樣的國家裡，民主的也好，極權的也好，總之，宦
海升沉的情形似乎是不可避免的。

II. Miscellaneous

A. 動手

1. 咱們應該耐心跟他講理，不應太衝動，隨便動手打人。

2. 我們這次的旅行，一共需要兩個月的時間，應準備的東西及事情很
多，現在我們大家就分別動手去準備吧。

3. 做比說難。意思是說單說一件事情比真的動手去做要容易的多。

B. 在...作祟

1. 一個人在創造事業的階段裡應該勇往直前，吃苦耐勞，不應允許金
錢，名譽在心裡作祟。

2. 宦途固然多刺，但如不使虛榮在自己心裡作祟，或可平安渡過。

3. 閱歷越廣，知識越豐，就應當越虛心。一旦讓自滿的思想在心裡作
祟，只有固步自封而別無他途。

c.以（...）為然

1. 因為一時悲觀而心情不好，是自然的事。但如從此就愁眉苦臉（frowning）我則不以此種態度為然。

2. 頓悟前非（ errors ）跟頓改前非不能混為一談。因為前者是消極的而後者是積極的，你以此為然否？

3. 整理國故是我們最需要的事，但是空喊口號，而不着手進行我則不以為然。

III.   Variations on Familiar Patterns

A.不...不...

1. 不徹底改善現行的公文程式和法規，公文的處理不能簡化。

2. 縱使有人控告那位牧師侵佔教會財產，但不經調查屬實不能輕易處理，何況可能是有人故意造謠呢？

B.即使...只要...就可...

1. 即使他態度鬼鬼祟祟，但只要沒有越軌的行動，他就可以享受一切應享的權利。

2. 即使你拖欠一點，只要你每月不停的還錢，就可以還清債款。

3. 即使傾家蕩產，只要能保全他的生命，讓他到達安全的地方，我就心滿意足了。

I. Structure Words

    不拘

        1. as VERB

            a. This man likes to put on airs but is not
               particular about little things.

            b. If after the lecture we do not stand on ceremony
               and can frankly exchange our ideas, the whole
               evening will be even more interesting.

        2. as CV/CJ

            a. I cannot make any exception no matter what the
               accused's background or position is.

            b. The constitution clearly states that everybody,
               whether young or old, male or female, rich or
               poor, literate or illiterate, has the right to
               vote.

II. Miscellaneous

    A. 動手

        1. New peaks in production can only be achieved when
           the whole body of worker comrades works whole-
           heartedly together.

        2.. The principle is very clear. What you work at
           personally will ultimately be clear to you.

        3. There are a lot of switches (機關) on this machine.
           If you are not certain about them, to avoid danger,
           please do not touch them at random.

    B. 在...作祟

        1. For so many years now the fear which has been eating
           away his self-confidence has increased his pessimism.

        2. Unless a person resolves not to allow stray thoughts
           to disturb his peace of mind, he will waste enormous
           time and energy and not get anything done.

        3. He finally discovered that it was sand in the gas
           tank (汽油桶) that was causing all the trouble.

C. 以 ... 爲然

    1. Whenever he comes to the Board of Directors meeting, he puts on the airs. His friends feel his attitude is not right but are too embarrassed to mention it to him directly. It really is a tough problem.

    2. A newspaper reading room is a place to read papers. It is of course necessary to maintain silence there but I do not feel that it is right for readers to have to pay a fee.

    3. He says that the contented (知足常樂) outlook of the Chinese has slowed the forward development of their material culture. Do you think this is right?

II. <u>Variations on Familiar Structures</u>

A. 不 ... 不 ...

    1. In anything, if one does not adopt a positive attitude, there can be no good results.

    2. If one does not have a sincere attitude in dealing with people, naturally one cannot win their trust. That's perfectly obvious.

B. 即使 ... 只要 ... 就可 ...

    1. Even if you can't go, you must let him know. So long as they know in advance, they can do it for you.

    2. Even if he is a reactionary, so long as he does not spread any dangerous rumors, he won't be interfered with.

    3. Even if you don't do it well, it doesn't matter; so long as you still bear the responsibility of leadership, we can help you.

III. <u>Review Sentences</u>

Use:

從事於   不 ... 而能 ...   有見於

其中   VERB 一步   與生俱來

無所不爲   受

1. He was born with that dull stupid look of his and he can't change it. But he is really not stupid.

2. In view of the need for trained personnel, the Survey Office will begin a large-scale program in the next fiscal year to train surveyors.

3. He has always been engaged in building bridges in the east.

4. In that pile are the most recently received petitions. Because we are short handed, we cannot deal with them quickly, especially since many of them are concerned with technical questions which we are not really qualified to answer.

5. I have never discovered a physicist without laboratory experience who could be called qualified.

6. People who roam around all day and will stop at nothing are a real menace.

7. 他那一段話是對儀仗隊而言的。大概的意思是說除了要講究各人的儀表以外，還得注意全體的精神。

8. 在宦途中不會做人就不能升官。在學術界則並不如此，即使不會做人但只要肚子裡有學問就有資格擔當較重要的工作。

9. 為了避免辦事拖泥帶水，藉以增加效率起見，我們才訂立了這一個標準以求劃一。

10. 這個家庭不獨已經到了盛極必衰的地步而且很可能從此一蹶 (fall) 不振了。

11. 要使一個人由一個無惡不作的兇手變成一個奉公守法的良民其難有如登天。

Write Sentences Using:

1. 只要...即可	6. 日益	11. 只要...總...
2. 從...入手	7. 出身	12. 只有...才...
3. 為...所 V	8. 一向	13. 甘心
4. 之所以能	9. ...不及	14. 不堪...
5. 大致	10. 幾乎	15. 寧可...也...

Fei Hsiao-t'ung, leading British-trained anthropologist famous for his studies of Chinese village life, here describes the importance of the soil to the Chinese peasant. In the early days of the Communist regime, Fei was head of the National Institute of Minorities. He was subsequently accused of being a rightist and forced to confess, but was later once again accepted.

From this opening chapter of his book, Rural China, one paragraph on the distinction between certain Chinese and German terms has been omitted.

Fei Hsiao-t'ung, Rural China (Hsiang-t'u Chung-kuo), Shanghai, 1948, pp. 1-7.

134:T	鄉土			Adj: rural, native (134:2; 138:1; 139:10; 140:9, etc.)
	本色			N: natural color or characteristics
	費孝通	--syàu--	1	N: Fei Hsiao-t'ung
2	基層			N: basic or lowest level (134:2,5; 136:9)
3	邊緣		NM1	N: rim, boundary, edge
4	不妨	--fáng	2,S1	AV: there is no harm in, might as well (134:9)
	土頭土腦		NM2	EX: rustic, simple, uneducated
6	土氣		NM2	SV: rustic, simple (135:6; 136:2; 140:3)
	藐視	myǎu--	3	V: to despise (135:6)
7	謀生			V: to earn or eke out a living (135:6; 136:3)
9	討生活		NM3	VO: to seek one's livelihood
135:1	放牧			V: to graze herds
	依舊			V/A: to be as of old (164:11)
	鋤地	chú--	4	VO: to hoe the earth (127:6)
	播種		NM4	VO: to sow

2	鑽	dzwàn	5	V:	to dig, bore or penetrate into
	史祿國	--lù--	6	N:	Shih Lu-kuo
3	下種子		NM5,NM4	VO:	to plant seeds (136:12; 137:2)
6	命根			N:	"life-blood"
7	占				alternate form for 佔 (135:11)
	土地(神)		NM2	N:	Earth God, local God
	人性			N:	human nature
	白首偕老	----syé--	7	EX:	husband and wife grow old together
8	閒事			N:	idle matters of no concern to oneself
	奶媽	nǎi--	8	N:	wet nurse
9	箱子	syāng--	9	N:	suitcase, trunk, chest
	水土不服			EX:	to be not yet physically adjusted or acclimated to a place (usually: 不服水土)
10	煮	jǔ	10	V:	to boil (as water, soup)
	竈	dzàu		N:	kitchen stove
	一曲難忘			N:	"A Song to Remember"
11	領略			V:	to understand, sense or "take in"
12	飄忽無定	pyāu-----	11	ex:	to move about without settling down
136:1	莊稼	--jyà		N:	crops
	侍候	shr--	12	V:	to tend, cultivate; attend to
2	插入	chā--	13	V:	to stick or insert into
3	張			N:	(short for) Kalgan (張家口)
5	墓碑	mùbēi	14,15	N:	tombstone
	家譜	--pǔ	16	N:	family records, genealogy
8	常態			N:	normal situation or state of affairs (138:12)

	變態			N: abnormal situation
	旱	hàn	17	N: drought
	拋井離鄉	--jǐng----	18	EX: to leave one's native place
11	飽和點	bǎu----	19	N: saturation point
	宣洩	--syè	20	V: to trickle or leak away (136:12)
	鋤頭	chú--	4	N: hoe
12	家族			N: clan
137:1	淘汰	táutài	21,22	V/N: to purge or wash away; to weed or wash out; displacement (by something better or more fit)
	猺山	yáu--		N: Yau Mountain
2	拚命	pàn--	23	V: to do something as if one's life depended on it
	長成	(jǎng)--		V: to grow to or into
	村落			V: village, settlement (138:7,8)
3	路斃屍體	--bì----	24	ex: corpses of those who have died by the wayside
4	隔膜	--mwó	25	V/SV/N: to be cut off or separated from; separation, distance between (137:4; 138:9)
6	插秧	chāyāng	13,26	VO: to plant young rice seedlings
7	與其 X 不如 Y		S2	PT: it's better to do Y than X
	忙不過來		S3	RV: to be too busy to see to everything
12	四川	--chwān	27	N: Szechwan
	梯田	tī--	28	N: terraced fields
138:1	屋簷	--yán		N: roof eaves (of a house)
2	鄰舍	--shè	29	N: neighbors
5	水利			N: water conservation
11	圈子	chywān--	30	N: circle, group

139:2	熟悉	--syī	31	V/SV: to be familiar with (139:3; 140:7,8)
	陌生人	mwò----	32	N: stranger (139:9; 140:5; 141:2,3)
3	麾擦	mwótsā	33,34	N: friction
	陶鍊	táu--	35	V: to refine (as metal in a fire) (鍊 is alternate form of 煉) (139:4)
4	論語			N: <u>Analects</u> of Confucius (140:10)
	陌生	mwò--	32	SV: strange
	不亦悅乎	----ywè--		EX: what a pleasure it is (when ...) (from the <u>Analects</u>)
5	描寫	myáu--	36	V/N: to describe; description
	從心所欲而不踰規矩	-----yù----	NM6	"I could follow what my heart desired, without transgressing what was right." (adapted from the <u>Analects</u> of Confucius)
	規矩	--jyǔ	37	N: custom; customary code (140:2)
6	從俗		NM6	V: to conform to custom
7	通了家			ex: to become connected (as families by marriage)
8	打(個)招呼			VO: to signal a greeting
	…就是了		S4	PT: ... and that's all
9	底細			N: real story; detailed background of; particulars about
10	畫個押	----(yá)	NM7	VO: to make a mark (as the signature of an illiterate)
	無從		S5	PT: no way to ...; no place from which to ...
	見外			V: to treat as an outsider (colloq.)
11	再可靠也沒有		S6	PT: nothing more reliable than ...
12	天生			ex: innate, natural; born of heaven
	磁器		NM8	N: porcelain

140:1 文   NM9   M: for coins and old Chinese cash
                                           (round coin with a square cut out in
                                           the middle)

       及早   A: on time; earlier

       契約   chì--   38   N: deed, contract

    2 思索   --swǒ   39   V/N: to think over; thought

    4 摸熟   mwō--   40   RV: to feel out, become familiar with

    6 表達   V/N: to express; expression of one's ideas

    7 螞蟻   mǎyǐ   N: ant (140:7)

   10 籠罩   (lǔng)jàu(VII:15)   V/N: (to) cover
                                 41
       萬有   N: universe; Nature

       孝   syàu   1   SV/N: filial; filial piety

   12 日常   Adj: daily (precedes a noun)

       性格   N: personality

       承歡   NM10   V: to please or give delight to (as to
                                           parents)

141:2 激速   jī--   42   A: rapid, fast

    4 詞彙   --hwèi   43   N: term, vocabulary

       衣錦榮歸   --jǐn----   44   EX: (lit. to return wearing brocade
                                           garments); to return home covered
                                           with glory

       去處   N: place to go; whereabouts

CHARACTERS TO BE LEARNED

1. 孝 syàu   (1) SV/N: filial; filial piety (134:T; 140:10; 162:3)

        愚忠愚孝 EX: blind loyalty and filial piety (162:3)

          孝敬 V/N: to be filial; to offer presents to
               elders or superiors; filial piety

孝順 V/SV/N: (to be) filial; filial piety

孝心　N: filial heart or mind

孝子　N: filial son

孝經　N: <u>Classic of Filial Piety</u>

(2) BF: mourning

孝服　N: mourning robes

帶/穿孝 VO: to wear mourning

脫孝 VO: to take off mourning

守孝 VO: to be in mourning

2. 妨 fáng   BF: prevent, interfere with or be an obstacle

不妨 MA: there is no harm in; might as well (134:4,9)

我們不妨先休息一會兒，等他囘來了再問他。
We might as well rest a while and then check
with him when he comes back.

何妨 A: What harm? Why not? (interrogative adverb
used in rhetorical questions)

我看完了再去又何妨！
What's wrong if I go after I finish reading!

無妨 V: (literary form of) 不要緊

你去也無妨　It doesn't matter if you go.

你不去也無妨　It doesn't matter if you don't go.

妨害 V/N: to be injurious to; to hinder; (to) harm

妨害治安/家庭/自由　EX: to be injurious or
detrimental to
peace/the family/
freedom

妨礙 V/N: to hinder; hindrance or obstacle

3. 藐 myǎu   BF: treat with contempt; slight

藐視　V: to regard with contempt; to despise (134:6; 135:6)

藐小　SV: insignificant; small

4. 鋤 chú　V: to hoe, uproot (171:1)

鋤頭　N: hoe (136:11) (把)

鋤地　VO: to hoe the land (137:6)

5. 鑽 dzwān (1)　V: to creep or bore into; to penetrate into (135:2)

鑽進　V: to bore or penetrate into (142:5)

(dzwǎn)　鑽木　VO: to bore into wood (in order to strike up a fire)

鑽木取火　EX: to strike fire by rubbing twigs together

(dzwàn) (2)　N: awl, drill

鑽子　N: awl or drill (把)

鑽石　N: diamond (顆)

6. 祿 lù　BF: official pay (135:2)

祿位　N: salary and rank

高官厚祿　EX: high rank and high salaries

7. 偕 syé　CV: together with

白首/頭偕老　EX: husband and wife grow old together (135:7)

偕同　CV: to go with, accompany

偕行　V: to go with, to accompany

8. 奶 nǎi　N: milk

奶媽　N: wet nurse (135:8)

牛奶　N: milk (of cows)

奶油　N: butter

奶奶　N: paternal grandmother

9. 箱 syāng (1) BF: box, trunk

　　　　　箱子　N: trunk, chest, suitcase, box (135:9) (隻)

　　　　　皮箱　N: leather suitcase (隻)

　　　　　車箱　N: the trunk of a car

　　　　廢紙箱　N: wastepaper basket

　　　　(2) M: for box, trunk, etc.

10. 煮 jǔ　　　　V: to boil, cook (135:10)
　(煑)

　　　　　煮飯 VO: to cook (rice)

　　　　　煮水 VO: to boil water

　　　　　煮開 RV: to boil

11. 飄 pyāu　　　V: float in the air; to be borne by the wind

　　飄忽無定 ex: to float or move around without coming to
　　　　　　　　rest; to drift (135:12)

　　　　　飄流　V: to float or drift about without settling
　　　　　　　　down; (here 漂 can be used for 飄)

　　　　　飄零　V: to fall (as leaves from trees); to decline
　　　　　　　　(as of family fortunes)

　　　　　飄揚　V: to blow into the air; to waft

　　　　　飄動 V/N: to move or flutter in the wind; fluttering

　　　　　飄蕩 V/N: to be fluttering (in the air); to be floating
　　　　　　　　(on the water); to be drifting (of people);
　　　　　　　　fluttering, drifting

　　　　　輕飄 V/SV: to wave in the air; light, floating

　　　　　　　　輕飄飄的　A: dizzily; wafting lightly

　　　　飄飄然　EX: to feel as light as air; to be walking on
　　　　　　　　air; happiness induced by compliments

　　　　飄雪/雨　V: to snow/rain (light snow/rain)

12. 侍 shr̀　　BF: serve, attend on

　　　　　侍候　V: to wait or attend on (136:1)

侍女　　N: maid servant

侍從　　N: followers; attendants; servants

侍奉　　V: to wait on

服侍　　V: to wait or attend on (as a patient, etc.)

侍者　　N: waiter, attendant

13. 插 chā

（插）

V: to insert or stick into

插入　　V: to insert into (136:2)

插圖　　N: illustration inserted in a book

插足　　V: to get a foot in; to get a foothold

插花 VO/N: to put flowers in a vase, to arrange flowers; flower arrangement

14. 墓 mù

N: grave, tomb

公墓　　N: public cemetery (座)

掃墓　　V: to sweep the graves (practice of tending and sacrificing at family graves, particularly at the springtime Ch'ing Ming festival)

墓地　　N: cemetery; graveyard

15. 碑 bēi

N: large stone tablet (used for commemorative purposes)

墓碑　　N: tombstone (136:5)

紀念碑　N: commemorative tablet, monument

碑文　　N: inscription on a tablet

里程碑　N: (lit. and fig.) milestone

有口皆碑 EX: everyone sings its praises

16. 譜 pǔ

N: record, register

家譜　　N: family tree or record; genealogy (136:5)

臉譜　　N: theatrical make-up or mask-like make-up of the characters in Chinese opera (168:2)

樂譜　　N: score for music

歌譜 N: songbook

譜子 N: music book

離譜 V: to be way off the subject

沒譜 V: to talk or act without plan

食譜 N: cookbook

17. 旱 hàn   BF: dry

大旱 N: severe or extreme drought (136:8)

旱災 N: drought

旱路 N: land route

18. 井 jǐng (1) N: well

拋井離鄉 EX: to leave one's native home (136:8)

離鄉背井 EX: to leave one's home town

井水 N: well water

油/鹽井 N: oil/salt well

(2) BF: orderly

井然 SV/A: in good order; orderly

秩序井然 EX: everything is peaceful (of society, situation)

井然有序 EX: everything is well-arranged in proper sequence

井井有條 EX: tidy, in good order; shipshape

19. 飽 bǎu   SV: to feel full of food; satisfied (of hunger)

飽和點 N: saturation point (136:11)

吃飽 RV: to have eaten sufficiently

飽暖 N: ample food and clothing

飽受 V: to be fully ...

飽受虛驚 EX: frightened by empty fears

一飽口／眼／耳福　EX: luck in having something good to eat/look at/hear

飽食終日　EX: well-fed all day without working

飽滿　SV: full, replete, saturated

精神飽滿　EX: to be full of spirit

飽學之士　N: learned person

20. 洩 syè　　BF: leak out, divulge

（泄）

宣洩　V: to melt, trickle away (of crowds, emotions, etc.); to leak (136:11,12)

洩漏　V: to divulge, to leak (as secrets)

洩氣 VO/SV: to lose interest; to discourage; become disheartened or discouraged (colloq.)

好好兒幹，別洩氣！
Keep at it! Don't give up!
大家都給他幫忙，他自己反而不努力，真使人洩氣。
Everybody helped him but he wouldn't make the effort himself. It really made you disappointed.

這一次你一定要把事情辦好，別再洩我的氣。
This time you must make a success of this. Don't disappoint me again.

洩恨　VO: to give vent to feelings of anger or vengeance

發洩　V: to give vent to

21. 淘 táu　(1) BF: scour, scrub; wash away (137:1)

淘米　VO: to wash rice

淘金　VO: to pan for gold

(2) SV: mischievous

淘氣　SV: mischievous, naughty (of children)

22. 汰 tài　　BF: scour, wash out

淘汰 V/N: to wash away or eliminate (as by time, progress, competition, etc.), to be displaced (by the

onward press of time, etc.); displacement
(137:1; 146:9; 148:3)

23. 拚 pàn   BF: stake all on ...

拚命 V/A: (lit. to disregard or risk one's life); to do
something as though one's life depended on it;
desperately, energetically (137:2; 142:5)

Note: 拼／拚命
are both in practice pronounced pīn mìng. 拼
though commonly occurring in this meaning, is
incorrect. 拚 though technically supposed to
be pronounced pàn is usually pronounced pīn.

24. 斃 bì   BF: kill, die a violent death (137:3)

斃命   V: to die a violent death

槍斃   V: to execute (by firing squad)

倒斃   V: to fall down dead

坐以待斃   EX: to wait resignedly for death

25. 膜 mwó   BF: membrane
   (mwò)

隔膜 SV/N: (to feel a) lack of understanding, distance,
emotional gulf, coolness between (137:4; 138:9)

耳／眼膜   N: membrane of the ear/eye

26. 秧 yāng   BF: young plants, seedlings; sprouts

插秧 VO: to transplant rice seedlings (137:6)

秧苗   N: sprouts of rice

秧歌   N: type of popular, rural folk song

秧歌舞   N: type of folk dance

27. 川 chwān   (1) abbr. for Szechwan

四川   N: Szechwan (137:12; 172:4)

(2) BF: river

山川   N: mountains and streams

川流不息　EX: to flow on without stopping

河川　N: river, stream

28. 梯 tī　　BF: ladder, stairs

梯田　N: terraced fields (137:12)

梯子　N: ladder

樓梯　N: stairs

電梯　N: elevator

雲梯　N: scaling ladder used in fire rescue work or in scaling walls

29. 舍 shè　　BF: cottage, shed

鄰舍　N: neighboring homes; neighbors (138:2)

草舍　N: thatched cottage (166:11)

宿舍　N: dormitory

舍下　N: my poor home (conventional)

舍妹／弟　N: my younger sister/younger brother

30. 圈 chywān (1)　N: circle

圈子／兒　N: circle (138:11)

圓圈　N: circle

圈套　N: (lit. and fig.) snare

圈點 V/N: to punctuate; punctuation marks

(2)　M: for "time around"

轉三圈兒　EX: to turn around three times

31. 悉 syī　(1) BF: learn about; know

熟悉　SV: familiar with; familiar (139:2,3,5,11; 140:2,7)

(2) BF: all, fully, entirely, altogether

悉知　V: to know fully

32. 陌 mwò
(mài) BF: raised path between fields

陌生 SV: unfamiliar (as of people, place) (139:4)

陌生人 N: stranger (139:2,9; 141:2,3)

33. 磨 mwó V: to grind or polish; to rub (139:3)

磨滅 V: to rub out, crush; obliterate (fig. applied to crushing of movements, spirit, etc.)

不可磨滅 EX: cannot be obliterated or denied; irradicable

磨米 VO: to grind rice

臨陣磨槍 EX: (lit. to start to sharpen your spear on the eve of battle); to cram (for an examination)

(mwò) N: mill, grindstone

磨房 N: mill

水磨 N: type of mill consisting of two grindstones wet by a steady drip of water

34. 擦 tsā V: to scour, rub in or off

磨擦 V/N: to rub; friction (between people and objects) (139:3) (also written 摩擦)

有磨擦 VO: to be at odds with

他們兩個人有磨擦。
There is friction between these two.

擦乾淨/亮 RV: to wipe or rub clean/polish

擦破/壞/掉/etc. RV: to scratch or nick/to break by rubbing/to rub out/etc.

擦皮鞋 VO: to shine shoes

35. 陶 taú (1) BF: kiln

陶煉 V: to fashion or refine (139:3,4)

陶器 N: pottery, earthenware

陶土 N: clay for pottery

(2) Surname

36. 描 myáu   V: to trace

描寫 V/N: to describe; description (139:5)

描紅 V/N: to practice writing Chinese characters (i.e. to trace along the red guide lines)

描畫兒 VO: to trace a picture

素描   N: sketching

37. 矩 jyǔ   N: carpenter's square

規矩 SV/N: well-behaved; rule, regulation (139:5,11; 140:2)

有規矩 SV: well-behaved, acting as expected (from original meaning of 規 as compass and 矩 as carpenter's square)

規規矩矩(的) A: properly; in keeping with appropriate or established norms

38. 契 chì   BF: contract, agreement

契約   N: written contract or agreement (140:1)

地契   N: land deed

房契   N: house deed

契合   V: to agree with, coincide with, correspond to

39. 索 swǒ   (1) BF: search into; inquire; think over or about

思索 V/N: to think or ponder over; thought (140:2)

索引   N: index

索隱   N: (lit. to search for what's hidden); commentary on the classics

逼索 V/N: to press forcibly for; to seek under pressure; to extort demand; demand, urgent pressure for

索取   V: to extort forcibly, procure

索性 MA: might as well (connotes more desperation and is stronger than 不妨) "What the heck"(索 swó)

索性忘記它吧。
Might as well forget about it.

這件事太難作，你索性別作了。
This is too hard to do; you might as well not do it.

(2) BF: large rope

繩索　N: large rope (條)

40. 摸 mwō			V: to grope, feel for

摸熟 RV: to practice, get the feel of, become familiar with (140:4,12)

摸索　V: to grope for; to feel out (142:5,8)

暗中摸索 EX: to grope about in the dark

摸清 RV: to make out, to get the feel (or hang) of something

摸着門兒 VO: to find the way or trick (to do something)

41. 罩 jàu			V/N: (to) cover, shade

籠罩 V/N: (to) cover (in the sense of to encompass) (140:10)

燈罩 (兒)　N: lamp shade

42. 激 jī			(1) BF: rouse, stimulate

激速　A: very fast; rapidly (141:2)

激起　V: to arouse, stir up (156:12)

過激　SV: radical

過激派　N: radical group (151:2)

激戰 V/N: to fight fiercely; a fierce fight

激動 V/SV/N: to stimulate to action; impulsive; impulse

感激 V/SV/N: (to be) grateful; gratitude

激增 V/N: to increase rapidly; increase

激發　V: to rouse to; to give a push to (as to stimulate to)

不偏不激　EX: moderate (in temperament, views, policy)

失之偏激　EX: to have the failing of going to extremes

激怒　V: to be in rage

(2) BF: overflow

激流　N: to flow strongly; turbulent flow of water

43. 彙 hwèi　　BF: class, series; classify

詞彙　N: vocabulary (141:4)

彙報 V/N: to report to superiors on conditions in one's group; report

字彙　N: vocabulary

44. 錦 jǐn　　BF: brocade, tapestry, embroidered work

衣錦榮歸　EX: to return home clothed in glory (lit. to return in brocaded garments) (141:4)

錦標　N: prize (in athletic competition)

織錦　N: tapestry

錦上添花　EX: (lit. to add flowers to embroidery); to add a superfluous touch of beauty or elegance

NEW MEANINGS

1. 緣　　BF: along; border

邊緣　N: edge or border of, hem (134:3; 142:7)

2. 土　　SV: rustic, native, simple

土頭土腦　EX: simple, rustic, uneducated (134:4)

土氣　SV: simple, rustic (134:6; 135:6; 136:2, etc.)

土地　N: Earth God, local god (135:7)

土地神／廟   N: local god/temple to local god

土人   N: aborigines; natives

3. 討   V: to beg, demand, to curry, to work for

討生活 VO: to work for a living (134:9,11)

討好 V: to curry favor, to please

討便宜 VO: to seek petty advantage (便 read pyán)

討人喜歡 EX/SV: to seek to please someone; to be ingratiating; pleasing (as a beautiful child)

討飯 VO: to beg for food

討飯的 N: beggar

討債 VO: to collect debts

自討苦吃 EX: to bring distress or suffering on oneself

自討沒趣 EX: to bring embarrassment on oneself

4. 種   BF: seed

播種 VO: to sow seed (135:1)

種子 N: seed (136:12; 137:2)

5. 下   V: to put down; to plant (135:3)

下種子 VO: to plant seeds (135:3)

下手 V/N: to put one's hand to something; to start to do something

先下手爲強 EX: it's best to get the jump on the other fellow

下工夫 VO: to work at, to spend time on

6. 從 (1) V/CV: to follow, comply with

從心 V/A: to follow one's desires at will (139:5)

從心所欲 EX: to follow the desires of one's heart

從俗 V: to conform to custom (139:6)

擇善而從 EX: to choose the good and follow it (148:3)

從善 V: to do what is good

從善如流 EX: to follow the good like a stream (148:4)

從簡/輕 A: simply/leniently

一切從簡 EX: to do things very simply (i.e. at minimum expense)

從輕處分 EX: to punish leniently

從優 A: liberally; exceptionally

待遇從優 EX: to offer handsome terms (as salary, etc.)

從權 A: to act according to circumstances

從權辦理 EX: to deal with a matter in the light of circumstances

從長計議 EX: to act deliberately

從一而終 EX: to die faithful to one husband; not to remarry

隨從 N: followers, attendants

從命 V: to obey a command

從犯 N: accessory criminal; accomplice

(tsūng) (2) BF: lax, yielding

從容 V/SV: (to be) relaxed, dignified

從容不迫 EX: in an easy manner

7. 押 yá BF: make a cross (as signature of an illiterate)

畫押 VO: to affix a signature with a cross or mark (139:10)

8. 磁 (瓷) BF: porcelain

磁器 N: porcelain (139:12)

細磁 N: fine porcelain

9. 文   N/M: a cash (an ancient Chinese coin); for coins (140:1)

10. 承   BF: please; flatter

     承歡 VO: to give delight (as to one's parents) (140:12)

     奉承 V/N: to flatter; flattery

STRUCTURE NOTES

1. Note that 何妨 and 不妨 are not conjunctions. In the following
    correlative structure they function as adverbs on the main verb.

    既然他知道的很清楚，你就 { 不妨 何妨 } 問問他！

    Since he is very clear on that, you might as well ask him!

2. 與其 X 不如 Y   PT: prefer Y to X; better to do Y than X

    與其 ...不如 ... is a variation of 與其 ... 毋寧 ...   (cf. XIV
    Structure 5)

3. 不過來   RE: too busy to; to be unable to get around to ...
                     properly

        忙不過來   RV: to be too busy

        看不過來   RV: to be unable to get around to reading (them
                       all)

    Note:

        The resultative complement 得／不過來 is attached to monosyllabic
        verbs.

4. ... 就是了   PT: ... and that's all

    A. 請你當面告訴他就是了。

    Please tell him to his face, that's all.

    Notes:

        1. In the above sentence the first clause can be construed
            as the subject of the predicate verb or expression 就是
            了 .

        2. 就是了 cannot be replaced by 罷了 here. (cf. IB Structure
            12)

    B. 我們大家是熟人，打個招呼就是了。

    We are all well acquainted; we just have to nod and that is all.
    (139:8)

Note:

    1. Here 就是了 can be expanded to 只要 ... 就是了 .

5. 無從   **A: to be in no position to ... ; to have no way to begin to ...**

    無從說起 **ex: to have no way to mention it**

    無從入手 **ex: to be in no position to begin**

Note:

    1. 無法 functions like 無從 .

      他無法說我。

      He couldn't (i.e. had no grounds on which to) criticize me.

6. 再 SV 也沒有了   PT: nothing more SV; most SV

```
┌─────────────────────────────┐
│  S + 再 + SV + 也沒有了       │
└─────────────────────────────┘
```

    金子再貴重也沒有了。
    Nothing is more valuable than gold.

```
┌─────────────────────────────┐
│  S + V + 再 + SV + 也沒有了    │
└─────────────────────────────┘
```

    你肯這樣做再好也沒有了。
    Nothing could be better than your being willing to do this.

Note:

    1. 不過了 can be substituted for 也沒有了 .

    2. S + 再 + SV +也沒有了 may be transformed into 沒有 + 東西/人 etc. + 再比 + S + SV + 了 .

✻　✻　✻　✻　✻

Note for Review:

    1. 雖則 ... 但... （134:6)

    2. 祇有 ... 罷了 （134:8)

3. 與其 ... 不如 ... 罷了   (137:7)

4. 既不 ... 也就沒有 ...   (137:8)

5. 無論 ... 總是 ...   (137:10)

6. 假如 ... 的話，就 ... (138:12)

7. 不是 ... 而是 ...   (137:5; 140:1)

8. 凡是 ... 老是 ...   (134:10)

9. 不管 ... 還是 ...   (135:3)

E X E R C I S E S

I. Correlative Structures

A. 與其 ... 不如 ...

1. 為了達到教育青年的目的，對於成績不良的學生，與其加以淘汰，令之退學，不如增設補習學校，加強他們的訓練。

2. 數學是一種推理的 (inductive) 學問，與其死背定義和定理，不如多做習題藉以熟習定理的應用。

3. 他們兩人之間已經發生很多次摩擦了，與其這樣下去，弄得隔閡日深，不如把話說清楚了，免去誤會而得到諒解。

B. 再 ... (也) 沒有 ...

1. 正在插秧時，下了一場大雪，結果損失很大。再慘也沒有的是他又因為這個打擊而病倒了。

2. 大旱逢甘雨，那是再痛快也沒有的事了。

3. 他這幾天心情惡劣，受不住刺激，假如我們再把他考試失敗的消息告訴他，那是再殘忍也沒有了。

II. Structure Words

A. ... 就是了

1. 他家的小女兒今年才一歲半，真聰明極了。甚麼都聽得懂，只是不會說話就是了。

2. 你說我那一點不如他？他會做的事，我都會；我會的他倒不一定會。只不過他有錢我沒錢就是了。

3. 我一定會來的，甚麼時候那就說不定了。到時候你們先吃，別等我就是了。

III. Miscellaneous

A. 不妨

1. 他所講的雖然只是一種造瓷器的土法，並不科學，但你不妨依照這種方法做做看，可能會減少很多成本呢。

2. 這本書的內容既然不易引起讀者的興趣，不妨多加一些插圖，或可藉以增加此書的銷路。

3. 這種燈光太強，刺激眼睛。長久在這種燈光下看書很容易損傷目力，不妨裝一個燈罩，把光減弱，也許會好一些。

B. 何妨

1. 你這樣的向他說明，已盡了你做朋友的心了，如果他還不信的話，何妨讓他自己去試試看。

2. 這個人雖不合我們的條件，可是他是王部長介紹來的，我們讓他參加考試，又有何妨？考得不好，我們就可以名正言順地不用他，到那時候王部長也不好意思說甚麼了。

C. 無妨

1. 今天休息，在家裡呆着也無聊，我們無妨上街走走，說不定還可以找到一點寫作的材料。

2. 這個讀者的來信內容很豐富，也很有風趣，可是和我們的主題沒有甚麼關係，我想，這樣的信我們無妨不予答覆。

D. VERB 得／不過來

1. 因為這兩天是限期最後的兩天，所以特別忙，連登記都忙不過來，怎麼能有工夫再從頭整理呢？

2. 每逢軍閥佔據一個城，他們雖然就說保城安民，其實搶東西都還忙不不過來呢，那有時間想別的事情？

3. 這麼多的考卷我改都改不過來呢，怎麼還能陪你一起去看電影？

E. 無從

1. 王先生有三個兄弟留在中國大陸，他們分別十幾年了，一直沒通消息，現在縱然想寫信，也無從打聽他們的地址。

2. 雖然有人想暗殺那位總理，可是戒備森嚴，防衞緊密，刺客簡直無從下手。

3. 因為黃河上流水勢很急而下流泥沙太多，倘若陰雨連天水流卽無從宣洩，（ drain off ）很容易造成水災。

F.索性

1. 他的生活起居一直飄忽不定，索性把房地產全部賣掉，到處爲家還
   可以省去許多麻煩。

2. 雖然他是富家出身，未嘗受過生活的折磨，但是如今遇到災荒流落
   他鄉，也就顧不得羞恥，索性靠乞討爲生了。

3. 既然你很同情我的處境，又瞭解我的背景，我索性跟你說個痛快，這
   樣幾年來的煩悶便可以發洩出來了。

I. <u>Correlative Structures</u>

A. 與其...不如...

1. It is better to manage one's own affairs well than to bother with other people's business.

2. Because it saves time and is easier, it is better to get advice from an expert than to try to figure things out yourself.

3. It is better to be filial to one's parents while they are still alive than to wear mourning and give them an elaborate burial after their death.

B. 再...（也）沒有

1. He witnessed the tragedy with his own eyes. Therefore his report is the most accurate of all.

2. The idea he came up with is absolutely perfect but it took him three days to work it out.

3. There is no harm in discussing this again with him. If he approves, that's fine. If not, then we will have to stop for the time being.

II. <u>Structure Words</u>

...就是了

1. He resigned his job and went home. It wasn't that he was under fire or underpaid. He was just very tired.

2. You ask me why I spend so much time travelling around the country side. I just enjoy looking at the terraced rice fields and watching them transplant the young plants. That's all.

III. <u>Miscellaneous</u>

A. 不妨

1. Although he does not know much about oracle bone inscriptions, he knows a lot about bronze inscriptions (鐘鼎文). If you are interested, you might as well ask him. Perhaps he can suggest some good reference material.

2. Since you are a student studying abroad for the first time and are not yet familiar with conditions here, there is no harm in taking only a few courses at first. Get acquainted with conditions at school and then plan your next step.

3. If the landlord is so unreasonable on this point, you might as well clarify all the other provisions in the lease. That will reduce misunderstanding and bother.

B. 何妨

1. You have always thought your family came from a village on the border between Italy and France. When you are in Europe this summer, why not check into the family registers of the village and study the tombstone inscriptions for any clues you can find?

2. Think it over, while you are here, what harm is there in trying your hand at sketching? You might even get so interested you would decide that you might as well go further and try carving wood-block illustrations.

C. 無妨

1. According to the provisions of the law, it does not matter if you don't pay your taxes on time so long as you report what you owe by the deadline.

2. They had some constructive suggestions they wanted to make but were afraid of embarrassing their host. I told them he would not be offended and that they should go ahead --it would not matter.

D. VERB 得／不過來

1. Even though we all came and helped him get the auditorium ready, he was still too busy. This really is too big a job for one person.

2. When country people come into the city, everything looks good to them. There are so many things that they can't even see them all, let alone buy anything.

3. As magazine subscriptions (訂價) are very cheap here, he subscribed to a number of different kinds, but in the end he could not read them all.

E. 無從

1. The monuments and wars of the ancient world have been pretty well studied but at the moment we really don't have a way to begin to study the sociology of ancient cultures.

2. Our discussions of Chinese rural society recently have become increasingly complex to the point where I simply don't know where to take hold.

3. Recently archaeologists have discovered a lot of old tombs in Shensi. They are supposed to be very old but there is still no way to determine exactly what the period of these relics is because the material unearthed to date is too limited.

F. 索性

1. I have so many questions that I don't know where to begin, so I might as well not ask any.

2. The plane is on fire, and since we probably won't come out of this, we might as well shut our eyes and let fate take its course (聽天由命).

IV. Review Sentences

Use:

上軌道	本身	祇有 ... 罷了	類似
年復一年	倘若 ... 則 ...	似乎	以 ... 而說
尤其	凡	一切	不是 ... 而是 ...
常軌	有意	終	歷次

1. When a society becomes excessively decadent and corrupt, it has lost its creativity and all anyone can do is to watch it go down to extinction.

2. People who make their living by farming all know the value of land.

3. He seems terribly depressed as though he has a lot of things on his mind he does not find easy to talk about.

4. The characters carved on this tombstone are similar to Han characters, so we can surmise that this is a relic of the period just before or after the Han dynasty.

5. People familiar with our local conditions all insist that the people here are extraordinarily polite and cordial to strangers.

6. In many ways the big-family system in itself is not an ideal social organization. Although it has persisted for several centuries, in modernizing societies the small-family system is replacing it.

7. After repeated years of disaster, nothing had returned to normal. The life of the peasants in particular was much more impoverished than it had been before.

8. A lot of people asked questions after the lecture. It seemed to me that some did not really have anything to say but were just deliberately trying to provoke trouble.

9. This is a newly established school. Nothing is working properly yet. No regulations exist to govern the students, the number of teachers seems insufficient, and no one really knows how to go about raising money.

10. 市上糧食的販賣多半以斗爲單位，但是佃戶每年繳給地主的糧食，則多以斤爲單位。

11. 宋代學者對於四書五經的研究旣精深，又有其獨到之處。

<u>Write Sentences Using</u>:

1. 在 ... 作祟   7. 不得

2. 不以爲然   8. 業已

3. 爲 ... 着想   9. 藉以

4. 介乎 ... 之間   10. 不拘

5. 一天 ... 就一天 ...

6. 無論 ... 總是 ...

T'ao Hsi-sheng and others

This declaration of January 1935 by ten university professors expressed concern that Chinese culture was being threatened by the spread of Westernization and called for a judicious synthesis of Eastern and Western elements. It was conservatism of this sort that called forth the statement on "Our Ideas on the Cultural Movement" which was presented above as Selection IX.

Chang Ching-lu, ed., <u>Source Materials on Contemporary Chinese Publishing</u> (Chung-kuo hsien-tai ch'u-pan shih-liao), Peking, 1955, Vol. II, pp. 155-160.

<u>142:T</u>	本位			N:	native basis (i.e. Chinese) (143:4,6; 146:2,6; 147:1,11, etc.)
	宣言			N:	proclamation, declaration
4	濃	núng	1	SV:	dense, concentrated, thick (as of liquids, fog, etc.)
	萬象			N:	Nature
	蜷伏	chywán--		V:	to crouch and curl up; to hibernate
	嚴寒	--hán	2	N:	severe cold
5	墳墓	fén--	3	N:	grave, tomb
	骷髏	kūlóu		N:	skull; skeleton (142:7)
6	眾生			N:	all living beings
	吊	dyàu	4	V:	to pull up (as by a rope)
7	溫暖			SV/N:	warm; warmth
	天堂			N:	heaven, paradise
	深淵	--ywān	5	N:	depths, abyss
	蕭索	syāu--	6	SV:	desolate
	凜冽	lǐnglyè		SV:	piercingly cold
	寒夜	hán--	2	N:	cold winter night
8	境界			N:	area, region; situation

	漂泊	--bwó	7	V: to wander about
	憧憬	chūngjǐng	8,9	V/N: to day dream, or reminisce; reminiscing
11	化育			V/N: (to) nurture
143:1	展望			V/N: to look out; prospect, outlook
4	嫌	syán	10	V: to find objectionable; to dislike
	刺目		NM1	SV: (lit.) irritating; (fig.) striking
5	強烈	--lyè	11	SV: strong, forceful
9	太古			N: early antiquity
	上進			V: to advance, go forward
10	隆盛	lúng--	12	SV: flourishing
	停頓		NM2	V/N: to cease, desist; (to) pause
11	儒(教)	rú(--)	13	N: Confucian (teaching)
144:1	巨艦	jyù--	14	N: large naval vessels
2	醒覺			V: to awaken (the mind) (usually 覺醒) (144:3)
3	曾國藩	----fán		N: Tseng Kuo-fan
	李鴻章	--húng--		N: Li Hung-chang
	洋務運動			N: modernization movement (lit. foreign things movement)
	梁啓超	lyángchǐ--	15,16	N: Liang Ch'i-ch'ao
5	堅甲利兵			EX: good military equipment
	聲光化電			N: (used here as a general term for) science
	模仿	--fǎng	17	V/N: to imitate; imitation (145:6,8,9; 147:7)
6	變法			V/N: (to) reform (political reform of governmental system)
	見解			N: understanding, explanation; idea, opinion

7	使命		N:	mission, responsibility
	畢竟		A:	after all; in the last analysis
8	迎頭趕上 (去)	S1	EX:	to try to catch up with the front
10	…之交	S2	PT:	at the juncture of (usually time)
	不已	NM3	V:	to have no end (literary form of 不停)
12	遂 swéi	18	A:	於是 (145:1)
	爲之一變		ex:	changed by it; thus changed
145:4	當前	S3	Adj:	current, present
	更爲	S4	ex:	to be more SV
7	獨特		SV:	special, unique
	交嬗 --shàn		V:	to be in a stage of transition
8	除却			same as 除(了)
12	混戰		V/N:	(to be involved in) mixed and confused fighting
146:2	任其自然		EX:	"Let nature take its course."
7	贊美		V:	to praise (贊 in this meaning is normally written 讚) (146:7,8)
	咒詛 jòudzŭ	19,20	V/N:	to curse or imprecate; imprecation (146:9)
9	卑劣 bēi--	21	SV:	low, base
	務盡	NM4	ex:	must be completely
	吝惜 lìn--	22	V:	to begrudge
10	渣滓 jādž		N:	sediment, siftings; refuse (148:3)
147:3	珍貴 jēn--	23	SV:	precious, valuable
4	大同		N:	cosmopolitanism (147:5)
6	要而言之		EX:	to sum up in a word
	眼光		N:	vision (as to have vision)

閉關自守   bì-----   24   EX: to stay in seclusion; to shut the gate and keep to oneself (used of China trying to repel the West)

度量   N: capacity

7 決心   V/N: to determine; determination

9 守舊   SV: conservative (148:3)

148:3 精英   N: essence

取長捨短   ----shě--   25   EX: to accept what is good while discarding what is bad

7 最勁最強   --jìng----   26   ex: most vital and most forceful

生力軍   N: reinforcements, new strength

CHARACTERS TO BE LEARNED

1. 濃 nùng   SV: dense, thick, concentrated (of tea, smoke, color, atmosphere, fog, etc.) (142:4)

     濃茶   N: strong tea

     濃度   N: density

     濃厚   SV: intense (as of interest, sentiment)

2. 寒 hán   SV/N: cold, wintry, in poor circumstances (142:7)

     嚴寒   N: extreme cold (142:4)

     性寒   EX: "cold" nature (of Chinese medicine)(163:8)

     寒心   SV: to cool off (usually from disappointment); disappointed; to be afraid (167:8; 168:2)

     寒冷   SV: bitterly cold

     受寒   VO: to catch a cold

     貧寒   SV: poverty-stricken

     寒假   N: winter vacation

     傷寒   N: typhoid

     膽寒   SV: fearful, lacking in moral courage

寒流　N: cold current/stream/front（股）

3. 墳 fén　　N: grave

墳墓　N: grave (142:5)（座）

墳地　N: cemetery

上墳　VO: to visit and tend graves

祖墳　N: ancestral tombs

4. 吊 dyàu　(1)　V: to pull up by a rope; to hang (142:6)

吊起來　RV: to hang up

吊死鬼　N: spirit of one who has committed suicide by hanging

上吊　V: to hang oneself

吊橋　N: suspension bridge（座）

吊床　N: hammock

(2)　M: for a string of money (like old Chinese cash)

(3)　V: to console, condole, to mourn (correct form in this meaning is 弔)

吊喪　V: to send condolences

5. 淵 ywān　　BF: deep pool, abyss

深淵　N: abyss (142:7)

淵源　N: source, origin

淵博　SV: profound and learned

學問淵博　EX: to be very learned

天淵之別　EX: extreme differences; the difference between heaven and earth; poles apart

6. 蕭 syāu　(1) BF: desolate, mournful

蕭索　SV: desolate (142:7)

蕭條　SV: desolate, pitiful

(2) Surname

7. 泊 bwó   (1) BF: moor; ripple; anchor

飄泊   V: to live aimlessly; to wander about (142:8)

飄泊不定   EX: roving, unsettled

泊船   V: to anchor a vessel

停泊   V: to moor or anchor

(2) BF: lake

湖泊   N: lakes

8. 憧 chūng   BF: unsettled

9. 憬 jǐng   BF: rouse, awake

憧憬 V/N: to day dream or reminisce; reminiscing (74:11; 142:8)

10. 嫌 syán   V/N: to find objectionable; to dislike; defect, fault (143:4)

私嫌   N: personal dislike

嫌疑   N: suspicion

涉嫌疑   ex: implicated in or involved, suspected

嫌疑犯   N: suspected criminal

嫌少/多/大/小   V: to object to a thing as being too less/many/big/small

嫌貧愛富   EX: to slight the poor and pay attention to the rich

11. 烈 lyè   BF: violent, turbulent

強烈   SV: strong, violent (of wine, wind) (27:8; 143:4)

猛烈   SV: fierce, ferocious (150:12; 166:2)

轟轟烈烈   ex: grand, imposing, world-shaking (175:2)

熱烈   SV: enthusiastic, ardent

劇烈　SV: severe, intense, violent (劇 here means intensely, very)

激烈　SV: extremist, radical

烈日當空　EX: with a fierce sun overhead

烈火　N: fierce fire

烈士　N: martyr

先烈　N: martyr

忠烈　SV/N: loyal, loyalty (of persons dead or willing to die for a cause, country, etc.)

壯烈　SV/A: glorious(ly) (as of one who bravely sacrifices himself for his country, etc.)

一九一一年中國革命有很多人壯烈犧牲了。
There were many brave martyrs who died in the 1911 revolution.

12. 隆 lúng　BF: glorious, prosperous

隆盛　SV: brilliant, prosperous, flourishing (as of an age) (143:10)

興隆　SV: prosperous, glorious, flourishing

隆厚　SV: generous

隆重　SV: impressive; solemn

13. 儒 rú　BF: Confucianist

儒（教）　N: Confucian teachings (143:10)

儒生　N: Confucian scholar (167:12; 172:9)

儒道　N: Confucian Way (168:7)

儒家　N: Confucianist

14. 巨 jyù　BF: great, enormous

巨艦　N: large naval vessels (144:1)

巨頭　N: major figures (149:10)

巨頭會議　N: (one term for) summit meeting

巨大 SV: enormous (150:11)

巨人 N: giant

巨盜 N: powerful robbers

巨浪 N: heavy seas; huge waves

巨禍 N: major disaster

巨款 N: enormous sum of money (筆)

15. 梁 lyǎng (1) Surname (144:3)

(2) can be substituted for 樑 in the meaning of bridge pole or beam

橋梁 N: bridge

梁上君子 N: nickname for a burglar

屋梁 N: beam

16. 啓 chǐ   BF: begin, start, open; inform (144:3)
(啟)

啓蒙 V: to enlighten; to instruct the young

啓蒙運動／時期 N: enlightenment movement/ period (151:6)

啓發 V/N: to stimulate, arouse; to open up man's mind and intelligence (163:7) (In Chinese Communists usage: to stimulate people to think critically about themselves and their past)

啓程 V: to start on a journey

啓示 V/N: to reveal, to unveil; revealing

啓示錄 N: Book of Revelations

啓事 N: announcement (as public notice)

17. 仿 fǎng   V: to follow the pattern of; to imitate
(倣)

模仿 V/N: to imitate; imitation (144:5)

仿照 CV/V: like, according to; to imitate

仿效 V: to imitate or follow (as fads or fashions)

仿古　V: to imitate the past

仿造　V: to make according to pattern (as to imitate antiques, etc.)

相仿　SV: similar to each other

18. 遂 swèi (swèi)　(1) A: in the end; eventually; consequently (67:2; 144:12; 145:1)

由於他研究科學上的許多問題，後來遂成爲一個有名的科學家。

Because he had studied many scientific problems, he finally became a famous scientist.

遂即　A: and consequently, then

他們研究了問題的性質以後，遂即商議解決的辦法。

After having investigated the nature of the problem, they (forthwith) discussed its solutions.

遂告失敗／完成　ex: to have eventually failed/been accomplished

(2) V: to follow, obtain, comply with (as wishes)

遂心／意／願　VO: to meet one's hope or desire

家裡有很多事他覺得不遂心。

Many things at home are not according to his liking.

未／不遂　ex: not to be in accord with one's desires

這個賊不但偷盜未遂，反而把自己的東西丟了。

The thief not only did not get what he wanted but he even lost his own things.

他受傷以後到現在還是半身不遂。

He has been paralyzed ever since he was wounded.

得遂　ex: to achieve what one wants

經過不斷的努力，他終於宿志得遂，成了舉世聞名的畫家。

By unremitting effort he finally achieved his long-cherished ambition and became a world famous artist.

19. 咒 jòu (呪)　V/N: to imprecate; (to) curse (146:7)

咒語　N: curses, imprecations

念咒 VO: to recite incantations

咒罵 V: to curse, abuse

賭咒 VO: to swear that dire consequences will follow (upon such conduct)

20. 詛 dzǔ BF: curse, imprecate

咒詛 V/N: to curse, imprecate; to rail at; imprecation (146:7,9) (usually 詛咒)

21. 卑 bēi BF: humble, low

卑劣 SV: low, base (146:9)

自卑 SV: self-deprecating

自卑感 N: sense of inferiority

卑賤 SV: base, mean, humble

22. 吝 lìn BF: stingy, sparing of

吝惜 V: to begrudge (146:9)

23. 珍 jēn BF: precious, rare

珍貴 SV: precious or valuable (147:3)

珍重 EX: "take care of yourself" (in letters, etc.) (161:6)

珍惜 V: to value or cherish; to prize (as time, opportunity)

珍本 N: rare book

珍寶 N: precious thing

珍奇 SV: rare, precious

24. 閉 bì BF: close, shut

閉關自守 EX: to keep in seclusion; to close the gates and keep to oneself (used of China in trying to keep the Western powers out) (147:6)

緊閉 V: to be tightly shut (152:9)

閉會 V: to close a meeting, adjourn

倒閉 V/N: to fail (of a business); bankruptcy; failure

禁閉 V: to detain under house arrest

閉口無言 EX: to say nothing, to keep mum

閉眼／口 VO: to close the eyes/mouth

夜不閉戶 EX: not to have to lock the door at night (connotes high level of social stability and order)

閉塞 SV: isolated (of a place); unenlightened (of thought)

關閉 V/N: to close, to shut up; to blockade; closing (of harbors, air fields, etc.); barrier

封閉 V/N: to close, to seal up, to blockade; sealing off of

停閉 V: to close (of stores)

閉門造車 EX: stubbornly to carry out one's idea irrespective of external circumstances (lit. to fasten the door and make carts) (車 read jyū)

25. 捨 shě V: to give up

取長捨短 EX: to choose the advantageous or strong points and reject the disadvantageous or weak points (148:3)

捨棄 V: to reject; to give up; forsake, abandon

捨命 VO: to sacrifice one's life for others

捨(不)得 RV: to be (un)willing to give something up

施捨 V: to dispense charity

捨已爲羣 EX: to sacrifice oneself (to the benefit or interests of others); to yield to the wishes of a group

捨生取義 EX: to sacrifice one's life for righteousness

窮追不捨 EX: to pursue to the end without yielding

捨己從人 EX: to yield one's wishes to those of others

26. 劲 jìn (jìng)   (1) BF: strong, energetic (148:7)

                强劲 SV: strong, powerful

                劲敵 N: well-matched foes

      (2) N: strength, energy

          有劲 (兒) SV: to have the physical strength to

(jìr)   起劲兒 SV: full of pep and spirit; to do things with spirit

        使劲 (兒) VO: to put forth or exert effort (physically)

(不) 對劲 (兒) EX: (not) "right" (in the sense of (not) "ringing true," "corresponding to the facts." The negative is also a colloquial expression for "to feel slightly under the weather.")

        他的態度有些不對劲兒。
        His manner seemed a little queer (i.e. had something queer or not right about it.)

NEW MEANINGS

1. 刺   BF: irritate

    刺眼／目 SV: (lit.) irritating to the eye; (fig.) striking to the eye

      刺耳 SV: jarring or grating on the ear

      刺激 V/N: to provoke, to stir up, incite; provocation, stimulus

2. 頓   BF: pause

      停頓 V/N: to cease, desist; (to) pause (143:10)

3. 已   BF: finish; come to an end

      不已 ex: unending, without end (144:10)

      無已 ex: without end (literary form of 不停)

4. 務   (1) must (literary)

      務盡 ex: must be completely (146:9)

務使　V: to have to cause or enable

務必／須　AV: to be necessary to; to be required that
(literary form of 一定要)

(2) A: earnestly

務請 ex: earnestly request

務期 ex: earnestly hope

STRUCTURE NOTES

1.   <u>迎頭</u>

    A.   迎 (BF) "meet," "receive," means "against" in such compounds as:

        迎面 (against the face) 來了一部汽車 .   (cf. 對面)
        Here was a car coming towards me.

        迎面 (against the head) 亂砍 .   to chop off heads right and left **in combat**

      迎風而去   to go against the wind.

    B.   Also notice the use of 迎 in the following phrases:

      迎上來   to go up to (someone)

      迎頭趕上   to try to catch up with the front; to press eagerly ahead

2. $\left\{{當 \atop 在}\right\}$ A B 之交   PT: at the time when ...

    A.   交 here functions as a localizer.

    B.   Cf. 當 ... 之際 / 時 , etc. (VI Structure 9)

3.   當前   <u>Adj: (at) present</u>

    A.   當前 is used most commonly to modify nouns:

      當前 (的) 任務   present tasks

      當前 (的) 困難   present difficulties

    B.   當前 is also now used as an adverb but apparently only in a pre-subject position.

      當前我們主要任務是努力建國。
    At present our chief responsibility is to work to build the nation.

    C.   當前 is also used as a verb meaning "to confront (us)," "to face us (as a problem)"

      大敵當前。
    The enemy confronts us.

4.   更爲 SV

Note use of 更爲 as emphatic expression before a bisyllabic SV.

        更爲迫切   more urgent

        更爲重要   more important

cf. 甚爲迫切／重要   very urgent/pressing

        ✻   ✻   ✻   ✻   ✻

Note for Review:

1.   固然 ... 也 ... (143:1)

    固 ... 但 ... (145:6)

2.   要 ... （就）必須 ... (143:3)

3.   既 ... 亦／也 ... (145:4)

4.   不僅 ... 並且 ... (147:2)

5.   無所 Verb   (146:9)

E X E R C I S E S

I. Miscellaneous

A. 迎頭趕上

1. 青年處在日新月異的二十世紀中如果不迎頭趕上，一定會被時代的巨浪吞沒的。

2. 每個人都應該有迎頭趕上的決心，不應該抱着閉關自守的態度。

3. 你應該珍惜你過去光榮的歷史，所以經過這次失敗後仍應該迎頭趕上重振你的聲威。

B. 聽／任／順／憑其自然

1. 教育兒女一定要任其自然的發展，我們只能在旁邊加以啓示性的指導，除此而外，不能作別的。

2. 儒家的思想特徵之一就是樂天知命，也就是順其自然。這是一種消極思想，我可不贊成。

C. 當前／面

1. 觀察當前世界大局，紛紛擾擾，人類頗有陷於悲境的可能。

2. 當前最重要的教育問題，不是課程內容的改良而是如何輔導青年，使他們有一個正確的人生觀。

3. 買賣房屋既然是屬於契約行為，雙方當事人應該先當面談好條件，然後再進行簽約。

D. 甚／更為

1. 五年沒有到過台灣，我發現台灣工商業比以前更為繁榮，社會更為進步。

2. 台灣的公共汽車甚為方便，票價也甚為便宜。

3. 他穿上這套衣服就顯得更為年青，更為美麗。

4. 現在公佈的新辦法中的各項規定都甚為合理。

I. Miscellaneous

A. 迎頭趕上

   1. The reason I do not approve of Taoist thought is because it does not have any "get up and go" spirit.

   2. I feel that we ought to increase our emphasis on the study of other cultures in order to try to catch up with the new currents in art and music.

   3. Even the most advanced nations of the Communist bloc are imitating the methods of capitalist countries in a determined effort to equal or surpass their accomplishments.

B. 聽／任／順／憑其自然

   1. Because of the strong opposition of such people, the work has not gone too smoothly. The only way to eliminate the opposition is just to let things go.

   2. Most people, when faced with something unpleasant, either curse without stopping or let things take their course. Very few take a middle-of-the-road position.

C. 當前／面

   1. Since the situation is that serious, it would be best to discuss it with him face to face.

   2. If we avoid our present responsibilities, we will not be qualified to undertake anything more important in the future.

II. Review Sentences

Use:

甘心願意	固有的	只 . . . 而已	與其 . . . 毋寧 . . .
之所以	是否	由於 . . . 所致	過於
在於	既 . . . 亦 . . .	至於	

1. The traditional education system has already been undermined by new forces, but no new educational system is being established.

2. Beginning today a system of signing in will go into effect to avoid a repetition of such evil practices.

3. Probably the reason for such corruption is the fact that there is no one to take the actual administrative responsibility.

4. If you want to reach the public, posting slogans is not as effective as publishing propaganda in the newspaper.

5. He is excessively self-deprecating. He is always insisting that he can't do anything.

6. Whether or not he will succeed will depend entirely on the effort he makes.

7. They lost money, not because business was slow (清淡) or because their management was poor, but simply because they could not cooperate.

8. This is not considered a big wharf. It can only handle ships weighing less than 10,000 tons.

9. To achieve his purpose he is willing to let people criticize him unfairly rather than to argue with them or rebut their accusations.

10. 儒道之創始人是孔子。其歷史背景是當春秋戰國之際各國爲了爭奪名利而騷擾不安，因此孔子遂有修身，齊家，治國，平天下的主張。

11. 他對於這個問題不僅是孤陋寡聞，而且還有盲從之嫌。

12. 全城的屠宰商有見於私屠的風氣很盛，特地發起取締無稅私屠的運動。

13. 要想使啓蒙運動發生效力，必須不遺餘力地埋頭苦幹。

Write Sentences Using:

1. 每逢 ... 就 ...　　　　7. 無從

2. 終於　　　　　　　　　8. 不拘

3. 跟着 ... 而 ...　　　　9. 固然 ... 也 ...

4. 果然　　　　　　　　　10. 要 ... (就)必須 ...

5. 不分　　　　　　　　　11. 除却

6. 玩 ... 把戲　　　　　　12. 不得

A leftist historian traces some of the events that lead up to the May Fourth Demonstration and gives a brief description of events that day and their aftermath in Peking and Tokyo.

T'ao Chü-yin, Historical Narratives of the Pei-yang Warlord Period (Pei-yang chün-fa t'ung-chih shih-ch'i shih-kua), Peking, 1957, Vol. IV, pp. 33-40.

149:2	和會			N: peace conference (149:3,8,10; 151:10; 155:11)
	一場春夢	--(cháng)---NM1		N: fleeting dream
5	時効			N: effective period
	綁	bǎng	1	V: to tie, bind
6	無恥	(--chǐ) (VII:14)		SV: shameless
7	勢不兩立			EX: (lit. of two persons or situations of such opposing interests that they cannot exist in the same place at the same time); cannot exist together
8	巴黎	(bālí) (VII:44,45)		N: Paris (151:9)
	專斷			SV: arbitrary, despotic, tyrannical
	抹殺	mwǒ--	2	V: to wipe out, obliterate
	面貌	--màu	3	N: face, features (lit. and fig.)
10	專橫地	(--hèng--)(VII:NM1)		A: arbitrarily
150:1	狂風驟雨	kwáng -----	4	EX: wild storm with raging winds and pelting rain
2	朕兆	jènjàu	5	N: omen
6	章宗祥	----syáng		N: Chang Tsung-hsiang (153:2,4,7)
	送行			V: to see someone off
8	下旬	--syún	6	N: last ten days of the month
	街頭			N: streets (156:8)

10	大風起於萍末	-----píng---		ex:	(here) beginning of a storm
	最高學府		NM2	N:	the leading educational institution
11	大本營			N:	headquarters
	爭鳴	--míng	7	V:	to sing competing songs (fig.)
	園地			N:	(lit.) garden; (fig.) arena (150:12)
12	鼓舞			V/N:	to encourage, cheer up; encouragement
	生根發芽	-----yá	8	ex:	to take root and sprout
	北大			N:	abbr. of 國立北京大學 (National Peking University) (151:3,8,11; 152:1; 154:8,9)
	新青年			N:	New Youth magazine (151:2)
	每週評論			N:	Weekly Review
151:1	抨擊	pēng--	9	V/N:	to attack critically; to refute; refutation
	禮敎			N:	traditional code of ethics
3	迫使			V:	to force; to drive to
	主辦			V:	to run (in the sense of being the chief administrative agency or officer)
	辭職			V/N:	to resign; resignation
	阻擋	--dǎng	10	V/N:	to impede, block; obstacle
4	朝着	(cháu)--	NM3	V:	to face
7	國恥／耻	(--chǐ)	(VII:14)	N:	national disgrace (151:9; 156:7,10)
	最後通牒	-----dyé		N:	ultimatum
	袁世凱	ywán--kǎi	11,12	N:	Yuan Shih-k'ai
8	二十一條			N:	The Twenty-One Demands (152:2; 156:6)
	大專			N:	universities and special schools or institutes (154:3,4)
10	悲憤塡膺	--fèntyán yīng	13,14	EX:	full of aggrieved anger

	時			N: 點鐘 (152:1; 157:11)
	法科			N: law school (151:11)
11	捍衞	hàn--	15	V: to guard against
12	謝紹敏	----mǐn	16	N: Hsieh Shao-min
	斷指血書			ex: (lit. to cut the finger and write with blood); to write a blood letter (to show sincerity)
	青島	--dǎu	17	N: Tsingtao
	激昂	--áng	18	SV: excited (as from righteous indignation)
152:1	高師			N: abbr. of 高等師範學堂
	誓死	shr̀--	19	V: to swear to die, etc. (152:10)
3	東交民巷	-----syàng	20	N: Legation Street in Peking
	擬	nǐ	21	V: to plan, to intend to (152:7)
4	抗議			V/N: (to) protest (152:5)
	推舉			V: select; elect; put forward (157:2)
	接洽	--chyà	22	V/N: to negotiate; negotiations
5	例假			N: legal holiday
	公使			N: Minister (157:2,6)

公使館　N: Legation (157:11; 158:2,7)

大使館　N: Embassy

領事館　N: Consulate

7	憤慨	fèn--	13	SV: indignant (158:5)
	事故			N: incident; accidental event (157:5)
	王府井大街			N: "Morrison Street" in Peking
	東單牌樓			N: southeast area of Peking
8	曹汝霖	tsáu rǔlín	23	N: Ts'ao Ju-lin (152:8,9,10,12; 153:1,4,7,9)

9	曹宅	tsáu--	23		N: Ts'ao residence
	激怒	--nù	24		V: to infuriate
10	市民				N: inhabitants of the city (155:7; 156:1)
	鼓噪	--dzàu			V: to make a great clamor
	一時				A: (here) for the moment; (usually) for a moment
	不…不罷休		S1		PT: to determine not to stop until ... has been done
	懾于	jé--			V: to be afraid of (153:12)
					N: power, influence (155:4)
12	鼎沸	--fèi	25		V: to bubble like a cauldron (used fig. of insurrections, etc.)
153:1	忿無可泄	fèn-----	26		ex: to have no way to give vent to one's indignation
	客廳	--tīng	27		N: parlor, living room
	慌做一團				ex: huddled together in panic
2	不由分說				EX: to act impulsively without permitting argument or explanation
	飽以老拳	-----chywán	28		EX: to pound someone fiercely with clenched fists
3	躺	tǎng	29		V: to lie down
	裝死				V: to pretend to die
4	騰起	téng--	30		V: to rise
5	奢侈	shēchǐ	31,32	SV/N:	extravagant; extravagance
	放一把火			VO:	to set a fire to (note 把 as measure for fire)
	美奐美輪	--hwàn----			EX: to be very beautiful
	付之一炬	------jyù			EX: to put to the torch

	煙霧迷漫	-----màn	33	EX: (lit. and fig.) smoky confusion	
6	搶救			V: to rescue by force	
7	六國飯店			N: Wagon-Lits Hotel	
	創傷	(chwāng)--	NM4	N: wound	
8	漫無目標	màn-----	33	ex: (here) disorganized and aimless	
9	眷屬	jywàn--	34	N: dependents	
10	吳炳湘	wú bǐng--	35	N: Wu Ping-hsiang	
	率領	(shwài)--	NM5	V: to lead (as a delegation, army)	
	殿後		NM6	V: to fall behind; to guard the rear	
11	嚇	syà	36	V: to frighten (155:5)	
	心驚肉跳			EX: to jump out of one's skin with fright	
12	訓令			N: instructions from superiors	
154:1	拳頭	chywán--	28	N: fist	
3	滋事	dz̄--	37	V: to make trouble	
4	總統府		NM2	N: Presidential Palace	
5	國務院			N: Foreign Ministry	
	請願			V/N: to petition (154:5; 157:9)	
6	總長			N: cabinet minister	
7	閣員	gé--	38	N: cabinet members	
	傅增湘	fù----	39	N: Fu Tseng-hsiang	
8	副署	--shù	40	V: to sign for or in place of a superior	
	發急			V: to get excited; to be in a great fluster	
10	徐世昌	syú--chāng	41	N: Hsu Shih-ch'ang	
	段祺瑞	--chí (rwèi)	(VII:19)	N: Tuan Ch'i-jui	
11	閃爍其詞	shǎnshwò----		ex: (here) by indirect reference	

	譴責	chyǎn--	42	V/N: (to) reprimand, (to) blame
12	彈壓	(tán)--	NM7	V: to keep down or suppress
155:1	山東旅京同鄉會			N: (lit. assoc. of Shantung fellow provincials stopping in Peking); Shantung Association of Peking
2	函電	hán--	43	N: telegram, messages
	汪大燮	wāng--syè	44	N: Wang Ta-hsieh
	王寵惠	--chǔnghwèi	45	N: Wang Ch'ung-hui
3	呈請		NM8	V: to request, apply for (of an inferior to superior)
	警察廳	----tīng	27	N: police department (155:5,8)
5	是日			N: that day (literary form of 這一天)
8	冒名	màu--	46	A: under false name
	詭稱	gwěi--	47	V: to lie, to say falsely, to deceive
	空勞			A: uselessly, in vain
9	林立			V: to stand close together (of many people, policemen, etc., standing thick as trees)
12	巡捕	syún--	48.	N: patrols; police
156:2	竟然			A: (here) unexpectedly
	奉系			N: Fengt'ien clique
	張作霖	----lín		N: Chang Tso-lin
	轄境	syá--	49	N: limits of jurisdiction
3	扣留	kòu--	50	V/N: to detain; detention
	張敬堯	----yáu		N: Chang Ching-yau
	報導			V/N: (to) report
4	質問		NM9	V/N: to cross-examine; cross-examination; inquiry
	啞子	yǎ--	51	N: mute

	瞎子	syā--	52	N: blind person
7	幽靈	yōulíng	53,54	N: spirits of the dead
	盯住	dīng--		RV: to keep the eyes upon; to keep in sight
	容留		NM10	V: accommodate
8	地點			N: place or location (157:11)
10	化裝			V/N: to be disguised or made up as; disguise
	食客			N: customer (at a restaurant)
	追蹤	--dzūng	55	V: to tail, to follow, to shadow
11	刀劍	--jyàn	56	N: swords
	遍體麟傷	----lín--		EX: to be covered with wounds
12	警署	--shǔ	40	N: police office
	虐待	nywè--	57	V: to maltreat
157:2	莊景珂	----kē		N: Chuang Ching-k'e (157:3,4)
3	意外			SV/N: unexpected; accidental event
4	防線			N: defense line
5	公然			A: publicly (157:9)
	認賊作父			EX: (lit. to acknowledge a thief as one's father); submissive or obsequious to an evil party for personal advantage
	對待			V/N: to treat (a person)
	怒火中燒	nù----	24	EX: to burn with rage
6	投遞	--dì	58	V: to submit, hand in (158:2,7)
	日比谷公園	----gǔ----	59	N: Hibaya Park (157:12)
8	交涉員			N: negotiators
	故障			N: incident (disturbance or trouble); (now used for) mechanical trouble

9	太歲頭上動土			ex: (lit. to put dirt on the Star God's head) to have the audacity to (as with a mouse provoking a lion)
10	瘋狂	fēngkwáng	60,4	SV: wild; crazy (158:11)
	血腥	--syīng	61	Adj: bloody
11	襲擊		NM11	V/N: (to) attack
	側巷	tsèsyàng	62,20	N: side alley
	大手町	----tīng		N: Otemachi
12	迎頭亂砍	-----kǎn	63	ex: to slash around wildly with a sword
158:1	揚長而去			ex: to stride off proudly with one's head high in the air
	刀光劍影	----jyàn--	56	ex: the flashing of many swords
	馬蹄	--tí		N: horses' hoofs (158:8)
	蹂躪	róulìn	64,65	V: to trample on
	砍傷	kǎn--	63	V: to slash and wound
2	冒死	màu--	46	V: to risk death
4	拳足	chywán--	28	N: fists and feet
	吳英	wú--	35	N: Wu Ying (158:5)
	惡狠狠	--hěnhěn	66	A: cruelly
5	奮不顧身			ex: bravely without regard to personal safety
	吶喊	nà--		V: to cry out
7	瑞士	(rwèi--)	(VII:19)	N: Switzerland
8	殺氣騰騰	----téng téng	30	ex: extremely fierce (meant to kill)
9	杜中	dù--	67	N: Tu Chung
	體無完膚	------fū	68	ex: to be so badly battered there is no place on the body without wounds
10	腹部	fù--	69	N: abdominal region

公憤   --fèn   13   N: public indignation

11 遭受   dzāu--   70   V: to meet with, encounter

冒險   màu--   46   VO: to brave danger

中華青年會   N: Chinese Youth Association

159:2 忿怒   fènnù   26,24   SV: furious or angry

蓬蓬勃勃   péngpéng   ex: lively, bubbling; rapidly growing
          bwóbwó

CHARACTERS TO BE LEARNED

1. 綁 bǎng   V: to tie up, bind (149:5)

    綁起來 RV: to tie up

    綁票 V/N: to kidnap, seize for ransom; kidnapping

2. 抹 mwǒ   V: to rub, rub over, smear; to wipe out, obliterate
   (mwò)

    抹殺 V: to obliterate, wipe out (149:8)

    抹布 N: dust cloth; dish cloth (塊)

    塗抹 V: to blot out (as sins, etc.)

3. 貌 màu   BF: form, appearance

    面貌 N: face, features, mien (149:8)

    相貌 N: physiognomy, looks

    外貌 N: external appearance

    禮貌 SV/N: courteous; courteousness

    以貌取人 EX: to judge by appearances

    容貌 N: appearances, looks, countenance

    貌合神離 EX: apparently of one accord, but divided in
              intent

4. 狂 kwáng   SV: wild; mad

    狂風 N: wild wind (陣)

狂風驟雨   EX: wild storm with raging winds and pelting rain (150:1)

瘋狂   SV: wild; crazy (157:10)

誇大狂   N: megalomania (165:4)

狂歡   EX: to rejoice wildly; wild rejoicing

狂徒   N: profligate

狂人   N: madman

發狂   V: to go mad

5. 兆 jàu   N: sign; omen (150:2)

徵兆   N: portent

凶兆   N: evil omen

預兆   N: omen, portent

6. 旬 syún   N: period of ten days; (also "decade" when referring to advanced age of a person)

上／中／下旬   N: first, middle or last ten days of the month (150:8)

旬日   N: ten days

旬刊   N: periodical issued every ten days

7. 鳴 míng   V: to call or cry (of birds)

爭鳴   V: to "strive and contend"

百家爭鳴   EX: The various schools strive and contend with one another over their theories.

爭鳴園地   EX: area of intellectual contention or dispute (150:11)

自鳴得意   EX: to be pleased with oneself; smug

一鳴驚人   EX: to be a smashing success on the first try

鳴謝   V: to express thanks

8. 芽 yá   N: sprout, shoot

發芽 VO: to sprout, put forth sprouts (150:12)

生根發芽 EX: to put down roots and sprouts (lit. and fig.)

豆芽菜 N: bean sprouts

9. 抨 pēng   BF: attack, impeach

抨擊 V/N: (to) attack, criticize (of a person, policy, etc.) (151:1)

10. 擋 dǎng   V: to resist; to stop

阻擋 V: to impede, block (151:3)

擋住 RV: to block

抵擋 V: to block, obstruct, resist

擋箭牌 N: shield; something to hide behind (used fig.)

別拿我當擋箭牌。
Don't use me as a screen.

擋路/風/光/etc. VO: to stand in the way of or block the road/wind/light/etc.

擋駕 V: to decline to receive visitors; to be "not at home"

11. 袁 ywán   N: Surname

12. 凱 kǎi   BF: victory

袁世凱 N: Yuan Shih-k'ai (151:7)

凱旋 V: to return in triumph

凱旋門 N: triumphal arch

凱歌 N: song of victory

13. 憤 fèn   (1) BF: angry; anger

悲憤 SV: melancholy and indignant (151:10)

憤慨 SV: full of righteous indignation (152:7)

公憤　N: public indignation (158:10)

憤世疾俗　EX: fed up with the world (165:6)

憤恨 V/N: to hate, be angry; anger, hatred

氣憤 SV/N: angry; anger

(2) BF: zeal; ardor

發憤　V: to resolve firmly to

14. 填 tyán　V: to fill up; to fill in (as a hole, blanks, etc.) (151:10)

填滿 RV: to fill up; to fill

填表格 VO: to fill in blanks (as forms)

填空白/兒 VO: to fill in blanks (as in questionnaires, exams, etc.) (空 read kùng)

15. 捍 hàn　BF: defend against

捍衞　V: to guard against (151:11)

16. 敏 mǐn　BF: keen, acute; alert, quick-witted (151:12; 173:2; 174:4)

敏慧　SV: sagacious; quick of perception

敏感 SV/N: sensitive; quick; perceptive; sensitivity

神經過敏　EX: excessively nervous; oversensitive

17. 島 dǎu　N: island (座)

青島　N: Tsingtao (151:12; 152:1)

牛島　N: peninsula

島國　N: island kingdom

群島　N: archipelago

海島　N: islands (of the sea)

18. 昂 áng　V: to rise; to raise (as prices); to be lofty

激昂　SV: excited (as by righteous indignation) (151:12)

昂貴 SV/N: high priced; expensive; high price level

氣昂昂 ex: to be very angry; pompous

昂起頭來 VO: to square your shoulders and face the situation

希望你們從今天起，能昂起頭來，面對現實。
I hope that from today on you will square your shoulders and face the facts.

昂然 A: haughtily; dignified/exalted in manner

19. 誓 shr̀ BF: oath

誓死 A: to swear to do something or die in the attempt (152:1)

誓不罷休 ex: to swear not to desist until ... (152:10)

發誓 VO: to vow

對天發誓 EX: to take an oath before Heaven

宣誓 V: to take an oath

誓不兩立 EX: I swear that both of us shall not stand. (i.e. fight to the finish to eliminate one party)

誓死不降 EX: to swear that one would rather die than surrender

誓師 V: to harangue troops

起誓 VO: to take an oath

20. 巷 syàng N: alley; lane (152:3; 157:11)

巷子 N: lane; alley (usually off a main street) (條)

巷戰 N: street fighting

巷口 N: entrance to an alley or lane

街頭巷尾 EX: all over town (lit. the entrance of streets and the end of lanes)

大街小巷 EX: all the streets and roads in town (lit. big streets and small lanes)

21. 擬 nǐ (1) V: to propose; draft; plan; intend (152:3; 152:7)

擬定 V: to draft (as documents, blueprints, etc.)

擬定草案　VO: to make a rough draft of a proposal

擬具　V: to draw up a proposal

擬就　V: to have settled, finished

擬請　V: to suggest that

(2) BF: compare

比擬　V: to compare to

擬古　V: to imitate the ancient style

擬態V/N: to mimic; mimicry

22. 洽 chyà　BF: blend with; in harmony with

接洽V/N: to negotiate, to make contact or arrangements with; negotiations (152:4)

23. 曹 tsáu　N: Surname

曹汝霖　N: Ts'ao Ju-lin (152:8,9)

24. 怒 nù　BF: anger; passion; rage

激怒　V: to infuriate (152:9)

怒火中燒　ex: to burn with rage (157:5)

憤怒V/N: to be angry and resentful; anger, resentment

發怒　V: to be in a rage, display temper

怒罵V/N: to curse angrily

大怒　V: to be very angry

老羞成怒　EX: too great embarrassment turns to anger

眾怒難犯　EX: It is difficult to face the anger of multitudes. It is dangerous to arouse the anger of multitudes.

遷怒　V: to transfer anger to someone or something else

觸怒　V: to irritate, anger or infuriate

怒潮   N: raging tide (lit. and fig.)

怒視   V: to glare angrily at

怒髮衝冠 EX: to be so furious that one's hair lifts the hat off one's head

25. 沸 fèi   BF: bubble up, boil

鼎沸   V: to bubble up like a cauldron (used fig. of insurrections, etc.) (152:12)

沸水   N: bubbling water, boiling water

沸點   N: boiling point

26. 忿 fèn   BF: anger, indignation

忿無可泄 ex: to have no way to give vent to one's anger (153:1)

忿怒 SV/N: angry, indignant, furious; anger (159:2)

忿恨 V/N: (to) hate

忿忿不平 ex: angry over injustice

氣忿   V: to feel indignant (over an injustice)

忿慨 V/SV: to feel something is improper; angry

悲忿 SV/N: sorrowful and indignant; grief and indignation

滿懷悲忿 EX: full of sorrow and indignation

27. 廳 tīng   N: hall; room

客廳   N: parlor (153:1)

飯廳   N: dining room

廳堂   N: hall

辦公廳   N: office

28. 拳 chywán   BF: fist

飽以老拳 EX: to pound someone fiercely with clenched fists (153:2)

拳頭   N: fist (154:1)

赤手空拳 EX: barehanded

拳術 N: boxing

太極拳 N: Chinese boxing

打拳 VO: to box

打(他)一拳 VO: to cuff (him); to hit (him) a blow

義和拳 N: the Boxers (also 拳匪)

拳足交加 V: to attack with both hands and feet

29. 躺 tǎng   V: to lie down (as on a bed) (153:3)

30. 騰 téng   (1) BF: soar; hover (153:4; 158:8)

騰空 V: to soar (into the skies); to hover, to mount to heaven

沸騰 V: to boil and bubble (lit. and fig. of trouble and dissension)

騰躍 V: to prance; to rear up

飛黃騰達 EX: to make rapid advance toward success in one's career

(2) V: to empty out and make room for

騰出來 RV: to move out things (to make room)

給他騰地方。
Make a place for him.

31. 奢 shē   BF: spend, thrift; wasteful; extravagant (153:5)

奢華 SV: showy, extravagant

奢望 V/N: (to have) extravagant hopes

驕奢 SV: haughty and extravagant

32. 侈 chǐ   BF: wasteful; extravagant

奢侈 SV/N: extravagant and wasteful; extravagance (153:5)

奢侈品 N: luxuries

33. 漫 màn   BF: overflow; boundless; wild; inundate

        迷漫   V: to be confused; indistinct

                煙霧迷漫 EX: (lit. and fig.) smoky confusion
                         (153:5)

        漫無 V/A: (to be) completely without

                漫無目標 VO: to be completely without a goal;
                          to be disorganized (153:8)

                漫無限制 VO: to have no restrictions what-
                          soever

        漫畫   N: cartoons

    漫不經心 EX: careless

        散漫 SV: disorganized, casual

        漫談   V: to talk at random; to "shoot the breeze"

        浪漫 SV: unconventional; transliteration for "romantic"

                浪漫主義 N: romanticism

34. 眷 jywàn (1) BF: one's family, especially wife and children

        眷屬   N: family; dependents (153:9)

        家眷   N: family; dependents

        攜眷 VO: to bring the family

        (2) BF: love with special affection

        眷愛 V/N: (to) love with special affection

        眷念 V/N: constantly to bear in mind, yearn; longing

        眷顧 V/N: to care for with tenderness; consideration

35. 吳 wú   N: ancient kingdom (in the general Kiangsu area);
                     Surname (56:12; 153:10; 158:4; 174:4, etc.)

36. 嚇 syà   V: frighten, scare
       (hè)
        嚇倒 RV: to frighten (into submission) (155:5; 168:12)

        恐嚇 V/N: to threaten; fright; threat

嚇了我一跳　ex: to give me quite a start

嚇人　VO/SV: to frighten others; frightening

37. 滋 dz̄
(滋)
   (1) BF: stir up; excite

滋事　V: to stir up trouble (as gangland violence) (154:3; 166:1)

   (2) BF: nourishment

滋長 V/N: to thrive (of flora or attitudes); growth

滋養 V/N: to nourish; nourishment

滋味兒　N: flavor, taste

嘗滋味　VO: to get a taste of (as food, travel, fishing, etc.)

滋潤　SV: moist; rich

38. 閣 gé
   BF: cabinet; council; chamber

閣員　N: cabinet member (154:7)

內閣　N: cabinet (of a country)

內閣總理　N: premier; prime minister

閣下　ex: you sir (polite form of address in letters)

39. 傅 fù
   (1) BF: teacher, tutor

師傅　N: teacher, tutor

   (2) Surname (154:7,8)

40. 署 shù
   (1) V: to sign

副署　V: to sign for or in place of a superior (154:8)

署名 V/N: to sign one's name; signature

簽署　V: to sign (petitions, documents, etc.)

(shǔ)　(2) BF: office, bureau

警署　N: police department (156:12)

公署　N: public office (i.e. physical office, not rank)

部署 V/N: to adjust, arrange; arrangements, deployment

41. 徐 syú (1) BF: slow, dignified

徐步 A: with slow steps

徐徐 A: slowly and leisurely

徐來 V: to come on slowly and gently

徐徐而來 ex: approaching with slow and dignified steps

清風徐來 ex: the refreshing breeze blows gently

(2) Surname (154:10,12; 172:2)

(半老)徐娘 N: elderly woman whose beauty is fading (lit. Lady Hsu, a beautiful concubine of Emperor Yuan of the Liang)

42. 譴 chyǎn BF: reprimand, scold

譴責 V/N: to charge with the responsibility (for disaster); (to) reprimand (154:11)

43. 函 hán N: letter

函電 N: letters and telegrams (155:2)

函件 N: letters, correspondence

函授 V/N: to teach by mail; correspondence course

公/專函 N: official/specially written letter

44. 汪 wāng (1) Surname (155:2)

(2) BF: vast area of water

汪洋大海 EX: vast expanse of the seas; great seas

一片汪洋 N: sheet of open sea

45. 惠 hwèi BF: kindness, favor to (155:2)

恩惠 N: mercy, kindness

46. 冒 màu (1) BF: feign, falsely as ...

冒名　A: under a false name (155:8)

　　冒名頂替　EX: masquerading as someone else; to take another's place under false pretenses

冒領　V: to collect something (like salary) in another's name without his knowledge

冒功　VO: to claim the merit of others as one's own

冒充　V: to pretend to be; to act falsely as ...

假冒　V: to act falsely as ...

冒牌　V/N: to fake or forge a trade mark; forgery

　　冒牌貨　N: faked thing, fake; (sometimes) an impostor

(2) BF: take risks, to be brave

冒死　V: to risk death (158:2)

冒險　VO: to risk danger (158:11)

冒失　SV: rash (prone to quick but careless action)

　　冒失鬼　N: blunderer

冒犯　V: to offend against; to affront, insult

感冒　V/N: (to catch) cold

冒雨/風　VO: to brave rain/wind, etc.

冒昧　SV: ignorant; rash; brash; (in polite conversation) "to take the liberty of ..."

我很冒昧地打擾你。
May I take the liberty of disturbing you?

(3)　V: to spew forth

冒火　VO: (lit.) to break into flames after smouldering; (fig.) to get angry

冒煙　VO: to smolder (as of a chimney)

冒氣　VO: (lit.) to spew forth (as steam); (fig.) to be angry

冒號　N: colon

47. 詭 gwěi　　BF: sly, crafty, resourceful

詭稱　V: to lie, to say falsely, to deceive (155:8)

詭辯 V/N: to argue sophistically; sophistry

詭計　N: artful device or scheme

詭計多端　EX: full of artful devices and schemes

詭秘　SV: secret; strange; mysterious

詭雷　N: booby-trap

48. 巡 syún　　V: to patrol

（巡）

巡捕／警　N: patrolman (policeman) (155:12)

巡視　V: to go on a tour of inspection

巡守 V/N: imperial tour of inspection

巡夜　V: to be on night watch

巡查　V: to patrol

巡洋艦　N: cruiser

49. 轄 syá　　BF: linchpin of a wheel; (thus) to have jurisdiction over; under one's official direction

轄境　N: limits of jurisdiction (156:2)

管轄 V/N: to administer; (to) control; (to) rule

直轄　V: to be under the direct control of the Chinese Central Government; to rule directly

直轄市　N: city under direct jurisdiction of the Chinese Central Government

院／省轄市　N: city under the direct control of Executive Yuan/Provincial Government

統轄　V: to control, to administer

50. 扣 kòu　(1) V: to detain, rein in, fasten

扣留 V/N: to detain (under detention) (things as well as people); detention (156:3)

(2) V/N: (to) button

扣子 N: button

扣上 RV: to button up

(3) V: to deduct; discount

打折扣 VO: to give a discount

回扣 N: deduction, kick-back

扣錢 VO: to deduct money

扣除 V: to deduct (as money from a salary check)

51. 啞 yǎ   SV: dumb (mute)

啞子/巴 N: mute (156:4)

吃啞巴虧 ex: to be victimized in mute silence; to suffer loss without being able to complain

啞口無言 EX: to be caught in an embarrassing situation with nothing **to say**

啞劇 N: pantomime

52. 瞎 syā   (1) BF: blind

瞎子 N: blind person (156:4)

瞎了 V: to become blind

(2) BF: irrelevant, nonsense

瞎說 V: to talk irrelevantly (idiomatic expression for "nonsense!"); to say crazy or wild things

瞎鬧 V: to act capriciously or nonsensically

53. 幽 yōu   (1) BF: dark, secluded, quietness (156:7)

幽靜 SV: quiet

幽暗 SV: dark

幽會　V: secret rendezvous

幽閒　SV: carefree, leisured

(2)　V: to confine

幽禁 V/N: to imprison; imprisonment

54. 靈 líng　(1)　N: spirit, divine

幽靈　N: spirits of the dead (156:7)

心靈　N: one's spirit; mentality

生靈　N: living beings

靈魂　N: soul (of a person)

靈性　N: spiritual nature

靈性生活　N: spiritual life

聖靈　N: Holy Spirit

(2) SV: efficacious, alert, sensitive; in working order (of machines)

靈活　SV: lively; flexible; bright

靈活運用　V: to apply or use flexibly

靈機　N: cleverness, quick intelligence

靈機一動　EX: a clever idea strikes

機靈　SV: clever, quick

靈便　SV: convenient; handy; quick (of persons)

靈敏　SV: quick (of the movements of living things); responsive to use (as brakes, steering)

靈驗　SV: effective (in fulfilling expectation)

靈藥　N: effective medicine

消息靈通　EX: to be well-informed on the news

消息靈通人士／方面　N: well-informed persons/ quarters

55. 踪 dzūng   BF: footprint, trace
   (蹤)
                 追踪 V/N: to trail, tail or shadow; to follow the
                          traces of; pursuit (156:10)

                 踪影 N: vestige or trace; clue

                 踪跡 N: traces, marks (lit. and fig.)

                 行踪 N: vestige, trace (as of a person's whereabouts)

                 失踪 V/N: to disappear; disappearance (of a person)

56. 劍 jyàn   N: double-edged sword (把)
   (剱)
                 寶劍 N: double-edged sword (5:9) (把)

                 刀劍 N: sword (156:11)

            刀光劍影 ex: the flashing of many swords (158:1)

                 劍術 N: swordsmanship

                 劍客 N: knight-errant

57. 虐 nywè   BF: tyrannical, cruel, oppressive

                 虐待 V/N: to treat cruelly; cruel treatment (156:12)

                 暴虐 V/SV: to be harsh and cruel (of rulers, etc.)

                 虐政 N: tyrannical government

58. 遞 dì   (1) V: to hand over, transmit

                 投遞 V: to hand in or submit; to deliver (mail, etc.)
                         (157:6)

                      無法投遞 EX: undeliverable (stamped on
                                   letters, packages, etc.)

            遞過來/去 RV: to pass over (as across a table, etc.)

             遞眼色 VO: to hint with the eyes; to express something
                         through the eyes

                 傳遞 V/N: to pass on; to transmit (as messages, etc.);
                          transmission

                (2) V: to alternate, substitute, change

遞增/減　N: proportional increase/decrease

遞補　V: to fill a vacancy

59. 谷 gǔ　(1)　N: valley　Rad. 150

山谷　N: valley

虛懷若谷　EX: very receptive to other people's suggestions or instructions

進退維谷　EX: to be in a dilemma; to be in a difficult situation

(2) Used in names and transliteration (8:3; 157:6)

(3) Surname

60. 瘋 fēng　V/SV: (to become) insane, crazy, mad

瘋狂　SV: wild, crazy (157:10)

瘋子/人　N: madman

瘋人院　N: lunatic asylum

發瘋　VO: to go mad

瘋了　V: to become mad

瘋狗　N: mad dogs

瘋話　N: crazy words, gibberish

61. 腥 syīng　SV: foul smelling

血腥 Adj: bloody (157:10)

腥味　N: foul smell (of blood, meat, fish)

魚腥　N: foul smell of fish

62. 側 tsè　BF: side; sideways

側巷　N: side alley (157:11)　(條)

側面 N/A: profile; from the side; sideways

側面圖　N: side elevation

側門　N: side door

側重　　V: to emphasize

側室　　N: side room; concubine

側視　V/N: (to look with an) envious glance; to look askance

左/右側　N: left/right side

側翼　　N: flank (of an army)

63. 砍 kǎn　　　V: to cut or chop off (157:12)

砍傷　　V: to wound by cutting

砍下來　RV: to cut or chop down

砍斷　　RV: to cut in two

砍頭　　VO: to behead

砍伐　　V: to cut or chop down (of timber)

64. 蹂 róu　　BF: tread or trample upon

65. 躪 lìn　　BF: trample down or upon (158:1)

蹂躪　V/N: to trample or tread on (used fig. of violating rights, etc.); cruel devastation or oppression

66. 狠 hěn　　SV: fierce, cruel

惡狠狠 (的)　A: cruelly (158:4)

狠心　SV: cruel, savage

狠毒　SV: cruel; malicious; vitriolic

兇狠　SV: fierce

67. 杜 dù　　(1) BF: block, impede; shut out

杜口　VO: to silence

杜絕　V: to suspend intercourse with; to cut off

杜門不出/謝客　EX: to shut the door and not go out; to refuse to receive visitors

杜漸防微　EX: to nip the matter in the bud (in order to guard against an evil or disadvantageous outcome)

(2) Used in transliteration; surname

杜魯門 N: Truman (158:9)

68. 膚 fū   BF: skin

體無完膚 EX: (lit. so battered that there is no whole skin on the body); (fig.) badly battered (158:9)

皮膚 N: skin

膚淺 SV: skin-deep; superficial, not thorough, shallow (as reasoning, interpretation)

69. 腹 fù   N: stomach; abdomen

腹部 N: abdomen (158:10)

腹地 N: region served by and supplying a port

心腹 N: intimate; trusted friend

他們都是他的心腹。
They are all his trusted friends.

心腹之患 EX: a thorn in one's side or flesh, an internal evil or calamity (as a traitor)

70. 遭 dzāu (1) BF: meet with, encounter with (connotation of something unpleasant or unfavorable) (174:12)

遭受 V: to encounter or endure (as a catastrophe) (158:11)

遭難 VO: to meet with calamity

遭遇 V/N: (to meet with or encounter a) situation, one's fate (usually unpleasant in connotation)

他年老的遭遇很不幸。
His lot in his old age was very unfortunate.

當你遭遇到困難的時候，你應當設法克服它。
When you run into difficulty, you should figure out a way to overcome it.

(2) M: for time; trip; adventure

第/頭一遭 N: the first time

NEW MEANINGS

1. 場 cháng   M/N: for dreams; battles; debates; scene of a play

   一場春夢   N: fleeting dream (as in reminiscing) (149:2)

   哭了一場   V: to cry a spell

2. 府   (1) BF: palace; treasury or store house

   最高學府   N: the leading academic institution or
                institution of higher learning (150:10)

   總統府   N: Presidential Palace (154:4)

   府上   N: (polite expression for) "Your residence"

   王府   N: monarch's or noble's palace (座)

   (2) N: prefecture (historical)

3. 朝 cháu   V/CV: to face (as toward Mecca) (151:4)

   朝天／上 V/A: to look upwards; to face uppermost

   朝陽   VO: to face the sun

   坐東朝西 ex: to be situated on the east side and face west
                (as a house)

4. 創 chwāng   BF: wound

   創傷   N: wound (153:7)

   受創   V: to be wounded

   重創 V/N: to be seriously wounded; serious wound

   創痕   N: scar

   創口   N: open wound or sore

5. 率 shwài   (1) BF: lead, leader

   率師   V: to lead (as delegation, army) (173:2)

      率師親征 EX: (the emperor) leads troops for
                   a military expedition

   率領   V: to lead (as an army)

相率　A: successively; one after another

統率　V: to lead

親率　V: to lead in person

(2) SV: straightforward

直率　SV: straightforward, frank

草率　SV: careless

6. 殿　　　BF: bring up the rear of an army

殿後　V: to lag behind; to bring up the rear (153:10)

殿軍 V/N: to bring up the rear, rear of an army; third place in a competition; also now used for last place in a contest

7. 彈 tán　(1)　V: to press down upon

彈壓　V: to police, keep under control (154:12; 155:7)

(2)　V: to rebound

彈力/性　N: elasticity

彈力　N: tension; stress of elasticity

彈出去　V: to bounce away

(3)　V: to play stringed instruments; to snap the fingers

彈唱　V: to play and sing

彈指之間　EX: (lit. in the time it takes to snap one's finger); in a twinkling

8. 呈　　　BF: submit, present, reveal, petition

呈請　V: to submit (155:3)

呈現　V: to reveal, to appear

敬呈　V: to present something respectfully

呈遞　V: to present

呈報　V: to present an official report

呈文　N: statement or plea from a citizen or lower government office to a higher one

送呈　V: to submit

9. 質　　BF: cross-examine

質問 V/N: to question; questioning (156:4)

質詢 V/N: to question; questioning

質責 V/N: (to) reproach

質疑 V/N: to interrogate; interrogation

對質 V/N: to confront face to face in court; (legal) confrontation

10. 容　　BF: receive; capacity

容留　V: to accommodate; to provide a place for and take in (156:7)

容納　V: to receive, to accommodate (as to take in) (102:7; 111:11; 118:9)

容量　N: (general term for physical) capacity

容積　N: capacity (term used in engineering and such calculations)

容忍 V/N: to bear, to stand (an insult, etc.)

收容　V: to receive and accommodate (a person)

容身　VO: to have room for someone (lit. as room; fig. as job)

11. 襲　　BF: make an attack; raid

襲擊 V/N: (to) attack, (usually suddenly); (to) raid (157:11; 158:3; 174:12)

空襲 V/N: to make an air raid on; air raid

侵襲 V/N: to invade; (to) attack

突襲 V/N: (to make a) sudden attack

偷襲 V/N: (to make a) stealthy attack

STRUCTURE NOTES

1. 不 ... 不罷休   PT: to be unwilling to stop until ...

$$S_1 + VP \text{ (goal)}$$
$$S_1 + 不肯停止$$
$$(\text{determination})$$
$$\Big\} \longrightarrow \boxed{S + 不 + VP + (V) + 不罷休}$$

他們要到前線去。
他們不罷休。 } → 他們不到前線不罷休。

They won't stop until they have reached the front line.

大家不找到曹汝霖誓不罷休。

They would never stop until they had found Ts'ao Ju-lin.
(cf. 152:10)

Notes:

1. This is a variation of the 不 ... 不 ... pattern, "if not ... then not ... ."

    不到黃河心不死。
    To persist until one has reached the Yellow River (i.e. his goal).

2. 誓 here functions like an adverb. 決 / 一定 can replace 誓

3. This pattern is also related to 非...不可 .

*   *   *   *   *

Note for Review:

1. 不但不... 反而... (149:4)   6. 由於 as CJ (150:11;157:2)

    不但... 並且... (149:6)

    不但毫無... 反... (149:9)

2. 當然... 但是... (151:2)

3. 如 ... 即... (154:12)

4. 爲 + V + O + 而 + V (150:3)

5. 用以 (151:7)

E X E R C I S E S

I.   Miscellaneous

竟然

1.   戒嚴的時候，晚上八點以後，此地卽禁止通行。你竟然敢違犯法令，半夜裡在這兒聚衆喧鬧，豈不是自找麻煩？

2.   很多歷史上的暴動，只是一種叛亂而已。而共產黨竟然稱之爲農民革命，實在抹殺歷史事實。

3.   When the government could not figure out ways to solve the seaman's strike, it finally used force to compel the workers to resume work.

4.   I can't imagine what their standards really are if they could elect a stupid old roué like him as their mayor.

II.   Review Sentences

Use: 當 . . . 之交   是爲了   寧可 . . . 也不 . . .   爲 . . . 着想

      置於   親 . . .   諸   藉以

      一日 . . . 一日 . . .   迎頭趕上   依 . . . 而定   V＋不過來

1.   The Communist Party is a party which puts its interests above the interests of the state.

2.   Their aim in drafting this proposal was to prevent the pro-Russian clique from making trouble on the spot.

3.   You said it would be good preparation for the exam to finish reading these books, but we are so busy we don't even have time to learn the vocabulary to say nothing of reading reference works.

4.   To avoid any further dissension, I would rather endure their recriminations than refute them in any way.

5.   So long as the Minister of Education does not sign this law, it cannot be put into effect.

6.   For the safety of this capital ship, the Navy should first clear out the floating mines before it begins its training exercises.

7. Whether or not one has to sign his name when handing
    over important documents depends on the circumstances.

8. They plan on this trip to get into the Northwest heartland
    of the country to conduct a scientific survey (探 測)
    of timber resources.

9. In the present day world, when one state encounters
    serious internal difficulties, other states really have
    an obligation to help solve the problem because
    otherwise a threat to international cooperation and
    peace might develop.

10. The reason the government published that special letter
    was to warn all venal politicians that in the future
    they would face punishment.

11. 他連一日三餐都沒有着落，還有甚麼可以自鳴得意的？

12. 校長以他這麼大的年紀還每天練習太極拳，藉以提倡運動，所以在青年
    學生中起了很大的影響。

13. 一般說來一個人在出事以後首先想到的是如何保護自己的生命，隨即想
    到他的家屬。

14. 當一個國家由興盛轉入衰亡之際，必有很多暴動和叛亂發生。

15. 當一個人的生活困苦到了極點之際，就沒有甚麼羞恥可言了。

16. 縱使這是一塊肥田，但是你若不加以耕種，也不會有豐富的收穫。

Write Sentences Using:

1. 一致   9. ...也好...也好

2. 用以   10. 迄

3. 甚至   11. 以至

4. 予以   12. ...不堪

5. 處於   13. 異然

6. 用以   14. 只消...即可...

7. 加以   15. 如...即...

8. 不但不...反而...

In this essay Chou Tso-jen argues against the ornate style and artificial content of elite literature and praises the clear and honest content of the popular tradition. For him popular literature is literature that attempts to improve the lot of the masses without being condescending.

Chao Chia-pi, ed., Collected Essays on the Theory of Building a New Literature (Chien-she li-lun chi), from Anthology of New Chinese Literature (Chung-kuo hsin wen-hsüeh ta-hsi), 10 vols. Shanghai, 1935, Vol. 10, pp. 210-213.

160:T 平民			N:	common people (160:T,2,3,7,10; 161:10; 162:4,11, etc.)
2 字面上			A:	literally
5 眞摯	--jr̃		SV/N:	sincere; sincerity (161:10; 162:4)
6 頂		NM1	V:	(lit.) to wear on the head; (fig.) to bear
率土之濱 莫非王臣	-----bīn -----(chèn)	1 (VII:49)	EX:	within the whole realm there is none who are not the king's subjects
8 高下			N:	difference, discrepancy (in treatment)
11 修飾	--shr̃	2	V/N:	(to) ornament; to adorn (161:3,9)
161:2 雕章琢句	----jwó--	3	EX:	to polish phrases carefully; careful style (162:7)
相近			SV:	close (i.e. to be alike)
3 雕琢	--jwó	3	V:	to carve, shape or polish
銅鑄	--jù	4	V:	(to) cast in copper
5 花瓶	--píng	5	N:	flower vase
6 觀世音			N:	Goddess of Mercy
11 文體			N:	literary style (162:4)
英雄豪傑	------jyé	6	N:	heroes (161:12; 162:5)

	才子佳人	----jyā--	7	EX: gifted young man and beautiful woman (161:11; 162:5)
162:1	切己			SV: of personal interest/concern (162:6)
	交互			A: mutually
2	甲		NM2	N: A (as in A, B, C, D)
	乙	yǐ	8	N: B (as in A, B, C, D)
3	不消說			不用說
	殉節	syùn--	9,NM3	V: to die in defense of her virtue
	守貞	--jēn	10	V: to remain chaste (of women who do not remarry or never marry following the death of a fiance)
5	自命爲			V: to style oneself as ...
	下風			N: disadvantageous position
	頌揚	sùng--	11	V/N: to laud; (to) praise
6	單體			N: unit (usually 單位)
	渾	hwún	12	V: to be mixed in with
	說及		S1	V: to mention
7	顧及		S1	V: to take into consideration; to be concerned about
	美妙動人	(--myàu---)(VII:34)		EX: to be strikingly beautiful
8	謅	dzōu		V: to throw together at random (as a tune); to compose easily
	支		NM4	M: for song or composition
	小曲	--(chyǔ)	NM5	N: ditty, tune
	闐堂大笑	hùng-----	13	EX: the whole company laughed heartily
	沒卻	(mwò--)		V: to obscure, hide
163:1	通俗			SV: common, ordinary, usual
3	按下		NM6	V: to press/keep down

4	田夫野老			EX: simple rustics (163:5)
5	領會			V: to understand
6	高濱球三氏	--bīn-----	1	N: Mr. Takahama Tamazo
	本草綱目			N: <u>Materia Medica</u> (163:8)
7	費心力			VO: to expend thought or mental energy on
8	一味			A: persistently
	玉蜀黍	--shŭshŭ		N: maize, corn
9	何首烏	----wū	14	N: polygonum multiflorum (medicinal plant)
	封鬼傳			N: <u>Investiture of the Spirits</u> (this and two following are names of imaginary novels distorting the titles of three well-known novels) （封神傳）
	八俠十義	--syá----		N: <u>The Eight Knights and the Ten Worthies</u> （七俠五義）
	殺孫報			N: <u>Retribution for Killing Grandsons</u> （殺子報）
11	慈善	tsź--	15	SV: philanthropic; benign, kindly (163:12; 164:6)
164:1	施粥	--jōu	16	VO: to dispense gruel (to victims of famine or other disasters)
	施棉衣	--myán--	17	VO: to dispense padded garments
2	乞丐	--gài	18	N: beggar
	銅子（兒）			N: a copper (small coin) (164:3,4,5)
3	鈔票	chāu--	19	N: paper money (164:3,4)
	酬付	chóu--	20	V: to recompense, to repay
4	爲非			V: to do evil
5	贖得	(shú--)	(VII:40)	V: to redeem, ransom
9	擠	jĭ	21	V: to squeeze or push to one side

章回小說   N: novel (章回 N: chapters into which
                                                       the novel is divided)

誇張   (kwā--)   (VII:23)SV/N: boast, exaggerate; exaggeration

夠得╱不上   RV: (un)able to come up to; to be
                                                       unworthy of

10 玉梨魂   --lí--   22   N: Spirit of Yǜ-li (title of
                                                       early Republican novel)

範本   N: standard edition

11 喜劇   N: comedy

CHARACTERS TO BE LEARNED

1. 濱 bīn   BF: shore, brink (160:6)

              海濱   N: seashore

2. 飾 shr̀   BF: decorate

              修飾 V/N: to adorn, dress up; ornament (160:11; 161:3,9)

              裝飾 V/N: to adorn; ornament

                    裝飾品   N: ornament, decoration (personal
                                    or for a room)

              首飾   N: jewelry (usually that worn on the head or
                            hair) (件)

3. 琢 jwó   BF: cut, polish (as of gems)

              琢成   V: to cut and polish into (2:7)

              雕琢   V: to carve, shape or polish (161:3)

         雕章琢句   EX: to polish phrases carefully; careful style
                            (161:2)

              琢磨   V: to cut and polish (stones); to improve one's
                            virtue; to think over or consult oneself

         琢玉╱石   VO: to polish jade/stones

4. 鑄 jù   V: to cast metals, to coin (161:4)

鑄鐵 N: cast iron

鑄造 V: to make castings

鑄幣局／廠 N: mint (as Treasury)

鑄錢 N: coins that have been cast

鑄成 V: to form

鑄成大錯 EX: to make a great mistake

5. 瓶 píng N: vase, jug or bottle

花瓶 N: flower vase (161:5)

熱／暖水瓶 N: thermos bottle

瓶子 N: bottle or jar

守口如瓶 EX: to keep silent (to protect other people's secrets)

6. 傑 jyé BF: hero, heroic

豪傑 N: hero (161:11,12; 162:5)

英雄豪傑 N: hero(es)

傑作 N: masterpiece

傑出 SV: eminent, outstanding

7. 佳 jyā BF: good, beautiful

佳人 N: beautiful woman

才子佳人 EX: gifted young man and a beautiful girl (161:11,12; 162:5)

佳作 N: elegant literary composition

佳音 N: good news

佳賓 N: honored guests (used to refer to but not to address guests)

不佳 SV: sad or unfortunate (as of news, fate, luck)

佳話 N: beautiful story

佳期   N: happy day (usually wedding day)

佳節   N: festival

8. 乙 yǐ   N: second of the Ten Celestial Stems (used like B in the A, B, C, D sequence) (162:2; 166:8; 167:4)

9. 殉 syùn   BF: sacrificed with the dead

殉難／國   V: to die for one's country; to escape from the hands of the enemy through suicide

殉情   V: to die for love

10. 貞 jēn   (1) BF: chaste, virtuous

守貞   V: to maintain chastity (of a girl who remains unmarried although her betrothed dies before their marriage) (162:3)

貞操   N: chastity

(2) BF: upright or loyal

忠貞   SV/N: loyal (as to one's country, etc.); loyalty

忠貞愛國   EX: loyal and patriotic

11. 頌 sùng   BF: praise, commend

頌揚 V/N: to laud; (to) praise (162:5)

歌頌 V/N: (to sing) praises

歌功頌德   EX: to praise merit and virtue

12. 渾 hwún   (1) V/SV: to mix or be mixed in with; unclear, cloudy (as of liquid) (162:6)

渾水   N: turbid water

(2) BF: whole of; complete; the mass; entire

渾身   N: the whole body

渾然   A: completely, entirely

13. 鬨 hùng   BF: din, noise

鬨堂大笑   EX: the whole company burst into laughter (162:8) (here 鬨 can be written 哄 and read hūng)

鬨動 V/N: to have a great emotional impact on the public; impact (also written 轟動)

起鬨　V: to stir up a row, create a fuss

14. 烏 wū　BF: crow; black (163:9)

烏鴉　N: crow; rook

烏合之衆 EX: group of toughs; undisciplined mob

烏黑　V: to be black (as a crow)

烏雲　N: black clouds

烏龍茶　N: Oolong tea

烏魚子　N: caviar

15. 慈 tsź

(慈)

BF: kind, gentle, compassionate

慈善 SV: philanthropic; benign, kindly (163:12; 164:6)

慈善事業　N: philanthropy

慈善家　N: philanthropist

慈悲 V/SV/N: to be sympathetic and merciful; sympathy

慈愛 SV/N: kind; love, compassion

仁慈 SV/N: merciful, benevolent; benevolence

慈母　N: good and kind mother

16. 粥 jōu　N: rice gruel, congee

施粥 VO: to give out gruel (as in a soup kitchen) (164:1)

喝粥 VO: to drink (or eat) gruel

17. 棉 myán　N: cotton

棉衣　N: padded clothes (164:1)

棉花　N: cotton

棉紗／布　N: cotton yarn/cloth

棉織品　N: woven cotton products

棉織工業 N: cotton weaving industry

18. 丐 gài   BF: beggar

　　　　　乞丐 N: beggar (164:2)

19. 鈔 chāu   BF: paper money

　　　　鈔票 N: paper money (164:3,4,5,6)

　　　　現鈔 N: cash

20. 酬 chóu   BF: reward; compensate
　（酧）
　　　　　酬付 V: to recompense; to repay (164:3)

　　　　酬勞／謝 V/N: to reward for services; reward

　　　　　應酬 V/N: to entertain (socially); social entertainment
　　　　　　　　　　(often connotes an obligation)

　　　　　報酬 V/N: to compensate or reward; compensation, reward

21. 擠 jǐ   V: to squeeze or push (164:9)

　　　　擁擠 V/SV: to crowd; crowded

　　　　排擠 V/N: to exclude or discriminate against a person;
　　　　　　　　　　discrimination against

　　　　　　受排擠 VO: to be discriminated against

　　　　擠牛奶 VO: to milk a cow

22. 梨 lí   N: pear (164:10)

　　　　梨子 N: pear

<u>NEW MEANINGS</u>

1. 頂   (1) N: top, summit; knob on official cap indicating rank

　　　　　山頂 N: mountain top

　　　　屋／房頂 N: roof of a house

　　　光頭露頂 ex: bare-headed

　　　(2) BF: topmost; extreme

頂頭兒　N: opposite end; farthest end; top

從這一直走頂頭兒那間房子就是辦公室。

That room at the extreme opposite end
from here is the office.

頂大／好／高　V: to be the biggest/best/highest, etc.

(3) V/CV: wear on the head; push the head against (160:6)

頂住　RV: to prop up or against

頂風　V/N: to head into the wind; headwind

頂天立地　EX: (lit. to prop up Heaven with one's head while
standing on the earth); to act like a man

(4) V: to assume someone else's place (at examination, etc.)

頂名　VO: to take the name of another

頂替　V: to take place of, substitute for illegally

(5) M: for hat

2. 甲　N: first of the Ten Celestial Stems; used as A in the
sequence A, B, C, D, etc. (162:2; 166:7; 167:4)

3. 節　(1) BF: chastity, purity

殉節　V: to die in defense of virtue (162:3)

貞節　SV/N: chaste; chastity

節操　N: moral principles, high integrity; chastity

名節　N: moral integrity; reputation

守節　V: to remain unmarried after the death of a
betrothed husband; to maintain one's virtue

失節　V: to incur disgrace; to lose one's virtue

(2) BF: vows, promises (to oneself)

叛節　V: to betray one's vows; to be disloyal (as to
one's country) (175:2)

變節　V: to betray one's vows (as to one's country)
(more common than 叛節)

4. 支   M: for song or composition

    一支歌 (曲)   N: a song

     一支小調   N: a ditty

5. 曲 chyǔ   N: ditty, song, melody

    小曲   N: song; tune (162:8)

    歌曲   N: songs

   進行曲   N: march (musical)

6. 按   V: to place the hand on; to press down on; to repress, restrain

   按下   RV: to press/keep down (163:3)

   按脈   VO: to feel the pulse

   按住   RV: to repress; restrain

STRUCTURE NOTES

1. 說／顧及   V: to mention/consider

Note the use of 及 as a PV. 及 is a literary equivalent of 到.

❋　❋　❋　❋　❋

Note for Review:

1. 固 (然) ... 也 ... (161:1,5)

2. ... 不消說，即使 ... 也不 ...   (162:3)

3. 不是 ... 乃是 ... (163:2)
   並非 ... 乃是 ... (163:3)

4. 不單是 ... 乃是 ... (164:4)

5. 倘如 ... 那時 ... (161:5)
   倘說 ... 便 ...   (163:6)

6. 只能 ... 却不能 ... (161:6)

7. 既 (然) ... 自然 ... (162:3,8)

8. 除却 ... 以外   (160:8)

9. 更爲 SV (162:1)

10. 非 ... 不可 (162:11)

11. 正因 ... 所以 ... (163:7)

E X E R C I S E S

I. Correlative Structure

不消說 ... 即使 ... 也 ... (cf. IB Structure 2)

1. 不消說你赤手空拳打不過他，即使你全副武裝也不一定能敵得過他。

2. 精神散漫，自不消說，即使精神集中，也不容易應付這種艱巨的工作。

3. 不消說無知鄉愚，即使受過相當教育的人也不見得瞭解「浩然之氣」這句話的意思。

II. Miscellaneous

一味 (的)

1. 你倘若一味的依着你自己的意思行事，完全不採納別人的意見，那還談甚麼合作呢。

2. 這個報紙既然是一味的歌功頌德，對於當局的政策既不批評又不提出建議，那麼對於社會輿論會起甚麼作用呢！

3. 千萬不要聽他一味的胡說八道了，這個人說話一向是毫無根據，誇大其詞的。

I. Correlative Structure

不消說...即使...也...

　　1. The trend of the century is such that the whole world
　　　　is moving in the direction of radical change, not
　　　　just the Far East.

　　2. He can't even make enough to support his wife and
　　　　children, let alone help you support yours.

　　3. Even the stupid ones don't want to do such a dangerous
　　　　thing, let alone the bright ones.

II. Miscellaneous

一味 (的)

　　1. How can anything be solved by always making grandiose
　　　　statements without being willing to get down to work
　　　　realistically with one's feet on the ground?

　　2. No matter what you discuss with him, he'll never
　　　　accept anyone else's ideas.

III. Review Sentences

Use: 有見於   未嘗不可   就...說   與否

　　　加以   不如   夠不上   之所以

　　　固然...但...   類似

1. Correct or not, I have always felt that such traditional
    concepts as filial piety or chastity for widows are
    unreasonable, no matter what the time or place.

2. Of course language in itself reflects a specific
    historical and cultural situation but it is also quick
    to absorb new elements from other cultures and blend
    them with the old.

3. Of course the reason he can foot the bills for so many
    philanthropic enterprises is that he inherited such an
    enormous fortune, but that doesn't mean he would not
    have been interested even if he had not had money.

4. In view of the fact you feel that he does not have the
    qualifications to be a member of parliament why do you

still want to elect him? Isn't that a bit self-
contradictory?

5. What this essay says is rather challenging, and it is
very well stated. No wonder that everyone feels it's a
masterpiece.

6. Of course it is better to prevent incidents than to try
to find a way to deal with them after they have happened.

7. 他既然固執己見拒不接受別人的勸告，那麼你姑且敷衍他一下就是了，
何必如此認眞？

8. 股票市場受時局的影響情形頗爲混亂，當局已公佈緊急辦法以防止投機
份子乘機活動。

9. 與其拘泥於古文的文體，雕章琢句，不如直接了當用白話文寫文章，盡
量發揮意見，不受體裁的限制。

10. 雖然宗教上的迷信大部分已被破除，但是拘於傳統的習慣，每逢年節，
此地居民燒香拜佛的風俗，仍然到處可見。

11. 想把問題研究得透澈，並非只作一點表面工夫即可，而要尋根問底，探
求問題的究竟才行。

12. 凶殺案發生後警察局派出大批密探，從事調查，但迄今爲止，半年有餘
，仍然毫無線索可尋。

Write Sentences Using:

1. 如 ... 則 ...   6. 不拘

2. 就 ... 來說   7. 固然 ... 也

3. 爲 ... 起見   8. 不是 ... 乃是

4. 着手   9. 更爲

5. 如何 ... 才 ... 是   10. 雖 ... 也仍然 ...

In this 1918 essay in <u>New Youth</u> Magazine, Lu Hsun attacks various forms of what he considers Chinese smugness and conservatism. Blind, universally held conceit in China's past and heritage is for Lu Hsun a sign of weakness and a block to progress. If China were to survive, he argued, she must encourage individual effort, rid herself of outmoded points of view, and be willing to change.

Lu Hsun hsien-sheng chi-nien wei-yuan-hui, ed., <u>Complete Works of Lu Hsun</u> (Lu Hsun ch'üan-chi), Shanghai, 1938, Vol. II, pp. 30-34.

<u>165:2</u>	自大			SV/N: conceited; conceit (165:4,7,8; 166:3,5)
	合羣			SV: cooperative (of people and their attitudes); (here) collective (165:8; 166:3)
3	振拔	(jènbá) (VII:17,18)		V: to promote, raise up
4	宣戰			V: to declare war
5	見識			V/N: to learn from (a person); knowledge; insight; experience
6	厭世家	yàn----	1	N: misanthrope (Lu Hsun's term)
7	福氣			SV/N: fortunate; good fortune
	幸運			SV/N: fortunate, lucky; luck
9	影子			N: (here) symbol, shadow of the substance (165:11)
10	榮光			equals 光榮 (165:10)
11	蹲	dwūn	2	V: to squat
	張目搖舌	-----shé	3	EX: ranting and raving (lit. with eyes open and tongue wagging)
	長技	(cháng)--		N: special finesse or technique
	亂謀	--dzàu		V/N: to yell wildly; yelling
	制勝			V: to win
<u>166:1</u>	大凡			A: in general; generally

2	卑怯	--chyè	4	SV/N: cowardly; timid; cowardice, timidity
3	扶清滅洋	(fú-----)(VII:37)		ex: to support the Ch'ing and exterminate the foreigners
	領教			V: to seek advice (polite term)
6	根柢	--dǐ		N: basis; roots
7	云	yún	5	V: to say (literary) (166:8,9,11,12)
	自負			SV: complacent ; self-confident
9	丙	bǐng	6	N: third of the Ten Heavenly Stems: like "C" in A, B, C, D, etc. (167:4)
	某子			N: philosopher (子 used sarcastically to parallel 孔子 , 老子 , 墨子)
	云云	yúnyún	5	ex: etc., etc.
10	格言			N: maxim ; motto
11	娼妓	chāngjì	7,8	N: prostitutes
	臭蟲	chòuchúng	9,10	N: bedbugs
12	戊	wù	11	N: fifth of the Ten Heavenly Stems: like "E" in A, B, C, D, E, F, etc. (167:4,8; 168:12)
	野蠻	--mán	12	SV: barbarian; uncouth (169:3)
167:2	滅絕			V: to wipe out, eliminate completely
	以…驕人			PT: to be proud because of ...
	醜惡	chǒu--	13	SV/N: to be ugly; ugliness
	口氣			N: tone of voice (as hint of intent)
4	荒謬	--myòu	14	SV: absurd
	情有可原			EX: there is some reason or excuse for it; somewhat reasonable
5	好勝心	(hàu)----		N: will to win or to be superior
	子弟			N: sons
	興旺	--wàng	15	SV/N: flourishing; prosperity (169:3)

破綻	--jàn		N: flaw
6 解嘲	--cháu	16	V: to divert laughter from oneself
鼻子	bí--	17	N: nose
8 居心			N: intent
9 定理			N: rule (in the sense of law; inevitable sequence)
10 一舉一動			EX: every movement
11 萬不能敵			ex: (lit. cannot possibly triumph over); cannot possibly be compared with
12 定然			A: certainly
道學			N: ethics
陰陽五行			N: the dual principles and five elements of Chinese cosmology
煉丹		NM1	V: to prepare an elixir (over heat)
168:1 仙人	syān--	18	N: hermit; immortal
打臉			VO: to paint the face in the Chinese theatrical style
戲子			N: actor
2 不由自主			EX: not slaves of ourselves; not to be in complete control of oneself
丹田		NM1	N: loin region of the body
禍害	(hwò--)	(VII:1)	V/N: to bring disaster; calamity, disaster
3 梅毒	méi--	19	N: syphilis; venereal disease
竟至			A: even to the point of ...
六百零六			N: 606 (a medicine with disinfectant properties)
肉體			N: physical (i.e. "of the body")
4 七百零七			N: satiric play on 606 above
5 旗號			N: banner, flag

6 愈   yù   NM2   V: to recover

   立意   V: to swear to; to make it one's goal
                                    to ...

7 奏效   dzòu--   20   V/N: to have a beneficial result;
                                    successful use or application of

   羼淡   chàndàn   21   V: to weaken (as to add water to strong
                                    coffee)

8 轉機   N: turning point; improvement

10 長進   (jǎng)--   SV/N: enterprising; progressive; progress

   療救   lyáu--   22   V: to cure

11 唾罵   twò--   23   V/N: to spit on and revile; reviling,
                                    curses

12 效驗   N: effect; result; efficacy

CHARACTERS TO BE LEARNED

1. 厭 yàn   BF: disgusted, tired of

        厭世   V: to hate the world; be a misanthrope (165:6)

        厭惡   V: to abominate; detest (惡 wù)

        厭煩   SV: troubled, vexed

        討厭 V/SV: to detest, loathe; to be a nuisance;
                    detestable; annoying

               那個人眞討厭。
               That man is really annoying.

2. 蹲 dwūn   V: to squat on one's heels (common posture among Chinese
                    country people) (165:11)

        蹲下／伏   V: to squat down

3. 舌 shé   BF: tongue   Rad. 135 (165:11)

               舌頭   N: tongue

        箝口結舌   EX: to keep or be forced to keep mum/silent

舌戰　N: war of words

4. 怯 chyè (chywè)　BF: cowardly; timid

卑怯　SV: cowardly; timid; fearful (166:2)

羞怯　SV: bashful and timid

膽怯　SV: fearful; timid

5. 云 yún　V: to say (literary) (166:7,8,9,11,12)

云云　ex: etc., etc. (166:9)

人云亦云　EX: merely to repeat what others have said

6. 丙 bǐng　N: third of the Ten Heavenly Stems; equivalent to "C" in A, B, C, D. (166:9; 167:4)

7. 娼 chāng　BF: prostitute (166:11)

娼婦　N: prostitute

賣娼　V: (lit. and fig.) to engage in prostitution; to prostitute oneself

私娼　N: illegal or unlicensed prostitute

娼戶　N: house of ill fame

8. 妓 jì　BF: prostitute (166:11)

娼妓　N: prostitute

妓女　N: prostitute

妓院　N: brothel

9. 臭 chòu　SV: smelly; have a bad odor (166:11)

臭味　N: bad smell

腥臭　N: bad smell (as fishy, rancid, bloody)

10. 蟲 chúng　N: insects; worms

臭蟲　N: bedbug (166:11)

蟲子　N: bug or worm

害/益蟲　N: harmful/beneficial bug or insect

寄生蟲   N: parasite

微生蟲   N: microbe

11. 戊 wù   N: fifth of the Ten Heavenly Stems; equal to "E" in
                A, B, C, D, E (166:12; 167:4,8; 168:12)

12. 蠻 mán   (1) BF: savage, barbarous

                野蠻   SV: savage or barbarian (166:12; 169:3)

                蠻橫 SV/A: unreasonable, arbitrary; barbarous(ly);
                        savage(ly); arbitrarily

            蠻夷/子/人   N: savages, wild tribes

            蠻不講理 EX: utterly unreasonable; not to listen to
                        reason

                南蠻   N: southern savage tribes

                蠻荒 SV/N: wild, uncivilized or uncultivated (regions)

                蠻族   N: barbarous tribes

                蠻力   N: savage strength; wild force

                蠻邦   N: barbarous countries

            (2) BF: quite

                蠻好   ex: pretty good

13. 醜 chǒu   SV: ugly, shameful; distasteful

                醜惡 SV/N: ugly, repulsive, ugliness (167:2)

                醜行/事   N: disgraceful conduct/ugly matter

                醜陋   SV: ugly or disgraceful looking

            出/丟醜 V/SV: to disgrace oneself; disgraceful

14. 謬 myòu   BF: absurd; false, erroneous

                荒謬   SV: absurd (167:4)

    (nyòu)   謬論   N: fallacious reasoning

                謬語   N: nonsense; fallacious statement or position

15. 旺 wàng BF: vigorous; prosperous; bright

興旺 SV/V: prosperous; flourishing; prosperity (167:5; 169:3)

16. 嘲 cháu BF: ridicule, abuse

解嘲 V: to divert laughter away from oneself; to be freed from being the center of ridicule (167:6)

嘲笑 V: to laugh at or mock

17. 鼻 bi N: nose Rad. 209

鼻子 N: nose (167:6; 168:5)

被人牽着鼻子走 EX: (lit. and fig.) to be dragged away by the nose

鼻祖 N: founder of a family or religious sect

鼻音 N: nasal sounds

鼻孔 N: nostrils

鼻樑 N: bridge of the nose

18. 仙 syān N: immortals; fairies

仙人 N: an immortal (168:1)

仙人掌 N: cactus

仙人跳 N: badger game

神佛仙鬼 ex: Gods, Buddhas, Immortals, and Devils

八仙 N: The Eight Immortals

仙境/界 N: fairyland

神仙 N: fairies, immortals

仙藥 N: elixir of life

求仙 V: to seek to become an immortal

求仙拜佛 EX: to pray to the immortals and beg the Buddha

仙女／子   N: fairy lady

仙鄉   N: fairyland, (also a conventional term used by the speaker to refer to another person's native place)

修仙   VO: to strive to eliminate the grosser elements and become an immortal

半仙   N: clever prophet or fortune teller

水仙花   N: narcissus

19. 梅 méi   (1) BF: plum; prune

梅毒   N: venereal disease; syphilis (168:3)

梅子   N: prune

梅花   N: plum blossoms (朵)

(2) Surname

20. 奏 dzòu   (1) BF: present memorials to the emperor (171:6)

奏效 V/N: to have a beneficial result; successful use or application of (168:7)

奏章   N: memorial to the throne

奏請   V: to petition the emperor asking ...

上奏   VO: to present a petition to the throne

(2) V: to play music

前奏   N: prelude

演奏 V/N: to perform (music); performance

奏樂   V: to play music

獨奏 V/N: to perform solo (as music); solo

合奏 V/N: to play in concert; concert by several performers

節奏   N: rhythm time (music)

21. 淡 dàn   SV: tasteless, insipid, weak; light (color) (168:7)

       淡薄 SV: thin; insipid, tasteless

       冷淡 SV: cold, indifferent; dull (as with trade)

       淡季 N: off season

       暗淡 SV: dim, dark (of one's future, life, etc.)

       清淡 SV: pale (of colors); not oily (of foods)

       平淡 SV: insipid; ordinary, commonplace

       淡水 N: fresh water

     淡而無味 EX: flavorless; without taste

22. 療 lyáu   BF: cure, heal (of illness)

       療救 V: to cure (168:10)

       治療 V/N: (to) treat; (to) cure

       療養 V/N: to convalesce; convalescence

          療養院 N: sanatorium; convalescent home

23. 唾 twò   V/N: to spit at, expectorate; saliva

       唾罵 V: to spit on and revile (168:11)

       唾口水 VO: to spit

NEW MEANINGS

1. 丹 dān   (1) N: pill; elixir of immortality

       煉丹 V: to prepare elixir (over heat with proper rites and mysteries administered by priests, usually Taoist) (167:12)

       仙丹 N: pill or drug of the immortals

          仙丹靈藥 N: efficacious medicine

       丹方 N: prescription (of an herb doctor)

       靈丹 N: efficacious pills

(2) BF: lower body

丹田　N: (Taoist term for) pubic region (168:2)

丹田不足　EX: one's constitution was not strong

2.　愈　yù　　　V: to recover (from a disease); (usually written 癒 or 瘉) (168:6)

病愈　V: to recover (from a disease)

*　*　*　*　*　*　*

STRUCTURE NOTES

Note for Review:

1.　即使 ... 也...　　(168:3,7)

2.　既然 ... 自然 ...　　(165:10)

3.　至於 ...卻 ...　　(165:8; 167:2)

至於 ... 則 ...　　(166:2)

4.　... 還怕不及 ...怎敢 ...　　(166:5)

5.　大凡 ... 多　　(166:1)

6.　倘若　　(165:10)

倘使 ... 那 ...　　(169:3)

7.　不 ...反 ...　　(167:2)

8.　不但 ...實 ...　　(167:8)

9.　不至於　　(168:3)

10.　雖 ... 其實 ...　　(167:10)

E X E R C I S E S

I. Miscellaneous

   1. 目前災荒遍地，民不聊生，救災救民才是急待解決的問題，發展實業
      則尚在其次。

   2. 這個書呆子讀死書還來不及那能談到融會貫通呢？

   3. 不管你做的如何隱秘，假如你是以迷信來誘惑民眾的話，那麼你的秘
      密總有洩露的一天。

   4. 俗話說「功到自然成」，只要有志氣，肯下工夫，總有出人頭地的一
      天。

   5. 做文章主要的是靠自己的靈思妙想，倘若一味的模仿古人，即使模仿
      了外貌，也模仿不了它的神髓。

   6. 即使宇宙間真有上帝，那也要先能自助才能獲得天助。倘若自己不求
      上進，別人是無能為力的。

II. Review Sentences

   Use:

年復一年	寧可 ... 也不 ...	差異
有意	獨有	勝於
為 ... 所 ...	奉 ... 為 ...	豈
終於	不是 ... 而是 ...	

1. Every government selects a day to commemorate the founding
    of the country, and this date is then observed year after
    year.

2. The government intends to ask for a supplementary
    appropriation (追加預算) but is afraid that Congress
    will not authorize it, and therefore is temporarily
    economizing on administrative expenses.

3. The government's overall plan for the development of
    atomic energy has already been ruined by this riot.
    Whether or not the plan can be revived in a short period
    of time is a serious question.

4. What is important is not slogans extolling virtue but the elimination of corruption.

5. There are still some people who regard riots as the only way to solve political disputes.

6. Anything can be solved by peaceful negotiation. Why is it only this that cannot be solved?

7. Some things seem extraordinarily troublesome but when we have to we can adapt without trouble.

8. The differences in the value of these two textbooks are not very great, and so they are very hard to criticize.

Write Sentences Using:

1. 不消說...即使...也...

2. 當面

3. 再 SV 也沒有了

4. 無從　VERB

5. 即使...只要...就可...

6. 與其...不如...

Here in very brief compass is described the misery of the peasant
population at the end of the Ming, the excesses of cruel officials
like Wei Chung-hsien, and the rise of Li Tzu-ch'eng and Chang Hsien-
chung. The treachery of Wu San-kuei which helped to facilitate the
Manchu conquest of China is outlined.

Sung Yang, _Historical Tales of the Revolutionary Movement of the_
Chinese Peasants (Chung-kuo nung-min ke-ming shih hua), Tientsin, 1949.

170:3	朱元璋	jū--jāng	1	N:	Chu Yuan-chang
5	屠殺殆盡	----dài--		ex:	to kill off almost completely
	瞧得／不起	chyáu----	2	RV:	to look up to or down on
	文字獄	----yù	3	N:	literary inquisition
	株連	jū--	4	V/N:	to implicate, involve in guilt; involving in guilt
6	殺戮	--lù	5	V:	to slaughter, massacre
	跪拜	gwèi--	6	V:	to kneel in obeisance
7	西番		NM1	N:	western barbarians
	倭寇	wō--		N:	Japan (old term)
	西南夷	----yí	7	N:	southwestern barbarians
8	連年		S1	A:	year after year (171:9)
	尖銳化	--rwèi--	8	V:	to become sharper or more acute
	士大夫			N:	(collective noun for) gentry, officials, upper classes (general term for the educated upper classes) (171:3)
9	東林黨			N:	Tunglin Party (or faction)
	閹黨	yān--		N:	eunuch party (or faction)
	歸附			V:	to attach oneself to; to return to allegiance
10	誅除	jū--	9	V:	to wipe out

	左右			V:	to control
	賄賂	hwèilù	10,11	V/N:	(to) bribe; bribery
	劉瑾	--jǐn		N:	Liu Chin
	魏忠賢	----syán	12	N:	Wei Chung-hsien (170:11; 171:2,3, etc.)
	特務／工			N:	secret agent (171:3)
171:1	東西廠			N:	Ming secret service organization
	錦衣衛			N:	Ming imperial guards who served as secret police
	流氓	--máng	13	N:	rogues, rascals (174:1)
2	書院			N:	academy
	生祠	--tsź		N:	shrine erected to a living person
	叩頭	kòu--	14	VO:	to kowtow
3	下流		NM2	SV:	low-class, vulgar
	乾兒	(gān)--	NM3	N:	adopted son
	貪緣名利	yín-----		EX:	to seek fame and profit by attaching oneself to powerful high officials
4	偶語		NM4	V/N:	to talk together; (of two person in) conversation
	恐怖	--bù	15	SV/N:	terrifying, terror
5	閹患	yān--		N:	disasters caused by eunuchs
6	奏乞			N:	means by which Ming nobles encroached on private lands
	投獻			N:	another means by which the nobles of the Ming dynasty encroached on the land of the common people
7	兼併	--bìng	16	V:	to combine, amalgamate
	苛征	kē--	17	V/N:	(to impose) excessively burdensome taxes (171:9)
	江河日下			EX:	to decline steadily (fig.)

8	崇禎	--jēn		N:	Chungchen (reign title) (171:12; 172:4; 173:5, etc.)
9	飢荒	jī--	18	N:	famine (171:11)
	苛重	kē--	17	SV:	onerous (as of taxes)
10	人煙			N:	signs of human habitation
	催逼	tswēi--	19	V/N:	(to) dun (for debt repayment)
	糧餉	--syǎng	20	N:	provisions (military)
11	石粉	--fěn	21	N:	pulverized stone
	人糞	--fèn	22	N:	human night soil
	飢民	jī--	18	N:	famine sufferers
12	掘	jywé	23	V:	to dig out
	土坑	--kēng	24	N:	pit, trench
	掩埋	yǎn--	25	V/N:	to bury; burial
172:1	減饍	--shàn		VO:	to cut back on food
	罪己詔	----jàu		N:	imperial rescript or apology
	遏止	è--		V:	to prevent, stop
2	徐鴻儒	--húng--		N:	Hsu Hung-ju
	白蓮敎	--lyán--		N:	White Lotus Sect
3	燃起	rán--	26	V:	to ignite, burn
	烽火	fēng--		N:	beacon
	高迎祥	----syáng	27	N:	Kao Ying-hsiang (172:7,8)
	滎陽	yíng--		N:	district and city in Honan
4	營			N:	military unit of battalion size
	剿殺	jyǎu--	28	V:	to wipe out
7	米脂縣	--jr̄--	29	N:	Michih county
	善 (於)			V:	to be good at

	騎射	chìshè	30,31	V/N: to ride horseback and shoot, horsemanship ard archery
	舅父	jyòu--	32	N: maternal uncles
8	闖王	chwǎng--	33	N: Ch'uang Wang (172:9; 173:6)
	闖將	chwǎng--	33	N: the general of Ch'uang Wang
	部			N: abbr. of 部下
9	繼位		NM5	V: to succeed to the throne
10	死命			A: earnestly; deadly; "fight to the finish"; desperately
11	粗莽	--mǎng		SV: coarse
12	網羅	wǎng--	34	V/N: (to collect, gather or) search for talent
	修纂	--tswàn		V: to compile
	稱贊			V/N: to praise
	脫粟粗糲	--shù--lì		ex: (to eat) plain coarse fare (rare)
	士卒		NM6	N: soldiers
173:1	舉人			N: second-degree graduate in old examination system
	李嚴	--yán		N: Li Yen (174:7,11)
	羅汝才	--rǔ--		N: Lo Ju-ts'ai
2	屢經	lyǔ--	35	V: to have experienced many times
	挫敗	tswò--	36	N: upsets and defeats
	襄陽	syāng--		N: Hsiang Yang
3	潼關	túng--		N: T'ung Kuan Pass (174:11)
	永昌	--chāng	37	N: Yungch'ang
4	昌平	chāng--	37	N: Ch'angp'ing
	譁變	hwá--	38	V: to mutiny; to defect
5	煤山			N: Coal Hill (in Peking)

	自縊	--yì		V:	to hang oneself
6	均田			N:	land equalization
7	掠	lywè	39	V:	to pillage, loot
	淫	yín	40	V:	to rape; to lust for
8	宿	(sù)	(VII:29)	V:	to lodge or live at
	田禾	--hé	41	N:	growing grain
	處斬	--jǎn	42	V:	to sentence to beheading
	譽	yù	43	V:	to praise
10	清醒			SV:	sober, calm
	謹慎	jǐn (shèn)	44(VII:20)	SV:	cautious
11	防禦	--yù	45	V:	to defend against
174:1	成性			V:	to become habitual; to develop the habit of
	甚且	甚至於			
2	浮華		NM7	SV/N:	vain; vanity
	奢靡	--mǐ		SV:	extravagant, wasteful
	腐蝕	--shŕ	46	V:	(lit. and fig.) to corrode, erode
3	花天酒地			EX:	to indulge in gay debauchery
	丞相	chéng--	NM8	N:	premier (historical title)
	收攬	--lǎn		V:	to draw (as disciples)
	門生			N:	pupils; disciples; students
	朝服	(cháu)--		N:	court robe
	拜客			VO:	to pay respect to guests
	開科取士			ex:	to hold civil service examinations
	宰相	dzǎi--	47,NM8	N:	prime minister (historical title)
4	拷打	kǎu--		V:	to torture by beating

逼索		NM9	V:	to press for (as debts)
吳三桂	--gwèi		N:	Wu San-kuei (174:8,9)
愛妾	--chyè		N:	beloved concubine
5 及時			A:	on time; in time
耽溺	dānnì		V:	to indulge or wallow in
6 把			N:	handful
傾軋	--yà	48	V:	to try from envy or jealousy to squeeze out a rival
8 下坡路	--pwō--	49	N:	decline; downward path
慟哭	tùng--		V:	to cry from sorrow; to weep bitterly
縞素	gǎu--		N:	plain white silk (i.e. mourning)
紅顏			N:	(poetic term for a) beautiful woman (refers to Chen Yuan-yuan, beloved of Wu San-kuei) *
10 役		NM10	N:	Battle of ...
京師		NM11	N:	capital
11 連戰連敗		S2	PT:	to lose every battle
有見地			SV/VO:	to have a sense of perspective and proportion
12 武昌	--chāng	37	N:	Wuch'ang
175:1 夾攻	jyá--	50	V/N:	(to) attack from both sides
力蹙	--tsù		ex:	to be exhausted; withered

* The poetic quotation in line 8 is used sarcastically to criticize Wu San-kuei
for using mourning for the deceased emperor to cloak his sorrow over
the loss of his beloved Ch'en Yuan-yuan.

CHARACTERS TO BE LEARNED

1. 朱 jū   (1) BF: vermillion

朱紅   N: red (color)

丹/朱紅　N: red (color)

朱門　N: gentry or important families (who had their doors painted red)

朱筆　N: imperial notations (from "the vermillion brush" used by the Emperor)

(2) Surname (170:3; 171:8; 173:5)

2. 瞧 chyáu　V: to see, to look at

瞧得/不起　RV: to look up to or down on; to (dis)respect (170:5)

瞧見　V: to see

3. 獄 yù　N: prison

文字獄　N: literary inquisition (170:5)

監獄　N: prison

地獄　N: hell

獄卒　N: jailor

越獄　VO: to escape from prison

入獄　VO: to be put in jail

下獄　V: to imprison; to put into prison

議罪下獄　ex: to sentence and imprison

4. 株 jū　M: for trunk of a tree; stalk of a flower

株連　V: to implicate, involve in guilt (170:5)

株守　V: to keep, hold, or maintain firmly (of system, method, principle, etc.)

5. 戮 lù　BF: slay; massacre

殺戮　V: to slay, slaughter; to massacre (170:6)

6. 跪 gwèi　V: to kneel

跪拜　V: to kneel in obeisance (170:6)

跪下　V: to kneel down

跪求   V: to kneel down and beg (for pardon, serious request, etc.)

7. 夷 yí   N: barbarians

西南夷   N: southwestern barbarians (170:7)

夷人   N: barbarians

8. 銳 rwèi   BF: sharp, pointed, acute

尖銳   SV: sharp, acute (170:8)

精銳 SV/N: picked; best-trained, crack (as of soldiers or weapons)

銳氣   N: ardent spirit; morale

鋒銳   SV: sharp

銳利   SV: incisive, sharp

銳眼   N: keen eyes

銳意   A: keenly, valiantly

銳意經營/求進   ex: to be firmly resolved to succeed at what one undertakes

銳師   N: well-trained troops

9. 誅 jū   V: to kill, execute

誅除異巳   ex: to wipe out those not of one's own group (170:10)

誅滅   V: to exterminate

誅戮   V: to slay, put to death (of bandits, criminals, etc.)

伏誅   V: to be executed; to bow down to a decree authorizing one's own death

口誅筆伐   EX: oral and written accusation

10. 賄 hwèi   BF: bribe

行賄   V: to bribe

受賄 V: to be bribed

賄選 V: to buy votes

11. 賂 lù   BF: bribe

賄賂 V/N: (to) bribe; bribery (170:10)

12. 賢 syán   BF: nice; good; virtuous

賢人   N: man of excellent virtues; a worthy

賢能 SV/N: capable; high character, ability

賢明 SV/N: to be possessed of high character; clear
          intelligence (often used of government
          leaders)

先賢   N: former worthies

讓賢   VO: to yield to a qualified successor

求賢   VO: to seek for worthy men

傳賢   VO: to transmit ... to a qualified successor

招賢   VO: to invite or call for virtuous and capable
          persons

禮賢下士   EX: courteous to the worthy and polite to the
              scholarly

13. 氓 máng   BF: vagrant; fugitives

流氓   N: vagrant, loafer (171:1)

14. 叩 kòu   V: to knock, to bump the head; to ask or pray for

叩頭   VO: to kowtow; to knock one's head on the
          ground as a ceremonial rite or in pleading
          for (171:2)

叩門   VO: to knock at the door

叩上／啓 EX: respectfully yours (polite term for
            concluding letters to parents, superiors)

15. 怖 bù   BF: afraid, alarmed

恐怖 SV/N: terrifying; terror; fear (171:4)

16. 併 bing   BF: combine, amalgamate, equalize
    (倂)
                    兼併 V/N: to amalgamate; amalgamation (171:7)

                    併進   V: to progress forward together

                一併在內 ex: all included

                    吞併 V/N: to swallow up, amalgamate; amalgamation,
                                combining (also 併吞)

                    併滅   V: to exterminate together with

                    併入   V: to include in

                    合併 V/N: to combine or amalgamate; combining

17. 苛 kē   SV: vexatious, troublesome, burdensome

                    苛征   V: to impose severe taxes upon (171:7)

                    苛重 SV: onerous (as of taxes)

                        賦稅苛重 。
                        The taxes are onerous (171:9)

                    苛刻 SV: very harsh

                    苛政   N: harsh or cruel acts of government, tyrannical
                                government

                    苛求 V/N: to make harsh demands; harsh demands

                    苛待   V: to treat cruelly or harshly

                    過苛   V: to be over harsh or cruel

                好持苛輪 ex: fond of giving severe criticism

                    苛擾 V/N: to disturb, to trouble, to annoy

                    苛稅   N: onerous taxes

18. 飢 jī   BF: hungry (strictly 飢 is hungry and 饑 is famine but
    (饑)   in practice they are used interchangeably)
                    飢荒   N: famine (171:9)

                    飢民   N: famine sufferers (171:11)

                    飢餓 SV/N: hungry; hunger

飢不擇食　ex: in times of necessity one cannot afford
　　　　　　to be particular

飢寒交迫　EX: to suffer both hunger and coldness

19. 催 tswēi　　V: to urge, hasten, press

催逼 V/N: to expedite, press for; urging, pressure for
　　　　　(as repayment of debts, etc.) (171:10)

催命　V: to hasten the death of

催促　V: to press, expedite, urge

催賬　VO: to press for payment of an account

催請 V/N: (polite term) to urge someone to do something
　　　　　(as urging someone to run for president);
　　　　　sincere request

催辦　V: to urge action

20. 餉 syǎng　　N: military pay

糧餉　N: provisions (military) (171:10)

餉給 V/N: (to issue) soldiers'/military rations ('給 jǐ)

餉項　N: soldier's pay

關餉　VO: to draw pay (military)

領餉　VO: to draw pay

21. 粉 fěn　(1)　N: powder (171:11)

粉筆　N: chalk (枝)

粉末　N: powder

粉刺　N: acne

粉碎　V: to smash to pieces; knock to smithereens
　　　　　(usually used) of past actions

粉條　N: noodles (usually made of green beans)

漂白粉　N: bleaching powder; bleach

油頭粉面　EX: (lit. slicked hair and powdered face); dandy;
　　　　　　cheaply made-up woman

粉紅色   N: pink color
(2) V: to whitewash

粉牆 V/N: to whitewash a wall

粉刷 V/N: (to) whitewash

粉飾   V: to adorn; to put on an appearance of

粉飾太平   EX: to put up an appearance of prosperity (i.e. false appearance of prosperity or peace)

22. 糞 fèn   N: manure, dung, night soil (171:11)

糞夫   N: coolie who deals in night soil (107:4)

糞便   N: night soil

23. 掘 jywé   V: to dig out (171:12)

掘開   V: to dig up or out

發掘 V/N: to excavate; excavation

掘土／地 VO: to dig in the earth

掘井 VO: to dig a well

24. 坑 kēng   (1) N: pit, gully

土坑   N: ditch, trench (171:12)

火坑   N: fiery pit; conditions of great suffering (sometimes used of prostitution)

水坑   N: pothole (filled with water)

坑兒   N: pit

坑埋   V: to bury

(2) V: to injure (in abstract not physical terms)

坑人 VO: to entrap another; to involve another in trouble

坑害   V: to entrap; to involve in difficulties

坑騙　V: to cheat, to defraud

25. 掩 yǎn　　　BF: cover, screen, hide

掩埋　V: to bury (171:12)

掩蓋　V: to cover up, hide

掩護 V/N: to cover, conceal (usually military); cover, concealment

掩飾 V/N: to smooth over or hide (faults); covering up

26. 燃 rán　　　V: to burn, to light fire

燃起　V: to ignite, to light fire (172:3)

燃料　N: fuel, combustible materials

點燃　V: to ignite, to light

燃燒 V/N: to burn; combustion, burning

燃放　V: to ignite (firecrackers, etc.)

27. 祥 syáng　　BF: auspicious (172:3,7,8,9)

發祥地　N: place of origin

慈祥　SV: kind, propitious and merciful

不祥　SV: inauspicious

安祥　SV: peaceful (in mind)

28. 剿 jyǎu　　　BF: attack, destroy
（勦）

剿殺　V: to slaughter (172:4)

進剿　V: to attack; to advance in attack

剿匪　V: to destroy bandits or rebels (in Kuomintang usage it means to destroy the Communists)

圍剿 V/N: to surround or encircle and then attack; encirclement

剿滅　V: to exterminate

29. 脂 jr̄　　　BF: fat of animals; lard, grease; cosmetics (172:7)

全／脫脂奶粉　N: whole/skim milk

油脂　N: lard, fat

脂粉　N: cosmetics

脂粉氣　SV/N: feminine; (to put on) <u>sissified airs</u>

30. 騎 chí　V: to mount or ride (as a horse) (172:7)

騎射　N: horsemanship and archery (172:7)

騎馬　VO: to ride a horse

騎馬找馬　EX: to have a job and look for a better one

鐵騎軍　N: cavalry (騎 here can also be read jì)

騎牆派　N: opportunists (in sense of those who do not commit themselves); fence-sitters

騎兵　N: cavalry (騎 here can also be read jì)

騎上　RV: to mount, ride

騎虎難下　EX: hard to disengage from a difficult situation

31. 射 shè　V: to shoot, to aim at (172:7)

注射　V/N: to inject; injection

放射　V/N: to radiate; radiation

放射線　N: radiation rays

照射　V/N: to illuminate; illumination (in sense of lighting)

反射　V/N: to reflect; reflection

射擊　V/N: to fire a gun; shooting, firing

高射砲　N: antiaircraft gun　(座)

掃射　V/N: to strafe; strafing

射箭　VO: to shoot an arrow

射死／傷　V: to shoot and kill/wound

發射 V/N: to shoot; launch, shot

32. 舅 jyòu   BF: maternal uncles

舅父   N: maternal uncle (172:7)

舅舅   N: maternal uncle

舅母   N: wife of maternal uncle

大／小舅子   N: older/younger brother of one's wife

33. 闖 chwǎng   V: to burst in, to break in (172:8)

闖進來／去 RV: to burst or charge in, to break in (as into room)

闖入   V: to break or burst into

闖禍   VO: to stir up calamity or trouble

闖下大禍   ex: to stir up a major calamity, incident

34. 網 wǎng   N: net, web, network

魚網   N: fish net (5:10)

網羅 V/N: to assemble talent after an intensive search; unearthing and assembling of talent (172:12)

結網   VO: to make a net

一網打盡 EX: to capture all in one net

鐵道網   N: railway network

網球   N: tennis

打網球 VO: to play tennis

漏網   V: to escape the net or dragnet; to be omitted inadvertently

35. 屢 lyǔ   BF: repeatedly, often

屢經   V: to have experienced repeatedly (173:2)

雖然他屢經失敗但他的勇氣未減。
Although he has failed repeatedly, he is not disheartened.

屢次　　A: repeatedly, many times

屢敗　　V: to be defeated repeatedly

　　　屢戰屢敗　　EX: defeated in every engagement;
　　　　　　　　　　　to be defeated repeatedly

屢建奇功　EX: to pile up meritorious achievements

屢犯　　V: to violate repeatedly

屢年　　A: (for) many years

36. 挫 tswò　　BF: dislocate, bend back, dull, dampen

挫敗 V/N: to dash or be dashed in one's expectations;
　　　　　　upsets and defeats (173:2)

　　　節節挫敗　EX: to be defeated or dashed at
　　　　　　　　　　every turn

　　　遭到挫敗　VO: to encounter defeat

挫折 V/N: to have one's ardor dampened by obstacles
　　　　　and defeats; obstacles, frustration

頓挫　　N: interruption, setback

　　　遭受頓挫　VO: to meet with a setback

挫辱　　V: to humiliate, disgrace

37. 昌 chāng　　BF: prosperous, good (used often in names and place names)

永昌　　N: Yungch'ang (style of the reigning dynasty)
　　　　　(173:3)

昌平　　N: Ch'angp'ing (173:4)

武昌　　N: Wuch'ang (174:12)

昌明　　SV: glorious, brilliant (of governments, policies,
　　　　　　etc.)

昌盛　　SV: prosperous, abundant

昌隆　　SV: prosperous, on the rise

38. 譁 hwá　　BF: noise, clamor

譁變　V: to mutiny, go over to the other side (173:4)

輿論大譁　ex: the public clamor, protest fervently

譁然　V: to clamor

39. 掠 lywè　　V: to plunder, rob (173:7)

搶掠　V: to rob, plunder, loot

40. 淫 yín　　(1) SV: lewd, obscene, dissolute

荒淫　SV: profligate, dissipated

淫婦　N: women of easy morals

(2) V/A: to go to excess; excessive, very great

淫威　N: arrogant airs of authority (term has a bad connotation)

他總是顯他的淫威。
He is always throwing his weight around.

淫雨　N: excessive rain

41. 禾 hé　　N: growing grain; crops　Rad. 115

田禾　N: growing grain (173:8)

禾苗　N: fields; rice sprouts ready for planting in paddy, seedling

42. 斬 jǎn　　V: to cut; to chop; to behead or execute

處斬　V: to behead; to be sentenced to beheading (173:8)

斬草除根　EX: to uproot, destroy thoroughly

斬首　V: to behead

43. 譽 yù　　(1) V: to praise (literary) (173:8)

面譽　V: to praise (someone) in his presence

(2) BF: reputation, fame

揚譽　V: to spread the fame or reputation of

名譽　N: reputation; fame

信譽　　N: reputation; reliability; trustworthiness

榮譽　　N: honor; good reputation

譽望　　N: reputation

44. 謹 jǐn　　BF: cautious, attentive, careful

謹慎 SV/N: cautious; caution (173:10)

謹防　　V: to guard against

謹記　　V: to have constantly in mind

拘謹　　SV: reserved (of behavior)

恭謹　　SV: respectful; polite

謹上／啓　EX: respectfully yours (polite form for closing letters)

45. 禦 yù　　BF: withstand, resist

防禦　　V: to oppose; to defend against (173:11)

防禦條約　　N: defense treaty

共同防禦條約　　N: mutual defense treaty

抵禦　　V: to resist, oppose

禦敵　　V: to resist the enemy

46. 蝕 shŕ　　BF: eat up gradually; eclipse

腐蝕　　V: (lit. and fig.) to corrode, erode; to be corrupted by pleasure, etc. (174:2)

月／日蝕　　N: eclipse of the moon/sun

侵蝕　　V: to encroach upon

全／半／分／環蝕　　N: total/half/partial/annular eclipse

剝蝕　　V: to be dilapidated and worn out

蝕本　　V: to eat up one's capital

蝕損　　V: to injure

47. 宰 dzǎi   (1) BF: minister, ruler

主宰 V/N: to be in absolute control of (as of party, government department, social movement, etc.); ruler or controlling power

(2) V: to slaughter

宰割 V: to cut up (as of meat) (also used figuratively to describe a small country being chewed up by a big one)

屠宰 V: to slaughter

宰牲口 VO: to slaughter animals

宰殺 V: to slaughter

48. 軋 yà   V: to crush, grind

傾軋 V: to try from envy or jealousy to squeeze out a rival (174:6)

軋碎 V: to crush to pieces

49. 坡 pwō   N: slope, declivity, bank

下坡路 N: downward path (usually fig.) (174:8)

走下坡路 V: (fig.) to go downhill

上／下坡 V/N: to take an uphill/downhill path; upward/downward path (lit. and fig.)

山坡 N: mountain slopes; slope of a hill

坡度 N: angle or degree of incline

高坡 N: upper slope; long slope

50. 夾 jyá   (1) V: to pinch, squeeze, or press in between; to hold under one's arm

夾攻 V/N: (to) attack from both sides (175:1)

兩面夾攻 ex: to attack from two sides at once (lit. and fig.)

夾擊 V: to attack from both sides

夾牢　RV: to grip or hold firmly

夾雜　V: to mix up

文白夾雜　EX: to have <u>wen yen</u> and <u>pai hua</u> all mixed together

夾緊　RV: to press or wedge tightly

夾道歡呼　EX: to line the streets and shout a welcome (like a ticker-tape parade)

(2)　V: to pick up as with chopsticks, pincers, pliers, etc.

夾起來　RV: to pick up; to insert between (as a book mark in a book)

夾住　RV: to grip firmly

(3) Adj: lined (as of garments) (This expression is traditionally used to describe late spring and early fall when such garments are sufficiently warm.)

夾衣　N: lined garments (i.e. garments made with two layers of cloth) (also 袷／袷衣)

NEW MEANINGS

1. 番　　　BF: foreign, aborigines

西番　N: western barbarians (170:7)

番人　N: foreigners, aborigines

2. 流　　　BF: class or set of persons

下流 SV/N: crude, vulgar; lower class (171:3)

上／下流社會　N: upper-/lower- class society

3. 乾 gān　　BF: nominal, in name only

乾兒子／女兒　N: adopted son/daughter (171:3)

4. 偶　　(1) BF: mate

偶語 V/N: to talk together; (of two people in) conversation (171:4)

偶數　N: even number

配偶　N: spouse

喪／失偶　V: to lose one's mate

(2) BF: idol

木偶　N: wooden puppet

偶象／像　N: image, idol

5. 位　　N: throne

繼位　V: to succeed to the throne (172:9)

6. 卒　　N: retainer, soldier

士卒　N: ordinary soldiers (172:12)

獄卒　N: jailor

販夫走卒　N: lower classes

7. 浮　　BF: flighty, superstitious ; superficial

浮華 SV/N: dissolute, empty, vain; vanity (174:2)

浮華墮落　EX: decadent, dissolute (of people and cultures)

輕浮 SV: superficial, light weight (especially being flirtatious)

浮名　N: empty glory

浮雲　N: floating clouds

8. 相　　BF: minister of state

宰相　N: premier (historical term) (174:3)

首相　N: premier

外相　N: foreign minister (of Britain, Japan, etc.)

海／陸相　N: Minister of Navy/Army, etc. (Japanese term)

9. 索　　BF: demand or ask

逼索 V/N: to press forcibly for; to seek under pressure; to extort demand; demand, urgent pressure for (174:4)

搜索   V: to search for, to flush out (as an enemy)

索取   V: to extort forcibly

索性   A: might as well (connotes "What the heck!") (索   read swǒ)

這件事太難作，你索性別作了。
This is too hard to do; you might as well not do it.

索引   N: index

10. 役   BF: battle

山海關一役   N: Battle of Shanhaikwan (174:10)

戰役   N: battle, military campaign

11. 師   BF: capital city

京師   N: the capital city (174:10)

STRUCTURE NOTES

1. 連 N where N is a time word like "year," "day," or "night." This
    pattern divides into two different idioms as shown below:

    (1) A: N after N; several in a row

         連年   A: year after year; several years in a row

         連日/天   A: day after day; several days in a row

    (2) A: all through the N

         連夜   A: all through the night

         連日連夜   A: (all through the) day and night

2. 連 V_1 連 V_2 PT: to V_2 every time you V_1

    連戰連敗   ex: to lose every battle; to lose every time
                     you fight

    連賭連輸   ex: to lose every time you gamble

Note:

    1. 連 V_1 連 V_2 can be considered a variation of the colloquial
        (每) ... 一次就 ... 一次 .

                    *   *   *   *   *

Note for Review

    1. 連 ... 也/都 ...   (172:12; 174:7)

    2. 被 + V   (172:9)

        被 + O + 所 + V   (174:2)

        被 + O + V + O   (174:7)

        被 + O + CV + O + V + O   (175:2)

    3. (一方面 ...) 另方面 ...   (173:11)

4. S + V + O + 者 (173:9)

    V + O + 者   (171:11)

5. 甚且 (variation of 甚至)   (171:11; 174:1,4)

6. 既然 ... 又 ...   (174:5)

7. 屢經 + Vn ...   (173:2)

E X E R C I S E S

I. Miscellaneous

A. 連年／日／etc.

1. 連日暴雨後，即將收割的稻田，已爲雨水所傷，損失大半了。

2. 他雖然大學已經畢業又專修文學，但做起文章來仍是錯字連篇。

3. 國家建設雖然已有相當的成績，但是經過連年戰爭，悉被毀壞了。

B. 善於

1. 就戰略來說共產黨是善於打游擊戰的，但是在最近這幾次戰鬥中他
   們却是屢戰屢敗。

2. 他只是善於掩飾自己的缺點，對於做人做事却沒有多少改進。

C. 連 VERB$_1$ 連 VERB$_2$

1. 一支訓練不足，裝備不齊的軍隊，作戰起來，不是臨陣脫逃，就是
   連戰連敗。

2. 依照憲法的規定總統的任期爲四年，得連選連任一次。

D. 及時

1. 「今朝有酒今朝醉」這種及時行樂的態度使他終生一無所成。

2. 受時局驟變的影響，物價飛騰，股票猛漲，金融情形混亂不堪，倘
   不及時挽救，經濟恐慌即將隨之而來。

3. 「少壯不努力，老大徒傷悲」，這是古人的敎訓。青年人倘不及時努
   力，豈有前途可言？

II. Review Sentences

1. 善於投機取巧而不務實際的人，終歸是一事無成的。

2. 有人批評他所寫的文章只是離章琢句，文詞華麗而已，並沒有高超
   獨特的見解。

3. 國家的存亡和社會的治亂，關係着每一個國民的身家與職業。

4. 雖然他們都是我的朋友，但是關係有親疏遠近之分。

5. 在群眾中專門挑撥離間，在工作上又只敷衍塞責的人豈能擔負起領導青年的重任？

6. 評定文藝作品的價值其標準在作品本身的優劣，不在新舊，古代有價值的作品，均能歷千載而常新，不是幾個自命為文藝批評家之流可以一筆抹殺的。

7. 他們的教育程度不同，能力不同，如何能從事於相同的工作。

8. 社會階級雖有貴賤之分，但是人格的高低則不能以此來衡量。

9. 一般所謂人口問題，係指因為人口增加的遲速，分佈的疏密與品質的優劣等所產生的各項問題而言。

10. 倘若他對人總是虛偽而無真誠的友誼可言，你還願意跟他做朋友嗎？

I. **Miscellaneous**

A. 連年／日／etc.

1. Because of disastrous droughts year after year, the grain harvests have been meager and the peasants are extremely impoverished.

2. Working day and night, they have finished the five hundred military uniforms.

B. 善於

1. People who are good at talking are not necessarily good at getting things done.

2. He is good at sensing other people's moods.

C. 連 VERB₁ 連 VERB₂

1. Last night my luck was bad. Every time I gambled I lost.

2. If the army is victorious every time it fights, as reported, why do we cede territory, pay reparations and sign unequal treaties with the enemy?

D. 及時

1. This old artist is very ill. If they can't get him to a hospital in time, then I fear for his life.

2. After a major famine, bandits appear in great numbers and society is very disturbed. The government ought to take steps to calm the minds of the people in time.

Write Sentences Using:

1. 以此爲然   6. 無從   11. 索性

2. 不拘   7. 有見於   12. 一俟 . . . 就 . . .

3. 一味   8. 較之爲

4. 不妨   9. 不得加以

5. 與其 . . . 不如 . . .   10. 蓋 . . . 所致